MW01098727

International Federation of Library Associations and Institutions
Fédération Internationale des Associations de Bibliothécaires et des Bibliothèques
Internationaler Verband der bibliothekarischen Vereine und Institutionen
Международная Федерация Библиотечных Ассоциаций и Учреждений
Federación Internacional de Asociaciones de Bibliotecarios y Bibliotecas

IFLA Publications 106

Women's Issues at IFLA: Equality, Gender and Information on Agenda

Papers from the Programs of
the Round Table on Women's Issues
at IFLA Annual Conferences 1993 - 2002

Edited by
Leena Siitonen

K · G · Saur   München 2003

IFLA Publications
edited by Sjoerd Koopman

Recommended catalogue entry:

Women's Issues at IFLA: Equality, Gender and Information on Agenda
Papers from the Programs of the Round Table on Women's Issues
at IFLA Annual Conferences 1993 - 2002
[International Federation of Library Associations and Institutions].
– München : Saur, 2003, 256 p. 21 cm
  (IFLA publications ; 106)
  ISBN 3-598-21836-2

Bibliographic information published by Die Deutsche Bibliothek
Die Deutsche Bibliothek lists this publication in the Deutsche Nationalbibliografie;
detailed bibliographic data is available in the Internet at
http://dnb.ddb.de.

⊗

Printed on acid-free paper
The paper used in this publication meets the minimum requirements of American National
Standard for Information Sciences – Permanence of Paper for Printed Library Materials,
ANSI Z39.48.1984.

Printed / Bound by Strauss Offsetdruck, Mörlenbach

ISBN 3-598-21836-2
ISSN 0344-6891 (IFLA Publications)

TABLE OF CONTENTS

I   Changing Roles of Women Librarians

II   Professional Status as a Goal

III Library Managers and Gender

IV Information Services for Women: Access and Hindrances

V Women's Information Needs: A Societal and Feminist Issue

VI Key to the Future: Education

VII Information Society, Culture and Economy: Global   Challenges

APPENDIX

Acknowledgements

The Round Table on Women's Issues, as part of its mission, promotes the collection, research, publication and dissemination of information on the status of women in librarianship. To this end it has worked within IFLA with those groups and individuals whose interests include professional education and advancement within the profession. This book is one result of these efforts.

We thank each person whose paper is included in this book for their dedication to the advancement of women's issues at IFLA. We also thank each person who has helped a colleague to do research and write a paper and to attend a conference. We thank each person, officer or otherwise, who has worked on making the RTWI programs a row of successes.

Special thanks are extended to IFLA Headquarters staff, the IFLA Publications Committee, the Professional Board, whose advice, practical guidance and friendly help has been indispensable in the process of making papers available to the whole IFLA community. For this publication to have green covers around its contents we thank the editors at K.G. Saur Verlag GmbH. It has been only through their marvellous collaboration that this book has become a reality.

Leena Siitonen
Chairperson of RTWI

PREFACE

In 1990 a small group gathered during the IFLA annual conference in Stockholm, Sweden, to discuss the professional status of women in librarianship and, more precisely, to focus attention to the status of women within IFLA's organisation, divisions and programs. The group that assumed as its name Group on Women's Interests in Librarianship brought into existence not only what was to become the Round Table on Women's Issues (RTWI), in Division VI Management and Technology, but also a program that year after year has gained momentum and a growing interest among conference participants.

From the initiative of Suzanne Hildenbrand, Professor at the School of Library and Information Science, New York State University at Buffalo, the group has grown from 1990 to 2002 to attract, involve and activate members from over seventy IFLA member countries.

In 2002 the Round Table's status was changed to that of Section. It was time to have a look at the twelve years of activity. The proposal to publish a selection of papers given at the RTWI programs, some of them jointly with the Round Table on Government Libraries and Official Publications, got the support of the IFLA Publications Committee and approval of the Professional Board. The results of selection and editing are presented in this monograph, published by K.G. Saur Verlag GmbH.

The papers are organized under the themes that covered the main issues in RTWI's work. The topics of the annual programs always reflected the themes of IFLA conferences. Without any coercion or guidance the proposals for papers focused on the one hand on women librarian's education, advancement, career development and status both in libraries and in professional organizations; on the other hand on women's literacy, women's information needs, women's access to information, library and information resources and services for women, and women's access and use of information and communication technologies. Consequently many feminist issues were dealt with by focusing on women's work and salary, vocational training, status in society and education, i.e., issues of equality and equity. These papers reflect on hardships, perseverance and struggles as they also describe advancements, even victories. Women's share of a country's cultural development is growing with their raising level of education. International aspects of women's issues are researched in several comparative studies.

Every year there were more and more proposals from among which a selection was made for the program. Thus, the papers in this monograph form only a fraction from the possible universe. There were a few principles followed in the annual selection process, besides the main rule that the papers had to adhere to a given theme. There was every year a paper from the host country and others from different regions of the world, and very special interest was paid to papers from countries that had not presented any before. Once an important topic had aroused interest and was researched in depth, it was followed up in papers that linked it to a more recent period or continued research, often also in another region of the world.

Editor's task was to find as many papers as possible for this monograph. Although many papers were available in IFLA's archive, others could be located only by requesting authors and their colleagues to send a copy and, lamentably, some could not be found at all. Very few papers had been translated from English to other official languages of IFLA, while a few papers, although presented in English, existed only in other languages. The papers reflect the style of their authors and the references and footnotes are also those of the authors.

This monograph reflects women's advancement in the library and information field. One of RTWI's founding members, the current IFLA President H. Kay Raseroka wrote in her paper "Information Services for Women in Developing Countries" (1993):

> *Information services for women in developing countries and in Africa, in particular, are essential for empowerment of women who are the pivot of family life and communities. The barriers which hinder the provision of information to women exist but are not insurmountable provided that information specialists together with library, documentation and archive administrators and policy makers:*
>
> *- firstly recognise the moral duty to redress existing injustices;*
>
> *- secondly accept the pragmatism that women's empowerment through accessible information and its use has a substantial multiplier effect in the welfare of families and communities;*
>
> *- lastly, are sensitive and responsive to innovative approaches of facilitating the development of channels of information which recognise women's own networks of communication and organisational structures as information centres into which LIS professionals can plug;*
>
> *and recognise the centrality of communication as the base for information services in general and for women specifically.*

The work for women's empowerment and for access to information is a challenge for all IFLA members in the foreseeable future. The editor hopes that this monograph will give all readers a stimulus to join in this invaluable and significant work.

Leena Siitonen

Madrid, Spain, 24 June 2003

I. CHANGING ROLES OF WOMEN LIBRARIANS

INFORMATION SERVICES FOR WOMEN IN DEVELOPING COUNTRIES

H. Kay Raseroka

University Librarian

University of Botswana

Gaborone, Botswana (1993)

Abstract

The paper argues that there is a need to consider women as a category of special groups whose needs for information should be analysed and met. It analyses the potential for women's information systems within the broad socio-cultural contexts and barriers to information access are presented. Proposals are made towards the establishment of information services for women, in developing countries.

Introduction

The importance of information in the life of an individual has been so well articulated in the literature that the slogan "Information is power" no longer requires an explanation. Information is essentially seen as a tool that is valuable and useful to people in their attempts to cope with their lives. (1)

The role of information in an individual's life is to reduce uncertainty and increase a person's capacity for problem solving and assist an individual in the identification of available alternatives. Information empowers its user to make decisions on the basis of synthesis of newly acquired data with the individually held knowledge to create personally relevant information useful in a given situation.

Information services provision as an activity, then, must take into account the unique way in which data may have as many meanings as there are recipients thereof depending on their individual knowledge base, needs and the use to which it is put. Ideally, information services are needs based, dependent on the clarity of communication of those needs by the individual seeking information to a person or source (gate keepet of information) judged to be knowledgeable on the one hand on the relevance of the supplied data and on the other hand on the client's needs. Information services provision is satisfied when the data supplied provides direct help for an individual or community to address day to day problems, from the client's perspective. Thus, fundamental to information service provision is communication between the information specialist and the client.

Women's Information Needs

Women are part of a wider society, thus, from this perspective their information needs would overlap to some extent with those of the rest of the society, where problems are common and require cooperative solutions. There are, however, distinct areas of

1

responsibilitiy for women in all cultures. These are the areas from which derive the needs for provision of specific information services. Women are pivot for family units and the community. Core information needs, peculiar to them as a group, arise out of their responsibilities which

- impact heavily on every member of the family particularly in the process of bearing and bringing up of children as well as giving care to the family in general and the elderly in particular
- transmit and determine change of societal values
- sustain life physically and economically through heavy involvement in all aspects of food production
- contribute a sizeable percentage to national economics.

In addition to these roles women have been catapulted into positions of heading households and bearing the brunt of not only child bearing but autonomous decision-making for the nuclear and extended families. This is largerly due to rapid change occurring globally. It has been further exacerbated in Africa by wars whether civil or of liberation, migrant labor systems and environmental factors such as drought, which have removed the majority of adult males from day to day participation in the life of a family.

In spite of all the various roles, women are ill prepared to meet the challenges and demands expected of them. They are generally left behind in aducation and training in all Third World societies. For example, in 1985 it was estimated that of the 162 million adult illiterates (above the age of 15) located in Africa 60 per cent were women as compared to 40 per cent of men (2). Further data on the percentage population (in Africa) of possible pupils in school indicates that 43 per cent of girls between ages 4–11 years as compared to 59 per cent of boys of the same age attend primary school (2). The situation at higher levels of education is more skewed against women. This situation arises from the belief that is deeply entrenched in cultural and social patterns in most developing countries that an investement of education and training should be bestowed on boys and men rather than girls and women. As a result of this inhibited approach to girls' and women's access to education, status and other means of realising their full potential, their contributions to national economies fall far below their capabilities. The seriousness of this neglect has been acknowledged particularly in agriculture, where women produce 90 per cent of the food grown in Africa, in family health welfare and services for which women are directly responsible. Yet, the majority of them are ill equipped educationally or lack relevant information or ability to improve their knowledge through reading.

From this perspective, then, targeting of information services to women is a matter of redressing injustice. Information services should empower women to take part in selfdevelopment which is the only realistic base for their sustained contribution to national development. Some of the areas in which information plays a major role for empowerment of women are in policy and in cultural interpretation of basic needs, such as access to land, shelter, food, water, fuel, health and education, awareness raising, leadership roles assessment of own need, management skills, division of labour between sexes, and control of factors of production.

Information services to women will by no means undermine those of other groups, but, instead, the knowledge gained will be used for the benefit of society at large, thorugh women's various roles and, especially, as their role as mothers. Trite as it sounds, there is truth in the saying "teach a man, you educate an individual, but teach a woman, you educate a nation".

Libraries and information services for women as a special group have yet to be proposed in the developing world. This is hardly surprising considering that national documentation and library systems are still grappling with infrastructural concerns, coordination, cooperation, and adequate human and financial resources, while at the same time searching for relevance in relation to the oral-based cultures. The analysis of and proposal for information services for women, then, should become an issue for serious consideration in the interest of justice and improvement of the quality of life for children and families.

Barriers to the Provision of Information to Women

Lack of homogeneity. The foregoing has concentrated on the need for information services targeted to women in general. It is important, however, to note that women, as a group, are not homogenous. There are various levels and subgrous within the broad category of women. Each level or group has distinct information needs. Sub-groups' information needs, like individual ones, are determined by the interaction of factors such as education environment, networks and economic conditions. Thus the type of information needs a sub-group of individual woman has would be influenced by whether they are rural or urban, wealthy or poor, illiterate or educated, and by their occupation and status within a given society.

Arising out of the above observations are questions which information specialists cannot ignore, if the aim is to provide relevant information services. Are individually determined services possible? Or are information services to be targeted to sub-groups?

In order to provide answers to these questions, it is necessary to

- understand the community and know its profile, including primary activities and the rhythm of women's life style within a given social system
- appreciate existing communication networks and channels within the community, among women as a group, and within the various sub-groups or organizations of women.
- last but not least, allow adequate time for marketing of possible new sources (through gate keepers) of information for women.

Availability of time enables changing ideas to be subjected to analysis, to be tested for relevance and accuracy before being accepted as useful and viable. Such a process is crucial for the women as participants in information seeking to have the opportunity to test new sources of information in their own practical ways, since more than any other group within the society they are aware, that the use of wrong untested data could be distraous not only for the individual woman but for the family.

Lack of Time. Women generally lack "free" time because of their various roles. Aarising out of this, culture has instilled in women as a virtue and expectation that they should occupy themselves productively at all times. In the rural areas "leisure" and information exchange is linked with routine communal activities, such as water fetching, fuel gathering, laudry, food production and processing among other things. With a rapid change of family structures, the absence of different generations of women (within the same household) has had a detrimental effect on trusted information pathways. Their role to act as a chain in the transference of tradition from one generation to the next has changed. In addition, because of the disruption of the extended family, information exchange networks within the safety of clan and family have been destroyed. Thus, even in the rural areas the communally based information system is no longer as effective as it used to be. Thus, there is room for intervention in the provision of needed information, within the context of rural women's life styles, since these include the new information networks.

The recognition of this gap has been well exploited by sectors such as health, nutrition, literacy, agriculture, and various subfields through provision of extension workers for each sector and subfield. Since, however, their information services are not coordinated, they have contributed to the increase in women's burdens and responsibilities. Each sector demands to be accommodated in women's schedules to a point where the services are ignored simply through lack of time or overload of information, and fatigue. Is this a niche which information specialist should investigate and perhaps exploit by providing coordination of information services?

Modern and urban living has tended to superimpose its owm structures and routines over the gradually changing traditional roles. The thrust of the change is towards maximization of economic power. The result has been the development of distinct women's information systems and networks which centre around

- self help organizations, such as general non-governmental women's organizations
- church-fellowship groups, such as mothers' unions of different denominations
- burial societies centered around villages and formal work places
- finance identification and maximization societies like revolving fund groups.

Any plan to establish information services for women has to to be based on the understanding of the inner workings of these communal informtaion networks, and voluntary organizations, being all the way understood and acceptable to the gate keepers. Consultations by library and information workers, information needs analysis and participatory means are the most viable foundation.

Illiteracy as a barrier to information use has been identified as a problem, which affects women more than men. Thus, information services provision to women needed to rely heavily on sound and visual transmission of information, such as the use of extension workers, radio, cassette taped information and video technology where available, as a medium of information services provision.

Traditional modes of information communication, such as those revolving around rites of passage ceremonies of puberty, marriage, childbirth and death, may still be viable channels for providing information services in some societies. They are, however, subject to taboos and are also undergoing such rapid change that other culturally acceptable channels of information have to be negotiated with women at all levels and locales.

Finding out What Women Know and What They Don't Know

Cultural conditioning of women lays a strong emphasis on self effacement, reticence, and absolute obedience of authority as being appropiate behaviour for women to accept a second class position to males, parents and, in some cases, to adult male offspring. These values have further engendered characteristics such as bashfulness about asking questions or seeking information outside of the immediate family. Women in Africa, thus, generally lack the confidence or courage and initiative for venturing outside the acceptable domains in search of solutions to problems. Inculcated reticence about self further encourages the undervaluing of skills and knowledge which women own, thus making it difficult for an outsider to assess needs for information accurately.

These culturally based constraints might prove to be the greatest barrier which has to be confronted by information specialists in facilitating broader access to information relevant to women. Fortunately, rapid change of traditional values may open up new and urgent demands for practical and survival information, thus encouraging faster processes for the search of solutions of day to day problems.

Relevant Information

Last but not least, there is the lack of relevant information to serve women in their various roles. While the desired information might be available somewhere, it is not collated and organized adequately enough to meet women's needs. The indigenous information arising from women's lives has not been collected and organized sufficiently to benefit all those who need to use it. It remains locked up with individuals or groups of women even now when traditional information networks are breaking down. Where data has been collected through researchers, it is presented as research reports and rarely repackaged for the benefit of the subjects of research. Data produced and collected nationally is rarely desegregated by sex, in such a way that issues affecting women can be easily teased out for use in specific information services. Further useful data is produced by sector and, for this reason, is scattered through all levels of national bureaucracies; they are subject to various controls within organizations and government departments, thus making it impossible to be accessed by those persons who need them most.

Information Specialist

Given the foregoing barriers, what are the expectations that should be met by an information specialist providing information services to women? The information specialists serving women cannot keep regular office hours, if they are to be accepted as a part of the information network: Information needs occur as part of conversation as women engage in routine work or group activities. In short, the first line information specialist who deals directly with the women must be part of the community or group of women.

How can library and information services (LIS) empower women to build their indigenous knowledge rather than be alienated from it? Is there a role for LIS personnel to be facilitators for self-empowerment of women rather than providers of an irrelevant service? What type of training will produce such facilitators?

I think, like Durrani (4), that appropriate information services must be based on a change of traditional concepts of librarianship (borrowed from the developed world) which emphasize books located in buildings to that which emphasizes information and is community based. The implications of community based information specialist pose serious questions for the type of persons to be recruited as information specialists serving as first line information service inter-actors or channels.

For example, would a community or group of middle-aged traditional women share their information needs with an unmarried young person who has no experience of motherhood? What level of education would be adequate to provide leverage but not be seen as elite to the detriment of the service? Should a first line information specialist be recruited from among the communities' gate keepers of information? Are there lessons to be learned from other extension agencies such as those serving as literacy teachers and family well-fare workers? These are some of the questions that have to be addresses in the research, planning and policy stages, if the establishment of appropriate information services for women has to be built on existing socio-cultural norms and create a community centered service.

The second line of information service – interpreters – would be based in library, documentation and information centres at the end of a telephone or radio phone, ready to receive information needs which have been referred by the on-the-ground first line information service facilitators. Their role is one of interpretation and matching of information needs to readily available data or repackaging various data to meet a specific information request. The source of data are not only those already collected, processed and coordinated through bibliographic control, but also those which are nebulous and located in specialist sources affecting all aspects of women's lives.

Information services for women cannot afford to be limited by the collections within the building; they will need to utilize all available sources of information suitably repackaged to meed local needs and conditions. Sources of information on or for women as well as networks and organizations generating and disseminating information for and about women are numerous. They need dedicated and innovative information specialists to collect, collate, process, create data bases, repackage and disseminate information to all who need it. In this role of committed information specialists who work closely with women we should aim and provide.

Conclusion

Information services for women in developing countries, and in Africa in particular, are essential for empowerment of women who are the pivot of family life and communities. The barriers which hinder the provision of information to women do exist but are not insurmountable, provided that information specialists together with library, documentation and archive administrators and policy makers

- firstly, recognize the moral duty to redress existing injustices
- secondly, accept the pragmatism that women's empowerment through accessible information and its use has a substantial multiplier effect in the welfare of families and communities
- thirdly, are sensitive and responsive to innovative approaches of facilitating the development of channels of information which recognize women's own networks of communication and organizational structures as information centres into which LIS professionals can plug.
- lastly, recognize the centrality of communication as the base for information services in general and, specifically, for women.

References

1. Dervin, B. (1977) Useful theory of librarianship. Drexel Library Quarterly, 13 (13): 16–32.

2. UNESCO Office of Statistics, quoted in Mueller, Josef. (1990) Literacy – Human Right not Priviledge. Development and Cooperation (2): 17–20.

3. University of Botswana. (1989) Gender and Education: Proceedings of a Workshop. February–March 1989. Gaborone: Faculty of Education Research Committee, p. 67.

4. Durrani, S. (1985) Rural Information in Kenya. Information Development, 1(3): 149–157.

Acknowledgement

This paper has been adapted from a paper presented by the author at the ninth Standing Conference of Eastern, Central and Southern African Librarians (SCECSAL IX) in Kampala, Uganda, June 21–29, 1990, under title: Constraints in the Provision of Information Services for Women in the Region.

HOW LONG DO WOMEN HAVE TO WAIT?

Tuula Haavisto

Secretary General, Finnish Library Association

Helsinki, Finland (1994)

Abstract

How long do women have to wait to become full-licensed citizens? And is it only to wait or is it to do something ourselves? One could think that the answer is obviously clear. But is it? The process of women towards being subjects is a dialectical process of our own activity and official actions while making laws and statutes, arranging national or local discussions and studies about equality. The mental process, women's collective and individual consciousness is also a complicated question. Men's opinions about equality are developing, too. Finland is a country, which has a long experience about majority of women working full-time outside home. Partly due to this fact the position of women in Finland is nowadays quite good. Nevertheless, we don't live in heaven yet. Women's salaries are lower than those of men. Women are not yet as high regarded as men. In the paper I will discuss the process of interaction between women's own activity and the society in formulating the present situation. As an example I use Finland and its libraries: 90per cent of its library staff is female, and the great majority of library directors are women as well. How does this influence our library policy, working methods, working atmosphere – or does it have any influence at all?

Introduction

How long to do women have to wait? The position of women is a process. This process has its own characteristics in every country and culture, but the main question always seems to be something like "how are the relationships and possibilities of women and men organized in society?"

In this paper I'll try to describe how the process has got further in one specific country, Finland. There is a dialectic relationship between women's own activities and the changes on the official side of the society, as in legislation. Both factors are important. Secondly, it is important to notice that women in Finland have managed to use the ages of transition in the history for their benefit. The same has happened in the other Nordic countries, too.

In Finland equality has developed rather far. This has happened in the framework of a Nordic welfare state, but it has also other roots. Not only the position and life of women has changed – men have participated in this process as well. Changes in legislation and ways of acting have covered the whole society.

Equality Was Born from Poverty

In certain sense the original root for the Finnish equality was the poor and non-independent history of the country. The majority of Finns lived even until the 1940's in countryside, cultivating small family farms. Compared with, e.g., latifundios in Latin America, the Finnish system was equally hard to everyone: Both women and men, even children, had to struggle extremely in order to survive. If there was any kind of upper class leading an easier life, it consisted mainly of foreign rulers. Finland was, until 1809, a Swedish province, and from 1810–1917 a Russian Grand Duchy.

In a farming family everyone had her or his "natural" role in the system. Everyone was needed, and every good worker, male or female, was respected. This fact is still alive in our everyday life: It is very clear that women participate strongly in the maintenance of families.

It is a Finnish peculiarity that a great majority of women is working and has worked full-time outside the home.

Having children doesn't change this choice. The state and the communities support women's work with long maternity leaves and day care system. During the recent recession these systems were threatened, but they still exist.

I must mention, too, that women's movements have been strong in Finland since the beginning of this century. Their activities have covered a large area from gymnastics to political women's organizations or the Martha Organization, that has enlightened women in household questions. The importance of these movements to the consciousness of Finnish women has been significant. I would argue that one or another women's movement has been near to each and every Finnish woman.

The State: An Enemy or an Ally?

Finland's existence under foreign rules has had other consequences. It is one reason for our women's movement's positive attitude towards the state as a social structure. Contrary to the Anglo-American feminist tradition, where the state has been considered as a paternalistic, negative power, women in all Nordic countries see the state more as an ally to women.

In Finland, during the last decades of the Russian rule, independence was a common goal of the whole nation. A lot of political, educational, etc. work was done to realize it. In this work also women's movements were active. When independence then was reached, in 1917, it was an achievement of everyone, including both genders. And thereafter, women had the right to have a clear role in "our common state".

In all Nordic countries, the public sector has from the beginning of the 20th century offered most working places for women. Researchers speak about a symbolic gender contract, although there is of course nothing in writing. Although it was generally accepted that women had their responsibility in public life, it was rejected yet still important: For women belonged education of children, health and social care on lower levels such as nurses.

Thus, librarianship, especially public libraries, was self-evidently a suitable area for women. Librarians also participated in the social mission which was mainly a responsibility of women: They were along with teachers refining the nation, uprooting bad manners from the common people. There are in existence impressive documents in our library history about this mission. In fact, the mission is still continuing.

Women, indeed, do have this mission of cultivating people in nearly every culture. What was exceptional in the Nordic countries was that women carried out this task largely in public life, not only at home. (But what also can be noticed is, that the enlightening movements in Finland were always started by men. After whose awakening speeches, women were allowed to continue, to implement ideas such as that of public libraries, in the everyday life, in every corner of the country.)

It was important that women occupied this large area of social activities. Eventually they reached also such specificity, which was badly needed in society. They could not be ignored. At the same time the male-dominated trade unions were negotiating better working conditions. According to a Finnish study on women (1) one could say: Over time two parallel welfare states developed. The men's state guaranteed traditional trade union benefits, and the women's state offered services and helped to organize everyday life.

In what ways these models survive or are reformed dur ing the present age of transition, is a challenge for their supporters.

Time for a New Gender Contract

Eventually, times were changing. Society was being modernized and, from the 1960's on, women were no more pleased with their "public maternity". They wanted conquer new areas, they wanted to be leaders. They wanted new respect – and better salaries – for their special skills, e.g., their social capability. As a result of great amounts of political work by women, and with more and more support from men, the formal equality got new pushes: The Council for Equality between Men and Women was founded in 1972 under the Ministry of Welfare to begin the official work for the gender equality. The first Act of Equality between Women and Men was accepted in 1987 (now under reform). Since then there has existed an Equality Ombudsman, too. Official groups for gender equality were founded in communities, offices and all kinds of working places. The last and previously "forbidden" profession, the clerical office, was opened to women in 1988. Until now, the army is not open for women in Finland, although there are demands for it. Interestingly, also a few men have used the possibility to seek for justice via the Equality Ombudsman's office.

In the last election, the Finns chose to the Parliament a larger share of women than ever before in any country (80/200). In the presidential election this spring, 1994, we had two strong candidates in the final round. The female one came second with 46% of votes. Finnish women see this situation as a turning point.

In the library world similar problems could be seen only partially. Libraries being a traditional women's area the majority of librarians has always been female and majority of chief librarians, too. Nowadays, 90 per cent of all public librarians and 80-85 per cent of chief librarians are women. However, in the research libraries the situation is different. There also ca. 90 per cent of all librarians are female but the chiefs are more often men than in public libraries. Among all the people active in the library field, in Finland, a great majority is female.

I think, there are two reasons for why women have occupied leading offices in libraries. Firstly, the tradition and the working culture have given women better support in their work than in most other countries. Secondly, and more wretchedly, the low salaries and the low status of librarians haven't locked men to these positions.

New Methods to Reach Equality

One element has been unchangeable during the whole process of the equalization. Appreciation of traditional women's work and their

capabilities has been lower than that of men. The 1990's has begun with efforts to find solutions to this problem. At least one methodological study (2) and some local studies have been done to find ways to balance different skills, responsibility, strain and working circumstances of a profession. These studies were requested by central labor market organizations.

Another recent gender question is how to implement quotas for both genders in certain institutions (educational, state and communal organs, etc). Preciously they were not actively demanded in Finland, but now, in conjunction with the reform of the Act of Equality between Women and Men, people are speaking about the good experiences with quotas in Norway, which have influenced positively especially politics.

As I've mentioned before, the appreciation and image of librarians in Finland is as poor as anywhere, but, amazingly, the image of libraries is not. According to my own evaluation, people in Finland are as conscious about the importance of libraries as one could wish. For example, this spring we collected easily more than 550.000 signatures (ca 11 per cent of the total population) in support of an appeal for libraries. We do not yet have clear ideas why librarians are not as well appreciated as their institutions. Maybe we have not popularized librarians' work enough. The old cliché about reading as librarians' work is still alive.

Differences

Which differences can be found between women and men as librarians? Nothing is very clear. It seems that differences between individuals are more remarked than between gender groups. Amongst both sexes persons who choose librarianship are more introvert people, also in Finland. First, I will present some criticism on women: They are slow to adopt new technical innovations. An acute problem in Finland is telecommunications. I would argue, that if we had more male librarians, our electronic network would be much further developed than it is now!

What is, according to my experience, very positive in most female librarians, is that they don't waste their time and energy in power struggles. Working groups, meetings, executive boards are concentrating primarily on the matter at hand and very seldom in prestige problems. I do meet such problems mainly when cooperating with "outsiders". But on the other hand this fact has also a negative side: I think women do even avoid power too much. When we come to a conflict situation, we are too helpless. Everything is OK, and most women are very capable, as long as all participants in a situation are willing to find a common ground. However such can not be the case always.

An interesting group to compare with librarians is that of information specialists, most of whom are working in the private sector. In Finland they have their own education, even their own culture. Again, the great majority of leading persons are female. In my opinion, these women are the strongest leaders in the field of libraries and information services. They have

learned more effective leadership in their private enterprises, and they have in many cases succeeded in conquering good positions through their own work. They are more goal-orientated, I think, than library leaders on average. Librarians have something to learn about here.

Important Issues

I have mentioned above that Finnish men have changed as well as Finnish women. Indeed, they have become more equal – through force of circumstances. But new generations, especially highly educated men, are ready to go further in this direction. When I think of men I know, their reason to adopt these attitudes towards equality is their democratic mind. They wouldn't feel at home in a paternalistic milieu either. They have found new elements in themselves; for example, they seem to be very keen, active and warm as fathers. A great majority of fathers nowadays take the possibility to use part of the legal maternity leave. This part naturally shortens the mother's leave. These important indicators were presented in a recent dissertation (written by a male researcher). It is very clearly different to co-operate with this kind of men than with traditional authoritative men. In international contacts one sometimes experiences this difference very strongly...

Of course we have a good selection of traditional paternalists in Finland too, but nowadays their fate is in my eyes more pitiable. In public discussions they are in a very bad position, even outlaws. The researchers and specialists on labor studies argue today, by a common consent, that the days of paternalistic bosses and small-scale tyrants are over. What is needed in modern working communities are quite different capabilities: team-working, equal negotiations, a really independent status for every working partner.

The last of demands above can be traced to a change in the work itself. Our society is on its way from an industrial society to an information society. In these new circumstances the quality of work becomes more important than mass production. Quality can only be produced by people who themselves are consciously responsible for their input in the working process. Subdued and controlled people are not such.

Another focus in the working life of the information society seems to be that different professions and branches compete for talented students. Since the importance of talent nowadays is found in the brain and not in the muscles, there is no sex limitation. I have read many articles and seen advertisements where industry tries to persuade girls enter into engineering and other traditionally male fields for education; companies want the best brains.

In my opinion, the need to get all the best brains to work will be the key element, in Finland as everywhere, in reversing the backlash against women's position. Problems caused by this new segregation according to talents will be, I guess, no more a problem of gender but that of social equality.

References

1 Liisa Rantalaiho. The Gender System of the Finnish Society. In: Liisa Rantalaiho (ed.). Social Changes and the Status of Women. Univ. of Tampere, Centre for Women's Studies and Gender Relations. Working Papers 3/1993. Tampere 1993.

2 Juha Vuorinen et al. What Does the Job Demand? A test study to develop job evaluation schemes. An English extract. Helsinki 1993.

LIBRARIES AND WOMEN LIBRARIANS: A CUBAN WOMAN LIBRARIAN'S POINT-OF-VIEW

Marta Terry

Director

National Library of Cuba

Havana, Cuba (1993)

Abstract

Many people think that librarianship is a feminine profession just as they think about teachers. Perhaps these two professions have common characteristics. There exit, however, some figures which will help to demonstrate the number of women librarians and women teachers in Cuba. This paper discusses some of the trends of women as librarians in Cuba.

Introduction

An in depth psycho-sociological study may be needed on the causes of why the common people are used to identifying certain professions with womanhood or femininity. It may also be necessary to include in the study the cause for retirement of men – as well as the advancement of women – in certain professions. Teachers, nurses, librarians, secretaries, tourists guides, among others, are considered women's occupations. Above all, woman is defined as that human being called mother, the reservoir of life. (1)

It may also be thought, parting from this truth, that all those jobs or professions in which profile there can be distinguished features such as caring for, giving shape, teaching, being kind, being patient, smiling, giving guidance, soothing – that all these be considered primarily feminine. I think, those features are valid and deserve an in depth study. It's very likely that there already exist hundreds of studies, but what I want to stress is that the same feature is valid in my country: Libraianship and teaching are professions in which woman has an almost omnipotent presence.

Libraries and Women Librarians – Teachers and Schools in Cuba

Taking into consideration the entire public library system, there are, in Cuba, 15 provincial libraries – one for each of the provinces, 168 municipal libraries – one in each municipality save one, and 201 branch libraries; all these together give a nationwide service. In the library system, that has as its methodological center the José Marti National Library – Biblioteca Nacional José Marti, are working 353 women and only 24 men at a level that requires a university degree. Unfortunately, we do not have the number of those librarians who have lower level education divided by sex. Yet by a simple observation we know that around 90 per cent of them are women.

As a part of information that I think might be of interest I present the following figures of the people who are working in the National Public Library System:

Librarians (university degree)	377
Technical personnel	1.220
Clerical workers	496

I think it is also interesting to observe the distribution of the managers: in the 15 provincial libraries, 13 directors are women and 2 are men. Women stay as directors on the average for 5 years.

At the José Marti National Library are working 295 employees: 243 are women and 52 men. Out of the 19 departments 13 have a female director and 6 a male director. Regarding the salary policy, there are various scales following a professional scheme: Librarians belong to the Group XI of University graduates. That means that their salary is regulated as follows: The first two years, after graduation and if a person has had a fair evaluation of his/her performance, he or she (shall we say 'she' all the time?) receives $231.00. A new evaluation of her performance after two years will make that librarian to reach a salary of $265.00. This salary scale is equivalent to that of Informático "B" and its abbreviated job description includes: Selection and acquisition activities; bibliographic description; primary attention to readers; attention to collections and stacks, etc. (2)

The category of Informático (computer specialist) "A" may be obtained only after working at least for 4 years as Informático "B" and, naturally, having a good evaluation of his or her performance. The corresponding salary is $265.00. After two years of following the pattern already described, the salary is raised to $280.00 and after other two years it may be raised to $295.00. A short job description in this category includes the following: To design selection and acquisition policies for the library collections; to make and apply information retrieval and processing languages; to have control of the application of standards for bibliographic description; to elaborate bibliographic catalogs; to establish and control preservation and conservation policies and technologies; and to apply, in general, new technologies in the library work. (3)

For a woman librarian, like for a woman teacher, the Cuban social system guarantees one month's paid vacation per year and, in the case of maternity, the present laws grant her the right to received 60 per cent of her salary and a non-paid license until the baby is one year old. The same right is granted for the mothers whose children are under the age of 16, in the case they fall ill or have any other impediment that prevents them from attending to their jobs. This regulation means that it is not allowed to nominate another person to a woman's position while she is on maternity leave.

It may very well happen that some of you ask whether all these regulations are kept even during the hard times in which we are living in Cuba. We shall answer this question with the following paragraphs from the *Proceedings of the Continental Meeting: The Cuban woman in the nineties: Realities and challenges. A solidarity encounter – Procedimientos del Encuentro Continental: La mujer cubana en los 90: Realidades y desafíos. Un encuentro solidario*, that took place from March 7 to 10, 1993 in Havana:

...Far from reducing the action field of social security this has been broadened... because social security is a non-renounceable responsibility of the Cuban State... particularly in the case of women since 1974. A specific law so launched which, among other benefits, grants a paid license for a term of six weeks before childbirth and twelve after childbirth. This paid license was widened recently, during a special period (July 10, 1991) until the child would be six months old, with the possibility of being extended non-paid for other six months. (4)

A working woman – that is to say a librarian or a teacher – has the right to retire from her job at the age of 55and, after 25 years of labor activity, she may continue to work beyond that limit until she wants or her strength allows. The salary she will receive would be equal to 50 per cent of the higher salary she has received during five years out of those ten during which she has been working. As retirement is not compulsory, for each year she continues working after the retirement age limit, the amount of money she will receive will be increased 15 per cent each year. That amount also will be increased by 13 per cent after five or more years she has continued working beyond the retirement age limit fixed by law.

Education

As it is well known, education has become one of the most outstanding successes of the Cuban society built after the 1959 revolution. Different types of schools and educational institutes are well spread throughout the country. According to the UNESCO Statistical Yearbook 1992, there were 9,417 schools; 71,887 persons are working in schools; 56,072 or 78 per cent are women, the figures corresponding to the year 1989. It is easy to see that the number of women was already reaching to 90 per cent. (5) It is not the objective of this paper to deal with the immense world of education in Cuba, instead our purpose is only to point out the similarities between librarians and teachers. I think that further studies should be done following this line of thought.

Women as Library Users in Cuba

I think it is of interest to look at the behavior of women as users of the public library system in our country. The research department of the National Library – Departemento de Investigaciones Histórico Cultural de la Biblioteca Nacional José Marti reports the following:

During the last years women attendance to the public libraries has been somewhat more numerous than that of men. This behaviour has a better correspondence with the sex composition of the Cuban population than the behavior observed in previous years. Women represent more than 50 per cent of the population. This information is obtained by the systematic research on the use of public libraries in Cuba that started in 1981. The latest figures from this research show an nationwide random sample of 9,664 readers or users out of which 4,927 or 51 per cent are women and 4,737 or 49 per cent are men. (6)

We have started this short paper by referring to the working conditions of our colleagues, librarians, and our sisters, teachers. It would be unfair though to think those achievements were not linked with the history of women in our country and their fight to get social acknowledgement and equality that only reached a full recognition with the revolutionary event of 1959.

As early as in 1869, during the First War on Independence, at the moment the Constitutional Assembly was to take place, a Cuban woman, Ana Betancourt, asked for the floor to address the Assembly and to state that in the same way that the Assembly had ruled that Cuba should be freed from Spain and there should be freedom from Negro slavery, the Assembly shoulöd take into consideration also to warrant the emancipation of Cuban woman. (7)

Mariana Grajales is the symbolic figurehead of Cuban mother and woman. She was the mother of Major General Antonio Maceo y Grajales, the warrior of our independence wars.

Historians have named him as "the Bronze Titan" because of his brave strength and intelligent performance during those 19th century wars and also because of his racial condition – he was a mulatto.. The story goes that when he was wounded in a combat and brought to his mother to be cared for, she exclaimed that she did not want any tears and commanded her youngest son to get on his feet and continue the struggle for independence in which the whole family was involved. Many stories can be told about Cuban women fighters who have become heroic revolutionaries and social fighters.

In the most recent history of the middle of 20th century Haydeé Santamaría and Melba Hernández constitute a symbol of feminine presence. They were the only women who took part in the assault to Moncada Caserne on July 26 in 1953. For their courage during those events they are known as "the Heroínas del Moncada", because "... never had such a high place of heroism and dignity the name of a Cuban woman ..." (8) Many librarians also contributed to this fight for our final independence according to their possibilities. Maria Teresa Freyre de Andrade, Blanca Bahamonde, Blanca Mercedes Mesa, Blanca Rosa Sánchez all fought for cultural, social and political goals. Their names appear also as founders of the library movement we have tried to describe in this paper.

We cannot leave outside our theme but must bring into your attention the role played by the feminine revolutionary organization called The Cuban Women's Federation – Federación de Mujeres Cubanas. founded in 1960, that has fought and continues to fight for the social welfare of Cuban women and children. This organization involves over 80 per cent of Cuban women, and its principal mission is "to carry out the health, education, labor and social security programs – to create new laws for popular benefit and specifically for women and children..." (9)

Conclusion

Finally, the Cuban women, a librarian as well as a teacher, engineer, farmer, unmarried mother, old woman, girl, young adult, black, white, they all are protected by a social system that has as a motto or a slogan the complete equality of its citizens; that discrimination by race, color of the skin, gender, national origin, religious beliefs and anything against human dignity is banned and punished by law; that all the citizens "have access in accordance to their merits and capacities to all State positions" and that they shall "receive equal salary for equal work".

The women librarians, as we have demonstrated, have the same status as any other professional according to their studies and their intelligence. They have a full opportunity to realize themselves as human beings.

Bibliography

1 Martí, José. Obras completas. La Habana: Editorial Nacional de Cuba, 1963-1973. 28 t.

2 Cuba. Leyes, Decretos, etc. Principales disposiciones sobre Seguridad y Asistencia Social. La Habana: Sección Territorial de Trabajadores Civiles de las FAR, 1989. 251 p.

3 Op. cit.

4 Cuba. Comité Estatal de Trabajo y Seguridad Social. Código de Trabajo / Comité Estatal de Trabajoy Seguridad Social. La Habana: Centro de Divulgación e Información Laboral de CETSS, 1985. VI, 100, 20 p.

5 Encuentro Continental de Mujeres (3° : 1993: La Habana) La mujer en los 90: realidades y desafios. Un encuentro solidario. s.n. 7–10 marzo, 1993. 15, 4 p.

6 UNESCO. Statistical Yearbook 1992. Paris: United Nations Educational, Scientific and Cultural Organization, 1993.

7 Setién, Emilio. Informe correspondiente 1 1992 del Problema Ramal Bibliotecas y Promoción. Informativa Cultural. 1993. 12 h.

8 Castro Ruz, Fidel. History Will Absolve Me. Havana, Cuba: Radio Havana Cuba, 196-. 176 p.

9 Espin, Vilma. Discurso ... La Habana: s.n.. Encuentro Continental... op. cit..

10 Cuba. Constitución de la República de Cuba. La Habana: Editora Política, 1992. 59 p. Esta Constitución proclamada el 24 de fébrero de 1976 contiene las reformas aprobadas por la Asamblea Nacional del Poder Popular en el XI Período Ordinario de Sesiones de la III Legislatura celebrada los días 10, 11 y 12 de julio de 1992.

TO MAKE WOMEN VISIBLE

L. A. Glinskikh

Municipal Association of Libraries

Ekaterinburg, Russia (1998)

Abstract

The idea of the creation of a Center for Women was shaped under the influence of a whole bunch of different factors – economical, political and social. Literally to say, this idea came from the air – the current situation with women's unemployment, health and their position in family and society is so disturbing and frightening that our library system could not let these problems to exist without any attempts to solve them. It is worth of mentioning that the overwhelming majority of librarians as well as library patrons are women, so the conceptual frame of a center sounded absolutely convincing for the Administration of the library system and for the library staff.

The Library was founded on the base of the public library in the distant city district, where there were no other organizations in any way linked with information, reading and culture in general. The first thing we did was to create the strategic documents, intended to help the library in its future work.

The main conceptual document among them was the library statute. This statute stated the main mission, goals and aims of the newborn center. The main goal of the center, for example was: To help the process of cooperation of women of this community in order to help them with the solving the problems of education, information access, recreation and social rehabilitation.

It was a suggestion by Library Administration and Committee, that the work of the Center could be organized in the following directions:

1. To investigate and study the needs and demands of women-patrons of the library.

2. To create of the specialized collection of books and other printed materials for women according to revealed necessities.

3. To create of the specialized system of informational service for women and members of their families.

4. To organize the consulting and information services for women with the help of professional lawyers, doctors, social workers.

5. To create the effective charity system, intended to help the families with the small income, 'one parent' families, retired patrons and patrons with disabilities.

The content of the work included both traditional and innovative (for our library system services for example:

- informational (selection of the literature on the special topics; preparation of the reference materials on special themes and topics, organization of book displays, the Days of Information and book reviews)

- recreational (different types of hobby-clubs, literary associations, and initiative groups)

Also, I would like to say some words about the library structure, management and staff.

Editor's note: The paper is available only in Russian on IFLANET; Conference Proceedings 1998. Code number: 122-122-R.

THE ROLE OF WOMAN LIBRARIAN IN THE DEVELOPMENT OF INFORMATION STRATEGIES AT THE UNIVERSITY OF HAVANA

Barbara Susana Sánchez Vignau

Department of Scientific-Technical Information

University of Havana, Cuba (1999)

Abstract

The use of information and communication technologies in the Cuban universities is a factor of vital importance for the development of these academic institutions. However, work in the process of computerization implies great changes in the current functions of our university libraries and their personnel. New times bring into development new modes of production, processing, access and transfer of information with the help of data suitable for the functions of our organizations, and in this process the woman librarian becomes a factor of vital importance.

This paper will consider the marked preliminaries and describe the process of change which has been initiated, in the Department of Scientific-Technical Information (DSTI) of the University of Havana including the Department of Strategy, with the participation of our female professionals.

1. Information in the Models of Change of the Universities

All the time we participate in a variety of changes in society which are all influenced by political, economic and technological currents entailing multiple effects in all organizations, including those of information. In them, however, the most important change of paradigm pertains to access. Access to information both from the qualitative and quantitative points of view implies certain social changes, as the inviduals who are best informed and have access to more information can take actions of major importance in more areas than individuals who have limitations in their access to information.

University as a social organization moves into new models, directed towards educating qualified individuals for professional functions, but it is also committed to generate useful knowledge for the development of society, thus the necessity to articulate information and knowledge in university at the end of this century and in the beginning of the next century. But – how to do it? This way of thinking results in working on different administrative viewpoints than before. It not only permits the incorporation in the society individuals whose education is based on a certain culture of training, but it also makes necessary to act in an articulated manner in the employment, in a rational and objective way, of information and communication technologies, in which university libraries occupy an privileged level.

Tendencies which operate in the information world in general and in organizations like universities in particular suggest the following: in a multifunctional university information and knowledge determine the basis of all processes and, in some more than in others, communication is the environment of interchange of knowledge par excellence. If information and knowledge are the key elements for the function of a university system, each thought or action related with them, their content, quality, opportunity, currency, pertinence, way of handling, transmitting, acquiring them, etc. plays an essential role in the betterment of the quality of higher education.

Change has appeared as subject in all the discussions, which have closely touched on the future. Their contents at the moment seem to include the power of information and the development achieved by the new information and communication technologies (NICT).

Universities as scientific and academic organizations have a double necessity: (a) to bring them up to date and include them in the production and diffusion of knowledge; and (b) the synthesis of the enormous quantity and variety in which information is presented, and the knowledge of current scenarios.

The modern society has become involved in one of the transformations, and the tiny driving engine of knowledge has, since a long time, had one name – universities. It's impossible to speak of advancement without mentioning the role these institutions have in the education of professionals who present the reality and turn into concrete results the long periods of preparation and improvement.

In this advancement of universities the library is a primary actor in the use of information and new medias of information, if the following is taken into consideration:

- Education and communication are the most secure medias for transporting information.

- Technology has created environments, which permit the interaction, transportation and dissemination of knowledge to the most remote places on the Earth.

- There exists truly surprising medias for maintaining, sharing and transfering knowledge.

- The modern world is a global village, where the barriers of time and distance are disappearing.

- It's possible to participate in the process of developing networks, which are completely transparent and highly competitive.

- The production of knowledge is becoming a decisive factor id the competitive position of a country, an industry, a company or an individual, and

- One must learn to utilize existing knowledge for problem solving.

From the quality of the process of information management depends the productive and creative insertion of academic communities into a society. which is advancing in an irreversible manner. From its strength and organization will depend, in the first place, the scope of the production of knowledge. Therefore, there is need for new types of information management models in libraries, which contribute to achievement of this objective, paving with it the way for an information culture, which contributes to the total quality demanded by organizations.

The library prototype has changed due to the massive entry of technology in all of its functions. The paradigms in the environment of information management have been destroyed opening up the entrance for new forms of interaction between the technology and the individual. The popularity of computers has allowed for a great number of users to have access to a PC, and this intense relationship of the society with technology has modified the design and offering of services. The way of interacting and communicating with users of information has transformed an conformist user into a demanding client who asks for a more systematic and efficient access to information.

University libraries must go, for the purpose of completing the tasks and demands of the scientific community, from the traditional model of management to a model of electronic library, in which a cooperative leadership will prevail having focus on client-user. There will exist also an interdependent structure and will stand out information resources managed basically in a working group and formed in such a way that the development of its components and quality are its foundational basis.

Library is a social enterprise whose mission it is to offer specialized services to students, professors, researchers and managerial staff in order to satisfy their educational and information needs by means of human and technological resources, which contribute to improvement of plans and programs for instruction – at pre- and postgraduate levels – and for research. This shows the peculiarity of spending money for producing something and then giving it away and, on the other hand, information is the only product which is used without paying for it: it is born to be shared. Without commercializing the subject, we would like to say that information with an added value will become the most important material of the most important products in the next millennium.

Our universities need to promote and support these new types of work projections relying for this purpose on their information tools or libraries, but there exists also need, in both cases, to implement and harmonize horizontal structures with the support from the new information and communication technologies (NICT).

For the new millenium, the university library is committed to centralize services to users, flatten its hierarchical structure and offer novel and better services just in time to satisfy the changing needs of the user-client. For all these reasons it is important prepare leaders to plan for initiating and carrying out the library's mission, in which nothing should be as certain as the satisfaction of the individual for whom we're working, because it is the leaders who determine the mission of an organization and the guidelines of a process.

In order to achieve efficient management, the university libraries must:

- guarantee their leadership role
- become the principal consultant or advisor in matters regarding information or, in the same way, the principal constituent of the decision-making system
- use adequately the technologies of information and communication (TIC)
- transform the information systems
- contribute to the immediate re-qualification of human resources to enable the required role in "the era of information"
- prepare information products of high added value in order to guarantee excellent services.

In this context important tasks are open for our libraries, which inevitably should abandon their historically passive role and assume a transformer's role; because on the one hand it is the universities where information is highly valued as a resource of resources, a product of developing the actual process for knowledge production. On the other hand, it is the universities, which own to a great extent the potential energy for proactive transformation which, in turn, the society should realize in order to meet the current and future challenges. The model library of the next millennium also needs to achieve new leadership positions where each generated process needs a coordinator and the library altogether a special leader who understand the past but doesn't let himself become limited by it.

For the next few years, it is not so important to take care of naming our organizations whereas the importance lies in not losing on the mission of their role while developing new paradigms. Libraries could continue as libraries although not as places where collections of books and other documents are kept and where dominates as well an organizational structure in support of the collection but as an organization which satisfies its clients knowledge, information and documental needs and has a goal a service culture. Use of technologies should amplify the client's options by offering new services, previously out of reach, and in this way to bring about the desired transformation.

There exist a direct link between the tendencies to employ the NICT and to apply new management models, in which can be identified as protagonists the human resources which facilitate the leadership of our organizations. This position has was traditionally occupied by a woman, who, due to the characteristics of activities in librarianship, became from the beginning chosen their fulfillment.

Whenever we recall libraries, we see a sweet woman appearing to guide and orient us to a book or a particular theme, and although times have changed with the appearance of the Internet, electronic mail or magnetic disks, woman continues to present the information activity of organizations, now with new preparation and new knowledge.

On the treshold of a new millennium, woman is getting involved in new activities in the computerization of libraries, combining in a balanced manner the execution of traditional activities with those which guarantee transition to the new model of an electronic library.

2. Occupations of Information Professional and Technician in the Information Department

The Department of Scientific-Technical Information (DSTI) is a member of the University Council of the University of Havana and is in charge of the methodological direction of the 20 libraries of the Faculties and Research Centers. It is responsible for acquiring, processing and distributing the information from the departments: technical services, information services, publications and printing and automation.

The university library and the network of libraries in the faculties and centers have been developed to the level which corresponds with the information needs required by the level of education achieved by the country and they make available traditional services as well as services assisted with information and communication technologies. Since the 1980s has been achieved a research plan in library and information science, programs for users, teaching information technology as a subject within the project on information culture which has been developed in the University of Havana for the preparation of professors and researchers of different faculties and research centers of the Institute of Advanced Studies.

There exists a plan for (self-) improvement for information professionals which covers the whole network of university libraries in the country and in which the Department of Information works as the leading organ of the information network of the Ministry of Higher Education, having the most experience in organizing periodically courses, seminars and consultancies for different Centers of Continuing Education and Centers of Higher Education. In addition, it is charged with a budget for purchasing documents, a collection for reference work, and tools for research by means of the Internet.

Starting in 1987, the first computers were acquired for processing in order to generate the first databases of the library with the introduction of CDS/ISIS. The collapse of the socialist system caused a deep economic crisis which had impact on the whole Cuban society; the country lost more than 75% of the import from socialist countries which affected purchase of petrol, food products, consumer products, raw materials, medicines, etc. Also it tightened the blockage of our country preventing in many occasions negotiations with other countries. Nevertheless the state directed all its efforts in keeping the educational centers and universities open and, in order to minimize the impact on medical services, some actions were taken in economic terms. However, this situation affected the libraries so that information centers of some enterprises had to be closed or they had to re-orient their services.

In spite of the mentioned situations, in 1992 there was acquired the minimal equipment for creating the first local network of the university library: two computers, one server and one modem; this network was connected with the XTs in the departments. The Ministry of Higher Education began to acquire the series of the Current Contents as one way to provide up to date documents for the whole system of higher education. This service was started in the library in a centralized manner for that segment of users who were in charge of the most prioritized research in the University of Havana, due to the fact that the faculty libraries neither had the necessary equipment nor the services available, and the reference personnel could not attend to all the needs of the university. The reference specialists began to realize interest profiles for 12 research groups for which were provided a search service and the entry of documents of personal character to date.

During these years was also started the introduction of other concepts in the library and information field's activities which, although they did exist, were not part of the vocabulary of Cuban librarians; for example, information management, strategic planning, management by objectives, marketing, mission, vision, added value products, reengineering, and others. When facing this new wave of terms it became essential to prepare specialists in new conditions imposed by globalization. Offering courses on strategic planning of information services, marketing, accounting, new technologies, and guidelines for information policies was initiated. Courses were started on planning strategies for information services, marketing, management, new technologies, and guidelines on information policies. This new culture was slowly incorporated into the language used by specialists and technicians, because in 1994 NICT began to establish bases for necessary change and prepared a development program for the University Library's network. This network included alleviating the library's problems and drawing up a legal document, which is being revised and outlines strategies needed to carry out the plan in new conditions.

2.1. Management Strategies at DSTI of the University of Havana

The definition of our mission – "To provide specialized information services to students, professors, researchers and administrative personnel in order to satisfy their professional and informational needs via those human and technological resources which contribute to the improvement of the plans and programs for instruction and research in the University of Havana" – together with management by objectives and establishment of criterias for measurement identify objectives for reaching agreement with the university's objectives. The proposed objectives aim: to achieve a situation in which by year 2000 eighty percent of users evaluate good the information services and information resources; to lead to an optimal use of the Current Contents service for professors, students and researchers; to provide academic journals in a current form and for work with their electronic versions. In addition, to guarantee for students, professors and researchers access to the services on Internet and electronic mail; to ensure that thirty percent of workers will be prepared through courses for diplomas, master's or doctorates; to facilitate the university library network's moving from traditional libraries to electronic libraries by offering to each library the necessary equipment and methodological attention, courses and advice. To realize projects for financing some activities and providing personalized service to those researchers who are engaging in the priority investigation at the University.

All these details have evolved from revival of the mode of action, because although the current changes in the libraries have a lot to do with new technologies, also the change in people's minds is decisive.

On the strategic planning of information systems CEPAL explains that "betterment of information units is focused in terms of:

- Earmarking greater financial resources, personnel, physical space, etc.

- Modernizing of operations, in general, by automation of technical processes, services and communications.

- Cooperating among the information systems units.

Although these aspects contribute to the betterment of the current situation, in many cases it has favored the patron of existing services without pointing our any change in the patron himself or herself. The use of microcomputers has been used to do the same things instead of doing them in a more efficient way and not for making the final outcome more flexible according to the need.

The concept of change covers modifications, foundations, and eliminations so that sometimes problems can be operational, political, institutional or related with performance. The idea of change consists of going from the current situation to a future situation, which supposes changes in processes, management styles, products and services. In this change environment has great importance.

The NICT-UH has to change its institutional paradigm due to being conscientious of the need to better its organization. For this end there are at work together number of activities, which have as their purpose to make better its participation as well in the top level of the university as within the system of scientific-technological information of the country's universities.

However, the work to measure anew the role of university library activities now does not cause reengineering of all the processes. It is not sufficient to know only the unavoidable need to reconfigure the library but to know those factors, which are leading to this change. Help from some circumstances is important even although they're not completely developed in the institution, because they assist advancement in this sense. They are as follows:

- Existence of an information culture inside and outside of the library which permits efficient handling of services and products:

- Developing information managers.

- Making possible awareness of information products as part of the result from the fundamental processes of institutions in higher education (research, teaching and extension work) .

- Including pre- and post-graduate academic programs, which will lead to the development of management of information.

The strategic management process in the NICT, thus, will result in a beginning of a phase of changes given the existing conditions. In the same way can be employed a strategy that within the organization allows to obtain relevant results, for which it's necessary to develop it together with strategic functions. These functions determine those areas in NICT-UH, which will become pioneers in the change process and, therefore, become susceptible to new levels of development.

Development activities affect four big areas which are: (a) organizational structure and linking system; (b) management of human resources; (c) Use and management of NICT; and (d) production of new products and services. The results of the change process have been mediated by the following strategies:

- Development of the library's organizational structure with a vision directed towards implementing horizontal structures, which permit harmonizing diverse processes as part of the informative library activity.

- Work for strengthening the network of faculty and research center libraries at the UH.

- Establish a linked system with the Faculty of Communication, especially with the area of Library Science and Information Science.

- Prepare a local network to guarantee the availability of and access to scientific, technical, corporate and electronic support, including the use of Internet.

- Develop products and services of a new kind in manual or automated form, which will ensure satisfaction of the user community's educational and informational needs.

- Establish cooperation and exchange programs with university libraries in Latin America and the Caribbean.

- Accelerate the education and development of the area specialists, as well as the strategic and applied research activity in this field.

- Improve work on publication, printing and commercialization of the scientific jperiodicals at UH. All the strategies listed above are in accordance with the mission of DICT and the operational objectives of UH and the Ministry of Higher Education in terms of the computerization of our universities.

To what extent have women influenced the results of the strategic project at DICT-UH?

The Department of information of the University of Havana employs the total of 60 personnel of whom 80 per cent are women. They are qualified professionals and technical staff with ample experience, which has made it possible for them to participate in the process of change with good quality work and excellent capacities in their functions. The process of change in the Information Society has prepared way for redesigning work in our libraries with a new meaning, which is special to those who work in universities. This has influenced the work realized by our institution by ensuring that specialists and technicians change into knowledge managers par excellence and make adequate use of new information and communication technologies in order to retrieve valuable and important results. The excellent work in information management performed by women in our department has guaranteed a good academic and research management of our university.

With the participation of our professionals and technicians and working towards the desired move, our organization could show the following results:

- The first CD-ROM was developed including Proceedings of the IV Seminar on Latin America and the Caribbean.
- Electronic mail service was provided as well as access to CD-ROM databases.
- Manual catalogue was converted into an automated catalogue with the possibility of immediate access via library network.
- It was made possible to offer new information services to privileged research groups through connection to the Internet.
- Work was started on reengineering of the synthetic analytical processing of information, with the help of NICT.
- There was enhancement in research and development in different areas of library work.
- A program on information culture was iniciated both within and outside of the organization for advancing quality in library management and for academic research activity of UH.
- Information professionals have acquired new levels of specialization for inclusion into managing their work.

An additional element in all this activity which involves women in the process of computerization of UH, can be identified their participation in a permanent manner in the Department of Women's Studies (Catedra de la Mujer), which is developed in the university environment, where have been developed varied services on the theme of women, and thereof, elaboration of informative products on the special subject, especially on a data base with approximately 1000 entries.

The Central Library as a member of the Department on Women's Studies contributes to the information assessment of investigation that is being developed not only by the UH but also by other organizations involved in women's studies in our country.

Conclusions

As it has happened in other areas of knowledge, woman in the library activity has occupied an important position. Librarian's professional image has moved from formal entering of document to participation as concultant and assistant in every organization. The introduction of new computer technologies has allowed the her better quality of management and thus greater excellence in her contacts with her clients. This reality has been a necessary paradigm for the woman in our Department on Information of the University of Havana, where without her participation and action it were impossible to perform the work realized through computerization in our Institute of Advanced Studies.

References

1. Alba. Luis. El profesional de información y los cambios globales. Temas para un debate. In CEPAL/CLADES. "Tres Enfoques sobre el nuevo gestor de la información".

2. Alvarez Martínez, Adrián. Administración del cambio: Un modelo integral de capatación. Soluciones avanzadas, 25–30, Junio, 1997.

3. Artiles, Sara; Adrián E. Cancino; Fidel García. La reingeneria de procesos en los sistemas de información. El caso de la Universidad de Camaguey. Octubre, 1998. 22 p. Paper presented at IV Taller de Bibliotecas de América Latina y el Caribe.

4. Benítez Cárdenas, Francisco (et al.). Calidad de la Educación Superior Cubana. Ciudad de la Habana, [s.a.]

5. Cornella, Alfonso. Los recursos de información, ventajas competitivas de las empresas. Madrid, McGraw Hill, 1994. 181 p.

6. CEPAL/CLADES. La información en contexos políticos y decisivos. Santiago de Chile, Naciones Unidas, 1993. 69 p.

7. CEPAL/CLADES. Planificación Estratétiga de sistemas de información documentales. Santiago de Chile, Naciones Unidas, 1991. 45 p.

8. Crespo, Manuel. La transformación de la universidad en cara al siglo XXI. In La Educación Superior en el siglo XXI. Visión de América Latina y el Caribe. Caracas, Venezuela, CRESAL/UNESCO, 1997 (vol. 2), pp. 31-146.

9. Cubillo, Julio. La búsqueda de nuevos liderazgos organizacionales en gestión de información en América Latina y el Caribe. In La Educación Superior en el siglo XXI. Visión de América Latina y el Caribe. Caracas, Venezuela, CRESAL/UNESCO, 1997 (vol. 2), pp. 997-1008.

10. Fernández-Aballí, Isidro. Nuevas Tecnologías de la Información y la Comunicación: Las transformaciones universitarias en vísperas del tercer milenio.

11. Caracas, Venezuela: CRESAL/UNESCO, 1996.

12. García González, Fidel. La Universidad del sigle XXI como un modelo de industria de la información y el conociemiento. Camagüey: Oficina de Promoción e Imagen, Universidad de Camagüey, 1998.

13. Conference organized by el Centro de Gestión de Información de la Universidad de Camagüey.

14. Guerrero, Liliana; Ma. Teresa Hernández. De la generencia de información a la inteligencia social. Ciencias de la Information (Cuba) 28 (4) diciembre 1997: 251-259.

15. Lafuente López, Ramiro. Conocimiento y uso de las nuevas tecnologías de la información y la comunicación. In La Educación Superior en el siglo XXI. Visión de América Latina y el Caribe. Caracas, Venezuela, CRESAL/UNESCO, 1997 (vol. 2), pp. 897-976.

16. McAnally Salas, Martha. INTERNET: una alternativa para el futuro de las bibliotecas. Octubre, 1998. 25 p. Paper presented at VI Taller de Bibliotecas de América Latina y el Caribe.

17. Morris, Daniel; Joel Brandon; Reingeniería, como aplicarla con éxito en los negocios. Santa Fé de Bogotá, McGraw Hill, 1994. 297 p.

18. Patterson Hernández, Mariela. Información y mercancía: En busca de una explicación. With Larissa Viciedo Tigera. Tutor: Lic. Radamés Linares Columbié, junio 1998. Thesis for the Licenciate decree in Información Científico Técnica y Bibliotecología. Facultad de Comunicación, Universidad de la Habana.

19. Ponjuán Dante, Gloria. Gestión de Información en las Organizaciones: Principios, conceptos y aplicaciones. Chile, Centro de Capacitación en Información, Universidad de Chile, 1998.

20. Rodriquez, Leida. Pasado, Presente y Futuro de la Biblioteca Central. Octubre, 1998. 5 p. Discussion paper presented at VI Taller de Bibliotecas de América Latina y el Caribe.

21. Rodriquez Reyes, Victório. Los servicios de información en el próximo milenio. In La Educación Superior en el siglo XXI. Visión de América Latina y el Caribe. Caracas, Venezuela, CRESAL/UNESCO, 1997 (vol. 2), pp.1035- 1058.

22. Tapscott, Don; Caston Art. Cambios en los paradigmas empresiales. Santa Fé de Bogotá, McGraw Hill, 199?.

23. Webb, T.D. La biblioteca "congelada": un modelo de cambio para las biblioecas del siglo XXI. Programa de gestión de información. Santiago de Chile: CEPAL/CLADES, 1996. Mimeographed material.

GOVERNMENT PROGRAMS AND PUBLICATIONS ON WOMEN IN CUBA

Mercedes Verdeses Vázquez

Director of the Information and Documentation Center

Federation of Cuban Women, Havana, Cuba (1994)

Abstract

A general overview of various programs organized by the Cuban Governemnt specifically for women. Campaigns originated by women themselves and products of information that by different ways reached women and the general public as means to involve them in these programs in order to achieve proposed results.

Government Programs Directed to Woman in Cuba and Their Effects

The 35 years that the Cubans have dedicated to construction of the social project that was initiated at the triumph of the revolution, on January 1, 1959, have made radical changes in the country, changes that distinguish it from countries in the so called Third World, also called developing countries, currently also called countries of the South, as their location in the southern hemisphere characterizes their economic and social underdevelopment. From the revolution's first moment onward the government focused its attention on finding answers to women's situation.

Cuban woman, present in all struggles, participated resolutely to ridding the country of colonialism, later of neocolonialism, and to reaching a revolutionary triumph in 1959. Women were 55 per cent of the illiterates, their incorporation in the work force was poor, according to the census of 1953 they were about 17 per cent of the work force, while many were domestic workers and helpers in bar; it was calculated that only 12 per cent were occupying productive and dignified jobs. Life expectancy of these women was 63.8 years and out of their children more than 60 in a thousand born alive died before reaching one year of age. Thirty-five years of common effort, political will to make social changes starting from a a decision to advance justice, achieved that, as our Chief Commander Fidel Castro said, "... there was a revolution within another revolution". For this reason, in spite of being a country blocked to live her worst economic crisis in our history, we can show advances reached for Cuban women. They now form more than 60 per cent of the qualified work force, their incorporation in dignified occupations and with all social rights is 39 per cent of the active labor force of the country. Their life expectancy is 77.6 years, and infant mortality is 9.4 per one thousand born alive, that makes them more secure and complete mothers.

In the following we will refer to some programs of the government that have had influence in these achievements and that through generated information resources allow us to show to librarians how they can find all this information via our network of libraries and information and documentation centers. Some of the programs created by the Cuban revolutionary govenrment for women are shown.

National Program on Maternal and Child Care

The purpose of this program is to raise the level of health and the rate of satisfaction of the population by means of prevention, promotion, protection and recovery of pregnant and not-pregnant women, the child and adolescent, provided by the National Public Health System in coordination with other state institutions, cooperation of mass organizations and active community participation. The general objectives are: to improve both quantitatively and qualitatively gynecological, pediatric and adolescent services by prioritizing risk groups as well as to decrease maternal, infant, preschool, school-age and adolescent mortality, to decrease the incident of low weight of recently born and to adapt the organization and function of health services to women, children and adolescent by following changes in the nuclear family. Among its specific objectives are: to link the family doctor's work with the activities of the program of services for mothers and infants; to increase health education for women in the community; to raise the quality level of gynecological services; to decrease mortality of mothers; to enhance services both prenatal and in child birth; to improve services during pregnancy; to advance services for abortion and to contribute to the development of research on maternity and child health.

Information generated in this program can be found in the annual reports on public health in Cuba and in annual demographic reports. Another manner of retrieving information are leaflets, books, posters and folders produced by the program as well as presentations and projects of specialists.

Program Hospital Friend of Child and Mother

The general objective is to achieve a situation in which all mothers breastfeed their babies with the mother's milk as the principal nutrition during four first months. Among the specific objectives are: to guarantee that the program is realized in strict relation and within the framework of the national program of services for mother and child of which it forms a part. Other specific objectives are: to adapt health services for gynecological services with facilities in proximity and breastfeeding at child birth; also action will be taken to allow for change of attitudes and behavior of the people in order to achieve completely the practice of breast-feeding.

This program, realized in Cuba since 1991, the year the country found itself in deep economic crisis, lacks sufficient resources from national sources and therefore libraries have leaflets that contain the definition and action plan of this program. Other materials available are projects and presentations created by our specialists, but at the moment reference materials are from international sources.

Program on Sex Education

The Resolution 293 of the president of the State Committee on Labor and Social Security 1989 authorized the creation of the National Center on Sex Education as an independent unit of the National Health System, in a unit under the central level of the Ministry of Public Health, exclusively for economic purposes from some insurance. In this governmental action women could see institutionalized the work performed since 1977 the National Working Group on Sex Education as an auxiliary structure of the Permanent Commission of Services to Infants, Youth and Equal Rights for Women of the National Assembly of Popular Power (Parliament).

The purposes of this program were directed towards preparing Cubans as to be able to distinguish that sex education is not only about intimate sexual relations or related activities that result from intimate sexual action like pregnancy, abortion, sexually transmitted diseases, but that they could identify the term sex as a sexual role. To have a desired child, to love him, to educate him according to his sex also is sex education. Thus, the main objective of this governmental effort is to give to an individual from childhood on "tools" and "instruments" to grow selfconfident and to know how to make decisions and to have an adequate self-esteem. In our libraries you can find books and leaflets on this theme published by the Group, videos, reports, specialists' presentations and projects, posters and folders and results from workshops of the community.

Program Early Diagnosis of Cervical Cancer

This program was established in 1967 in order to investigate the morbidity and to diminish mortality from cervical cancer by detecting it at its earliest stage possible to provide for early and efficient therapy. The program is basically based on primary services by means of inquiry on cervical cancer in the female population starting from 20 year olds who have had an active sexual life, and repeating the test every two years. The program has as its goal to rech 80 per cent coverage in 1995 and 100 per cent in 2000.

Until the creation of the service of family doctor in 1984 the bringing of women to get gynecological tests as well as the control of them was in the hands of the health officials of the Federation of Cuban Women. For this reason we can find in our libraries multiple materials on this subject created by women's organization and directed to women. Another way to find information on the results of the program are annual reports of the Ministry of Public Health, theses, specialists' works and presentations, as well as nationally produced books and leaflets.

National Program Early Diagnosis of Breast Cancer

This program with national coverage functions at the primary level of health services by means of questionnaire on risk factors to the female population with age 30 or more. Based on this questionnaire will be selected a risk subpopulation for mammography examination and the rest for an annual clinical examination. All women over 50 years of age also have a mammography test.

The objectives of this program are: to reduce the mortality from breast cancer in Cuba, to increase the survival rate of breast cancer patients, and to better the quality of life of these patients. This program has a system of statistical information where the program is controlled and evaluated. In libraries one can find annual reports of the Ministry of Public Health, books and leaflets on this theme, folders and videos that teach women themselves to do an examination of breasts. There are also works and presentations of our specialists.

Program on the Improvement of Women

Since women were at educational disadvantage, 55 per cent became literate in the literacy campaign of 1961 and 59 per cent of literacy workers at the end of the historic epic and when the country was declared free from illiteracy, it was decided to create the Program on the Improvement of Women. The first activities were performed by the Federation of

Cuban Women. In this way were created schools for household workers, a school for farm workers, "Ana Betancourt", that brought to the capital city daughters of farm workers and gave them minimal education at the same time teaching them dressmaking; at graduation they returned to their original homes with necessary tools and a sewing machine as to multiply the effect of their study.

Other areas in which this program worked was the creation of Pedagogical Institute Makarenko for teachers of primary school and also the opening of classes for the improvement of housewives. In these classes for the improvement our housewives studied to the 6th and 9th level in excellent campaigns until 1985.

With these achievements the program had other dimensions. Currently, the Adult Education in the Ministry of Education, with coordination of the Federation of Cuban Women, continues its wor in ways that are more in tune with current needs. Women that for some reason have no education are being rescued and given attention either at home or others in adult education classes. As result of this community work and based on the needs found dressmaking classes are offered in the regions as well as classes in office work, computation, etc., that serve as basis for incorporating housewives into work. The remaining women study in the national educational system.

This program has existed more than 30 years and has produced information in may different forms. Its results can be found in the reports on completed courses of the Ministry of Education. In addition, to learn about courses, forms and contents, one has manuals, readers, textbooks, study programs, etc., that are available in our libraries.

References

Cuba. Ministerio de Salud Publica. 1989. Programa Nacional de Atención Materno Infantil. La Habana, MINSAP, 59 p.

Cuba. Ministerio de Salud Publica. 1993. Programa de Acción para el Cumplimiento de los Acuerdos de la Cumbre en favor de la Infancia: Segundo Informe de Seguimiento y Evaluación. La Habana, MINSAP, 65 p.

Instituto Nacional de Oncología y Radiología. 1993. Informe del Departmento de Programa de Salud del Instituto Nacional de Oncología y Radiología.. La Habana, INOR, 20 p.

Interview/Entrevista: Realizada al Lic. Jaime Canfuz, funcionario de la Dirección de Educación de Adultos del Ministerio de Educación de Cuba, que atiende el Programa de Superación de la Mujer. La Habana, 27 de abril de 1994.

II. PROFESSIONAL STATUS AS A GOAL

THE STATUS OF LIBRARY WOMEN IN JAPAN

Yoko Taguchi

Professor of Library Science
Kyoto Seika University
Kyoto, Japan (1994)

Abstract

This paper outlines two surveys conducted on behalf of the Research Committee on the Problems of Librarians, the Japan Library Association (JLA). The first survey, among personal members of JLA, was carried out by FLINT (Feminist Librarians' Network) in 1987. The second survey, conducted in 1992, covered temporary workers in public libraries in Osaka Prefecture. The discriminatory status of library women in Japan was revealed through these two studies. Also discussed is FLINT: its origin, rationale, activities, and problems.

1 Introduction

Libraries have been expanding their services along with the economic development of the country. We have more libraries, more books and other materials and, maybe, more support from users. Now, libraries face the collapse of the "bubble" economy as well. As early as the 1980s, the national government adopted a policy of personnel reduction, which gradually spread into local governments. This resulted in a severe impact on libraries. At the same time, public demands regarding libraries had been increasing because of the modernization of library activities since the 1970s. The 1980s saw the introduction of the notorious "three no's": no increase in personnel, no increase in budget, yet no decrease in the services. Proposals to build local libraries were often campaign pledges made by politicians running for public office. People in small towns were demanding their own libraries.

How were these conflicting issues harmonized – dramatic increase in library services and comparative decrease in the number of public servants – in the 1980s and now? One solution was an increased employment of so-called "temporary" workers.

1.1 Definition and Background Information

Many institutions still retain the traditional lifetime employment system, with a seniority-based wage structure, under which employees are seldom dismissed. This has been understood as the best way to secure employee loyalty to the employer. This has contributed to the stability of the society. It has also maintained the status quo. Some employers have found that this arrangement is not always convenient in the current economic transition. The mass introduction of "temporary" workers gradually spread to the area of service professions. This happened at the time when many women – young and middle-aged – poured into the labor market.

It is necessary to understand what the term "temporary worker" implies. In Japan there are many titles for those who work under a "temporary" status. Many of them are not temporary workers in the full sense of the term. The Ministry of Education uses the term "non-regular assistant" versus "regular staff". The most generally used terms are "part-timer" or "part-time worker". Some workers call themselves "part-money workers", which may sum up the fragile status of these workers. They often work six to eight hours a day and 30-40 hours a week. They are paid per-hour wages which are often much lower compared to per-hour equivalent wages paid to full-time workers. They do not receive additional benefits. The majority of the "temporary" workers are women: usually those women who are returning to the labor market after some years of child rearing, and some young women who are looking for full-time or full-status library jobs. In general, they are well qualified and dedicated to the profession in spite of their fragile status. Patrons seldom realize who is "temporary" and who is not.

2 Invisible Library Women

There has been a general feeling among women librarians of their powerlessness and invisibility, despite their great number. An informal estimation figures that women comprise more than 60 per cent of the total library work force. There are more female students than their male peers enrolled in diploma courses of library science. We see many women working in libraries. Yet, very few women hold the top decision-making positions in many areas of our profession.

How many people are working in libraries and how many of them are women? How many female library directors are there? What is the ratio of women among "temporary" workers? We do not have sufficient data in order to answer these questions. There is a striking contrast between abundant data accumulation in the area of library collections and the services and the scarcity of data in the area of library personnel.

In a 1978 survey, 1.8 % of public libraries were headed by female directors, and the figure increased to 3.7% in 1985.(1) According to my rough estimate for this paper, this figure had increased to 7.6 % by 1992. (2) More than half of those women are heads of a branch library. Among libraries serving larger populations, the percentage of female directorship decreases sharply. There is no female head among libraries serving communities in which population exceeds 200,000. While women comprise 44% of full-time employees, more than three quarters (76%) of the temporary workers are women. (3)

According to the Ministry of Education's Library Statistics of Colleges and Universities, (4) there are 8.290 full-time and 4,335 temporary workers in 534 universities and colleges. Women comprise 53% of full-time employees and 77% among temporary employees.

As positions of academic library directors are traditionally and often as a rule occupied by professors, the number of female heads does not mean much for the purpose of status analysis. It simply shows the status of women academics. There exist no national data which show the composition of junior and senior management ranks by gender.

The school library is a typically feminized field. Women comprise 95% of employees in this type of library. About a quarter (24%) of people working in school libraries are employed as "temporary" workers. (5) Though this figure may appear to be better in comparison to other types of libraries, school libraries are not seen as enviable workplaces. Even full-time librarians are often underpaid.

3 Library Personnel Surveys

The absence of comprehensive statistics was our major concern. The FLINT (Feminist Librarian's Network) survey (6) is one of the earliest studies involving feminist consciousness from the very beginning of constructing the questionnaire. The survey of temporary workers (7) is more recent and seems to function as an encouraging documentation for some temporary women workers.

3.1 FLINT Survey

This was the first survey covering both male and female members of the most comprehensive library association in Japan. In order to carry out the survey we asked the Research Committee on the Problems of Librarians of the Japan Library Association (JLA) to give us official recognition.

In June 1987 we mailed questionnaires to 700 members of JLA. The membership directory, which lists 5,375 personal members, was stratified according to eight geographic regions. The total 700 random samples were chosen. We received 467 usable responses from 237 women (51%) and 230 Men (49%). They were analyzed from three points of view: all responses, full-time librarians, and full-time librarians with four-year college background. The questionnaire consisted of 33 questions covering four major areas: status and career, professional activities, demographic aspects, and two open-ended questions on the respondent's attitude toward librarianship and moral support received. The chi-square test and t-test were applied to the coded answers of the first three areas, while qualitative techniques were used for the last two questions.

Women and men were represented in different proportions in different types of libraries. About a half (n=107, 48%) of the men were employed in public libraries compared to 83% (39%) of the women. While 38 (18%) of women were working in school libraries, only one man was employed in this type of library. Of 22 library science faculty, 18 (82%) were men and 4 (18%) were women.

Of 467 respondents, 391 (84%) indicated they were employed full-time; 35 (7%) of the respondents were temporary workers. Of those full-time employees, 193 (49%) were female and 198 (51%) were male. Of the temporary employees, 19 (54%) were female and 16 (46%) were male.

Despite the general understanding that it is rather unmannerly to ask someone's income, the response rate was very high among the employed (98%). The median annual income of women was Y3.000.000-3.990.000 and of men Y.000.000-5.990.000.

As far as job rank was concerned, men had more staff members working for them than women did: 77% of women and 41% of men did not have subordinates. No women and 15 men (8%) in our sample were classified in the top administrative level.

Salaries in many Japanese bureaucratic institutions are based on age and seniority. The age limit (often 28 to 30) for the employment of full-time civil servants is a common practice, which is not generally considered to be discriminatory. Age is one of the major factors, which influence the income. The average age of female librarians was 38 years (median 37) and 42 (median 40) for male librarians. The age distribution of men showed the M-shape, which is often referred to as a typical age distribution of the female work force. A similar pattern was observed in another survey on public librarians. (8) This might indicate two different types among male librarians. One possible interpretation involves one group of people holding librarian's diploma and another group being without diploma but with more administrative experience in the parent institutions.

Significant differences in status between women and men were identified in all three groups. Among the full-time librarians significant gender-based status differences were observed, even though there were no significant differences in many other aspects including their professional involvement and years of work experience.

3.2 Temporary Workers Survey

The problems of temporary library workers are another serious concern.

Many of them are not members of any library associations, as we found very few in our FLINT sample.

A working group was organized on behalf of the Research Committee on the Problems of Librarians of JLA in order to conduct a survey on temporary library workers in Osaka. The purpose of the survey was twofold: firstly, to clarify the actual situation of the temporary workers, and, secondly, to grasp their views and opinions.

With the assistance of Osaka Public Library Association, two sets of questionnaires were sent to all public libraries in the prefecture of Osaka: one was an institutional survey and the other was to be distributed among the temporary workers in each institution. The report analyzed 255 usable responses (59%) from 216 women (85%), 34 men (13%) and 5 which were not gender-specified (2%).

Compared to the survey of public libraries in the prefecture of Osaka (1986) (9), this 1992 survey showed an increase in the number of temporary workers from 164 to 435. The working group suspects a further increase in the number of temporary workers flowing the subsequent full introduction of the five working day-week for local government employees.

Age distribution showed a sharp contrast between men and women. The median age of men was above 60 and of women 40-44. The age distribution of men suggests that temporary positions were chosen after mandatory retirement. In case of women, there were only 8 (4%) who were above 60, and 158 (73%) were between ages 25 to 54.

The survey of individual workers did not include wage questions. Though it was not easy to compare the real working conditions in different institutions based on job titles, the majority of men (n=22, 65%) were employed with favorable conditions compared to those of women (n=48, 22%). It also identified more than five titles for those temporary workers. Concerning the librarian's diploma, 10 men (29%) and 108 (50%) were qualified. Not much difference was found in the general educational background of men and women.

Frequent turnover was quite common. About three quarters of the responses (n=186, 73%) indicated less than 5 years of work. The seniority system usually does not favor temporary workers.

There was an open-ended question, which asked respondents describe "what one feels at one's work place". Among 233 responses, 155(61%) – including 19 men (56%) and 134 women (62%) – answered this question. The answers were analyzed and classified into three categories: working conditions (n=98), library services (n=78), and others (n=25). Respondents generally expressed high morale and commitment to the work in spite of their discouraging conditions.

The working group concluded that present library services depend heavily on the employment of those temporary workers. It insisted that the local governments should offer stable and agreeable working conditions to the temporary workers and transfer the full-time equivalent temporary workers to regular full-time employee status.

4 Conclusions

Since libraries ceased to be storehouses and librarians became more than mere guardians of books, public demand for better library services has been growing. Many young men and women have been employed during the period of library development since the 1970s. The FLINT study suggested that women might not be going up the library ladder at the same speed as men. The temporary workers survey indicated an increased number of such workers in Osaka Prefecture as well as their dedication to library services and anxiety about status at their work places. The majority of library women and in particular temporary workers, as the minority citizens of the country, comprise the base of library work force.

Library work is a labor-intensive field. Consciously or unconsciously, increased employment of temporary workers was a convenient solution to satisfy the so-called "three noes". It is essential to point out that such a practice is a simple case of discrimination.

Many tof the findings of these surveys were not at all new to us. Though they were shared knowledge among those who uphold more than half of the library services, it was important and essential for us to point them out as exact facts drawn out of scientific research. These are the surveys that professional associations like JLA should conduct more regularly together with their annual library surveys. The greatest reason that urged these groups to conduct surveys almost on their own may be their belief in the educational power of research and documentation.

5 Networking and IFLA

FLINT was established by twelve library women in 1984 (a year before the UN Nairobi Conference). It is intended to function as a nonhierarchical network for those who are interested in and committed to issues resulting to women's rights as well as library services.

The formation of FLINT was a result of our anger regarding women's status in our profession. We became organized in order to show our determination to make changes. In order to transform our anger into a healthier energy, we have meetings, lectures, newsletters, and some projects as instruments for networking. We are proud of our two projects: one is the membership survey of JLA, described above, and the other is a brief survey of female directorship.(10) Though it is more time-consuming and not always very successful, another important activity is consciousness-raising. There are members who have found their jobs through this grass-roots network.

Maintaining and expanding a network like FLINT is getting harder. Recruiting new and young members is one of our current problems. Many of us are in our forties now, and it is getting harder to put more of our time and energy into activities outside our immediate work. Taking the FLINT study as an example, we did almost everything by ourselves: preparing the survey, conducting it, coding the data, inputting, analyzing and, finally, writing a report as well as funding the study. We could barely manage the whole process for three years. I do not think I could repeat the whole process of the survey in the same way. I believe it is a legitimate task of the national library association.

I owe so much to the library women in other countries, especially the women in the United States for what they have done in the field of feminist librarianship. They have carried out so many surveys and documented cases for the improvement of the status of women in librarianship. As our societies and cultures are different, it is neither possible nor wise to copy what they have done. Yet our sisters overseas provide good examples. We have to invent instruments, which will be more functional in our society.

I have been investing a certain amount of energy and a little money into the development of the women's group in IFLA simply because I have hopes for its international influence. It may be possible for IFLA to pass some resolutions for the purpose of the promotion of library women's status. IFLA may be able to recommend member associations to carry out periodic status surveys in countries and regions where such surveys are needed. The Round Table of Women's Issues may function as a kind of catalyst in this respect. It is my sincere dream that this new Round Table be a meeting place as well as an international network of networks of library women with varying needs and dreams.

References

1. Kamitani, Nobuko. "Kokyotoshokan no shokuin kosei". Gendai no Toshokan 24 (1986): 231.

2. Nihon Toshokan Kyokai (Japan Library Association). Nihon no toshokan 1993 (Tokyo: Nihon Toshokan Kyokai, 1993): 281-340.

3. Kamitani: 228.

4. Monbusho (Ministry of Education). Heisei 5nendo Daigakutoshokan jittaichosa kekkahokoku (Tokyo: Monbusho, 1994): 3-12.

5. Zenkoku Gattoshokan Kyogikai(All Japan School Library Association). Gakkotoshokan hakusho (Tokyo: Zenkoku Gattoshokan Kyogikai, 1983): 193-211.

6. FLINT Librarianship Study Group. Nihon Toshokan Kyokai kojin kaiin jittaichosa hokoku (The status of women and men in Japanese librarianship). (Tokyo: Nihon Toshokan Kyokai, 1989).

7. Hiseiki Shokuin Jittaichosa Working Group. Toshokan de hataraku hiseiki shokuin (Temporary workers in the public library: a survey in Osaka Municipalities). (Tokyo: Nihon Toshokan Kyokai, 1993).

8. Maeda, Hideki. "Koritsutoshokan no josei shisho wa ima". FLINT Nyusu 9 (April, 1971): 4.

9. Maeda, Hideki, et al. Koritsutoshokan no shokuinzo. (Tokyo: Nihon Toshokan Kyokai, 1991).

10. Kamitani: 228-231.

TRANSITION OF LIBRARY AND INFORMATION SCIENCE EDUCATION IN CHINA: PROBLEMS AND PERSPECTIVES

Dong Xiaoying and **Zhang Shuhua**

Library and Information Science Department

Peking University (1996)

Abstract

Education of library and information science in China is in the period of transition and reformation. Development and application of information technologies have put forward new requirements to the professional personnel. The growth of information industry and expansion of labor market has motivated library schools to adjust their objective, curriculum and knowledge structure in order to meet social needs. The article discussed the changing of social environment in 1990s and their challenges to professional education, and the responses from library schools. The author made a survey on the curriculum of 17 schools in order to fine out their structure and cognition among teaching institutions. The difficulties and problems in educational reform are discussed and the trends of professional education in China are predicted.

Introduction

The development of education and training programs in the field of library and information science has been a common topic for international discussion. The wide application of information and telecommunication technologies and rapid growth of information industry has been leading the world into the information age. The technologies of information processing, the formats of information storage and channels of information dissemination have been changed so fast that updating knowledge and skill in the professional education are becoming a constant work. The new requirements and challenges from the profession and society have continuously driven educational institutions to refresh their curriculum and to expand teaching programs. The task is particularly urgent and serious for the fast changing country like China, since most curricula were established during 1980s, which can not meet the new environment of 1990s.

The first library school in China was found in 1920. During 1949 1979, there were only 8 library schools nationwide. Since 1978, the open door policy and reform have brought an unprecedented development of librarianship. According to the statistics of 1996, in the past 15 years, the numbers of public libraries have increased 105% (from 1256 to 2579), children's libraries have grown 110% (from 7 to 77), and the university libraries have risen 80% (from 598 to 1080). The requirement for qualified librarians has stimulated the growth of professional education at both university and college levels. Under the circumstance, the numbers of library schools have increased into 55. Among these schools, 19 are national universities which under the supervision of the National Education Commission, 21 are regional universities that are administrated by local educational bureau, 12 are financially supported and directed by the ministries affiliated to central government and 2 belong to military universities.

Since 1990, the increasing of library schools has slowed down. Education for library and information profession has shown the trends of paying more attention to quality than to quantity, and the programs are more diversify than unitary. The multi level education and training programs have been set up nationwide. There are 3 Ph.D. programs (Peking University, Wuhan University and Chinese Academy of Science), 11 Master's programs, 24 Undergraduate programs and many other continuing professional education programs. Some schools have provided part time undergraduate and graduate programs for experienced librarians and information specialists. Both the education and the academic status of Library and Information Science were recognized by the highest national academic institutions. In 1993, Library and Information Science was listed at the top level, at the first time, by the National Academic Commission. In 1994, the Guideline of National Social Science Foundation was first catalogue Library and Information Science and Documentation as an independent research area.

Social and Economic Factors Impact on Professional Education

During 1990's, the social and professional environment has experienced obvious changes compared with 1980s in following aspects:

Firstly, the emerging of information industry and new type of information services. China is the fast growing market in developing and application of information technologies in the world. The profits of information industry, for instance, have increased 10 times in 1995 compared to 1990 (from 50 billion yuan to 500 billion yuan). The hardware sold in 1994 increased 54% compared to the year before. Since 1994, the global upsurge of information highway has also strongly impacted on Chinese decision makers. Chinese information superhighway, which consists of "Eight Golden Projects", CHINANET, CHINAPAC and CERNET are involving in construction of information networks among banks, customs, enterprises and educational and research institutions. The expansion of market economy has stimulate d the growth of more efficient information services. Consultant companies, which cover many specified information service areas, have reached into 40,000 in 1994. The openness and repackaging of information resource for more efficient dissemination under networking environment are catching higher attention by both government and users.

There are 1200 Chinese databases and some on line services are available. The importance of information resource has been generally recognized as a strategic resource by government, industry and general public. In April 1994, when China got its first direct Internet link, there were only 1,000 users. Now there are 8 Chinese networks connected with Internet and the users have increased into 100,000 and keep growing. Following the rapid application of information technologies and telecommunication in social sectors, many professions are required information management expertise. The emerging of new information sectors has changed the profession into a multifarious situation. It is a new occasion for the expansion of library and information education, particularly to re-modify multilevel objectives and to update core curriculum in order to provide student's abilities of wide adaptability in job market and in life learning.

Secondly, the labor market of library and information institutions is becoming stable. During 1980s, because of the rapid growth of library schools and many opportunities of part time study and in service training available to practice librarianship, the educational backgrounds of library staff have changed a great deal. The proportions of library staff who had university degrees (as Table 1 indicated) have increased from 10% to 40 64%. The large and urgent requirements for personnel are no longer existed.

(Editor's note: *Table 1: Educational background of librarian in different libraries, not available, please contact Author.*)

Thirdly, the social value inclines to more emphasis on commercial benefits. During the transition period from planned economy to market oriented economy, the non-profit institutions, which mainly depend on government budget, have involved in a very difficult situation. In spite of the annual budget increase, many libraries are still faced with the problems of funding shortage resulted from the price increase of publications. The annual collections are getting smaller and some experienced librarians are looking for higher pay in other professions. Government has made a new policy to encourage libraries to find ways to support themselves. Some libraries have successfully gotten donations from business or from overseas, others are trying to make profits by the ways of renting space, offering public entertainment or providing fee-based information services; the rest are struggling for survival. The commercialized, social atmosphere has also had influence on students' attitude toward job selection. As Table 2 indicated, during 1986 1988, 90% of graduates from the library school of Peking University chose to work in various types of libraries. During 1990 1992, the students who voluntarily went to libraries and information centers took only 22%. In 1994, 16% of students chose to work in libraries and information centers. While more than one third would more like to work in joint venture enterprises, computer companies or higher pay professions.

(Editor's note: *Table 2: Job selection of graduates from Peking University from 1986 to 1994, not available, please contact Author.*)

Fourthly, the pressure from economical and market factors on education. During 1990s, Chinese universities have been adjusting their structure and composition in meeting with the new requirements of society. The emerging professions, such as law, economy and business, management and computer science are attracting more students while humanities and basic sciences are shrinking. Moreover, the change of university policy from free of charge to tuition required have pushed students and parents to considerate more carefully about the cost effective of educational investment and future options in job market. If educational institutions cannot meet the social requirement and can not provide good job opportunity, students would be reluctant to enter the subject field. All these factors, no matter positive or negative, have impacted on the educational reform in library and information science. There is pressure from surrounding on universities, that if you keep still, you will be left behind of the time.

The Adjusting and Reform of Library and Information Education in China

The first indication of changing came from the rename of the educational institution from library and information science into information management. In 1992, The Department of Library and Information Science, Peking University, first changed its title as Department of Information Management. Until March 1995, there are 26 schools or departments changed names as information management, information resource management, information technology and decision-making etc. Some schools, without changing their names, also start to update their curriculum.

It was a controversial issue in discussing whether the school name should be changed. The scholars who support the change suggested that information management, which broaden original coverage of library science into "wild adaptable areas related to information production, information collection, information sorting, information storage and information dissemination. The aims of information management are to provide services for different sectors, professions and users, including library, information center, archive, consult, business, enterprise, news agency and government institutions. The area of information management should include scientific information management, business information management, government information management and cultural information management. Although the subject areas are different, the basic principles and methods are general applicable". Some other scholars expressed their worries about the change. They appealed to keep sober mind in transition period, while many thing are still confusing and indicated that changing name is a of lost confidence on the profession.

The changing name not only brought in fresh air and opportunities of development, but also induced some confusion and problems. After establishing a stabilized teaching system and curriculum, the changing and updating of established ones, increasing equipment and information material, bringing up to date faculty's knowledge are becoming very difficult and money consuming. The other problems, such as how to adjust structure from library and information science into information management, and how to integrate modern technologies into traditional courses are still heavy tasks to be solved.

After renaming, some schools started to adjust and expand their objectives from just affording personal to library and information center to "provide senior information management staff who will take responsible to information collection, system design and analysis, information processing, information services for government, science and technology, culture, education, industry and business institutions" (Peking University). Since adaptability to new emerging professional sectors and long term development are becoming more important, the teaching program should "strengthen student's ability on understanding and using the basic principles and methods of information dissemination and communication in various environments and to apply information technologies to handle different information systems" (Nanking University).

The Survey and Evaluation of Curriculum of Library and Information Science

The change of name is only a prelude. The updating of the curriculum is the substantive progress of educational reform. Based on the 17 curriculums from different schools nationwide, Table 3,4,5 has listed required courses, specialized elective courses and non specialized elective courses according to the frequency of a course appeared on the curriculum. The survey aims at finding the curriculum composition, cognition and whether these courses can match with information management.

(Editor's note: *Table 3: Frequency of required courses in 17 schools, not available, please contact Author. Table 4: Frequency of specialized elective courses in 17 schools, not available, please contact Author.*)

The curriculums from 17 library and information teaching institutions have shown that

(1) three groups of courses, which cover rather comprehensive fields of library and information science, are demonstrated to be mixed with both tradition and modern technologies;

(2) the current courses on information management mainly based on library and information science. As Table 3 indicates th at traditional course, such as classification or

cataloguing, are still take very important position in core courses. The coalition between old and new programs is not established;

(3) there are certain level of cognition on core curriculum among different teaching institutes;

(4) the framework of curriculum, particularly the inherent connection between courses and the sequence in proper order, which develop from general to more advanced ones, are still not very clear;

(5) subject orientations are not solid enough to training students to become a subject specialist.

From Table 5, we can find that non specialized elective courses include mathematics, economics, sociology and other subjects. Since most undergraduates only major in library and information science, it is very important to encourage them to have a solid background and training in either social sciences or sciences and technologies. Since 1980, many educational experiments have been tested in Chi nese library schools, which try to provide a more comprehensive training at undergraduate level, but very few continued. In 1979 1980, Peking University, for instants, had required students to study in other schools or department, such as biology, computer science, economics, history, economy etc. for two years before they start to learn library and information science. The department also set up a Master's program, which was offered to the students who already had a degree in other subject fields. The experiment did not last long because of management difficulties. Now, undergraduates can study for double degrees in bachelor level, with extra one year longer, in the fields of law, intellectual property or computer science. The program should expand to many other subjects, but the decision will be depended on university administration.

(Editor's note: *Table 5: Frequency of appearance of non-specialized elective courses in 17 schools, not available, please contact Author.*)

When the objectives of professional education and frameworks of curriculum have been established, it is very important to deepen and expand it based on the development of information technology and social need. So the whole courses be more organic, solid and systematic rather than scattered. For library and information science, constantly assimilating the knowledge and methods from relevant a nd periphery subjects is inevitable, while keeping the identity of library and information science in an interdisciplinary environment is also very important. Considering the special need in China, the framework of information management should consisted of following parts.:

Information management. The management from macro point of view will include information policy, information legislation and law, information systems and structure. The method and theory of micro management will focuses on certain type of institutes where special circumstance should be considered..

Information technologies and their applications. The courses on information and teleco-mmunication technologies should be consolidated in order to help students no only able to use and understand the system, but also can maintain and operate on them. That means, they need more strict scientific training rather than just eliminating illiterate computer knowledge.

Information processing and access. To be the mean of effective information manage-ment, the basic principles and methods of information processing and retrieval are always core and basic part of the professional education. Information technologies are changing the way of information processing, but the nature and target are still the same. Any new theories and technologies are targeted for mo re efficient management of information should be included.

Communication and telecommunication. Networking has changed the traditional patterns of communication, information dissemination and sharing. There are many new research areas appeared following the expansion of international networking, from both technical, human to social aspects.

Management and use of subject information resources. Tremendous growths of different formats of information resource have made information retrieval more complex and difficult. More subject specialists are required in information management and reference services. The subject information that can be divided by subjects (such as social science information, science information, law information, business information, government information), by types (such as serial, rare books, tradition Chinese document) and by formats (such as printed material, CD ROM, on line and multimedia) is still very important part in core curriculum.

User studies and information marketing. It is necessary to let students keep in mind that no matter what kind of technologies has been developed or what kind of interface has been designed, to satisfy user's need are always our aims. These concepts should be particularly emphasized in China, where former planned economy used to neglect user's need and orientation, which also influenced on library and information services.

The Problem and Trends of Professional Education

The educational reform on library and information science is a long-term process that never reaches a final settlement. The process should keep balance between considering both need of job market and establishing a solid foundation in academic environment. In the meantime, the library and information science is facing with a more severe competition and challenges situation from both professional practice and university education, since information industry is becoming the backbone of national economy and highly demand in market. Educators in library and information science in China should be more sensible to the social environment in order to hold on their position and to strengthen the ability in replenishing the subject. Here are some suggestions:

• Establishing a comprehensive objective for education and training programs. The department of information management should establish a more clarified and concrete multi level objectives that can be put into practice step by step.

• Setting up a systematic and integrated curriculum. The framework of curriculum in information management should cover the most important knowledge and technologies in the procedures of information collection, information processing, information storage and retrieval, information dissemination and communication, information service and system evaluation.

• Combining research, teaching and practice and establishing a close relationship with all of them. Traditionally, theoretical studies published in Chinese professional journals are used the method of philosophical thinking. Since there are many new topics appeared during professional development, problem solving is more important. Researchers should come out from ivory tower and to face with reality by establishing closer relationship with practitioners.

• Strengthening national administration and coordination between educational institutions. The National Education Commission has selected 12 courses as required ones for professional education. Scholars in each field are invited to compile a guideline for each course. But the guideline might not meet the special interests and local requirement of each institution. In spite of the contradiction between national unified program and diversified of local needs, quality control and evaluation of curriculums from a national level are still necessary.

Based on the current situation in China, we may predict that

- the programs of professional education will be more diversified in meeting with various needs in society;

- the popularity of information network will promote Chinese educational programs and curriculums approaching to international standards;

- the changing of job market and application of information technologies will have stronger impacts on education system;

- the curriculum will becoming more comprehensive and harder after continuously updating and assimilating of knowledge and techniques from relevant subjects fields.

References

1. Jin Feng, The Objectives and curriculum for the higher education of library science in China. Dissertation of Master's degree. Peking University. 1995.

2. Chinese information policy on science and technology, Chinese Information Report, June. 1995.

3. Wang Wanzong, Training information specialists for the professional development. Proceeding of 2nd Seminar on Library and Information Science Education Between China and Taiwan. Aug.1994.

4. Li Jinzheng, Information management: The inevitable trends of library science education, Journal of Chinese librarianship, Vol.1, 1995.

5. Peng Peizhang, Education reform of library and information science and discipline building. Proceeding of 2nd Seminar on library and Information Science Education between China and Taiwan. Aug.1994.

6. Wang Shiwei, The puzzle and solution after changing the name in library and information science. Library Journal (Chinese), Vol.1, 1995.

7. Chen Shaonang (transl.) Educational reform of Library and information Science in Britain. Library and Information Work. Vol. 2, 1995.

8. June Kinoshita, Scientists hope competition will improve Internet access, Science, Nov. 1995.

PROPPING UP "HALF OF THE SKY" IN THE LIBRARY
PRESENT SITUATION AND PROSPECTS OF CHINESE FEMALE LIBRARIANS

Huang Xin

Deputy Director of the Library at Guangdong University of Foreign Studies,

Guangdong, P.R.China (1996)

(Translation into English by Professor Yiding Lee)

Abstract

Female librarians make up 60 per cent of the professionals in China's libraries. These huge human resources demonstrate an important standing and play a significant role, known as "half of the sky" in library service. They are the main force of the library, achieving excellent results in helping the success of teaching and scientific research. Chief librarians, shouldering heavy administrative tasks, are particularly brilliant stars with style and features of the era. The achievements of women librarians are admired by all the people.

However, due to the influence of feudalistic ideology and restrictions of subjective and objective factors, the overall quality of Chinese librarians is yet to be enhanced, and their talents and potentials are yet to be brought into a full play. Facing the near 21st century and opportunity and challenge in social reform, people should, starting from education, give female librarians more care, show more solicitude and support so that they can develop their spirit of self-esteem, self-confidence, self-reliance and self-improvement. Chinese women librarians should go all out and usher in a brighter future for China's library service with their wisdom and loving hearts.

A legend in Chinese mythology is widely circulated: In remote antiquity, when the columns holding up the heaven were broken, the sky was falling, a mountainous fire was burning, and a flood was surging, an empress called Nuwa made five-colored stones to mend half of the sky which had fallen down, and blocked up the flood with reed mortar. Thus, the Humanity had a narrow escape. From that time on, Nuwa has received the admiration of all Chinese peoples of various dynasties.

This is a myth. But in reality, on the vast Chinese territories a factual coincident with the myth has appeared: The Chinese females, making up 48.48% of the total population of China and having both talent and power, are creating wonders greater than the ancient empress Nuwa in every sector of social and economic life. They are propping up "half of the sky" in China, and they are metaphorically referred to as China's "half of the sky".

Half of the Sky: the Position and Role of Female Librarians

It is not an overstatement, if we describe the position and role of Chinese female librarians as "half of the sky" in China's library profession. From the point of view of quantity, according incomplete statistics, there are 2,200 staff members in Guangdong's public libraries, among them 1,400 are females, making up 63.63 per cent of the total staff. A spot investigation shows that females make up 73.03 per cent of the total librarians in 40 colleges and universities in the province of Guangdong. In Guangdong Sun Yatsen Library, the biggest of the province, the number of females is twice that of males; while in the library of Sun Yatsen University, the Number One Library among all the colleges and universities in the province, the ratio of female to male is 6.5 to 1, that is to say, females make up 86.57 per cent of the total staff.

In China today female librarians make up more than 60 per cent of the library professionals, being a really decisive force in the human resources. For investigating the quality, I recently made a questionnaire investigation, which showed the following:

In the libraries of the 40 colleges and universities, there are 322 females with a background of higher education, making up 64.95 per cent of the total staff of the same educational level; there are 680 females with medium level professional titles, making 72.04 per cent of the total staff of the same title. Over the past several years, female advanced workers of collegiate level make up 63.85 per cent, and those of the provincial or ministry level, 40.48 per cent.

The data presented above epitomizes the quality of Chinese female librarians. Besides, their potentials are expressed in the fields of teaching, scientific research and administration. Surveying the libraries of Guangdong's institutions of higher education mentioned above, female division directors count for 64.82 per cent, being the backbone of library services; scientific research prize winners of the collegiate level amount to 29 persons, 60 per cent of the total; those of the provincial or ministry level, 23 persons, 53.49 per cent. Since 1993, 188 female librarians have published their theses and monographs, the number of females higher than that of males, which is 135 persons, in the same period. Another example taken from the Editorial Department of "Work and Research in Libraries" sponsored by Tianjin Library Society presents an interesting contrast between fe male and male contributors. Over the past three years, this journal has published 296 articles, 35 per cent of which are from 105 woman authors. A third example to illustrate female librarians' potential in teaching is this: At Wuhan Institute of Library and Information – China's top institute of higher education for training senior librarians and officers – six woman professors and five woman associate professors have been promoted since the country's open policy was adopted.

Looking back into the 46 years since the founding of New China and, especially, the 15 years of reform and opening campaign, each foot-print they stamped on the soil, together with growing and expanding contingent, opens up before the eyes of people all over the world a picture that "China's female librarians are able to prop up half of the sky in the library".

A Glittering Group: Features and Deeds of Female Directors and Specialists

Just when the woman stars in the circles of literature, arts, education, and science and technology rose to the sky, shining with dazzling splendour, the circle of China's libraries pooled the wisdom and efforts of everyone and shot its stars into the sky, shedding luster on the land. Representing this glittering group are the female directors and specialists, particularly those in the province of Guangdong, the front area of reform and opening campaign in China, who are most imbued with the rich flavor of the day and graceful bearing of the southern part of the country. Here are a few shining examples of this glittering group:

• Wu Zehong, Director of Wuyi Library in the City of Jiangmen.

Six years ago, Ms. Wu left her comfortable office in the City Bureau of Culture for the most difficult job to run a poor, messy and shabby library. She invited people of talent, took vigorous measures on management and worked diligently and ingeniously. She persuaded the Representatives of the Provincial and Municipal People's Congress and Political Consultative Committees and won the support of the city authorities to help her with the necessary funding. A new library building covering a floor space of 8,400 square meters has been built, cars and motorcycles were bought, and computers have been used. The shabby library has taken on a completely new look. Ms. Wu was not satisfied with these achievements. With the support of the local government and joint effort of compatriots of Hong Kong and Macao, she established a "Golden Key" Foundation for her library and raised funds amounting to RMB 700,000. Then she began to initiate a computer company resulting a profit of several thousand a year. She is good at managing money matters: in hard times starting an undertaking through thrift and in prosperous times maintaining what has been achieved through thrift. In order to make the surroundings of the library green with less money, she led the staff members to carry pond silt by themselves, spending only RMB 50,000 to 60,000 but saving RMB 200,000 from the original budget. She has won an honorable title of "Advanced Librarian" awarded by Ministry of Culture for her brilliant achievements.

• The honourable title also went to Li Wenying, Director of Panyu City Library in Guangdong. Ms. Li graduated from the Library Science Department at Wuhan University, Hubei, in the sixties. During her tenure of office, she changed a shabby small library with only a floor space of 200 square meters, a staff of nine persons, and a book collection of less than 50,000 volumes, even without a telephone, into a medium-sized modern library with a floor space of 4,000 square meters, a staff of 21 persons, a book collection of 150,000 volumes, also equipped with TV sets, video recorders, theft-proof monitoring devices, laser projectors and computers. Li's public library was graded as a first-class public library in an evaluation sponsored by the Ministry of Culture.

• The Integrated Library Automation System (ILAS) developed by Shenzhen Library has won three prizes: a first prize awarded by the Ministry of Culture, a third prize by the Nation and a Sci-Tech Innovation prize (1994) by the United Nations. Nowadays in China there are more than 180 organizations using this new system. To appraise its achievements, the Ministry of Culture once again awarded the project a Sci-Tech Achievement Promotion prize in 1994. This project that has expedited the modernization of China's library services reminds us of a female librarian Zhang Zhenwen, a computer expert and senior engineer, who is the mainstay of this project. In appreciation for her significant contribution to the country, the Ministry of Culture awarded her the first prize of Sci-Tech Improvement in 1992.

How many female directors and experts like these are there in Guangdong, or in China? Nobody knows their number. They change the challenge simply into opportunity, shouldering with their slender shoulders the heavy task the people entrust them. With wisdom and boldness, they stride across one goal after another. It is gold that glitters. It is they, the female directors and specialists, that form this glittering group in "half of the sky" among other stars.

Quality Problems: Barriers to and Worries About the Growth of Female Librarians

It is not an accidental change from the myth of Nuwa mending the sky to the reality of women "propping up half of the sky". This is the inevitable outcome of social progress and the inexorable trend of national rejuvenation. It has been a long journey, a crusade, during which how much the Chinese women have paid and endured, and how often they have changed themselves to reach perfection i n their inner mind. However, the boundless sky cannot possibly always be clear and bright and spotless. There is dust and fog. People might expect a blue and clear sky, but we should look squarely at these "dust" and "fog". As mentioned earlier, the position and role of female librarians are very important, but it does not mean that their role has been given full play and their potentials fully developed. From the macro point of view, they are required to improve themselves psychologically, ideologically and professionally. In other words, their overall quality is not up to the standard. Many female librarians have no enterprising spirit either ability to think independently; they occasionally reveal their feelings of inferiority, negligence and narrow-mindedness. Some of them even never think about "Why am I working in a library?" and some of them do think about this question but the answer appears ridiculous: "Library work is leisurely and carefree, and I have many books to read and a lot of time to rest". Also, some of them treat library work as an simple job. "Lend and collect books, open the doors and keep an eye on books. It's a kind of attendance and sort of inferior job". These feelings make them muddle along and have no eagerness to improve their professional skills.

This unsatisfactory quality has been caused by many factors, which include not only influences from conventional feudal-mindedness but also confinement of many subjective and objective factors. For example, in Chinese traditional culture, the view of "Female taking care of internal housework and male taking charge of external affairs" has become a stereotype. The role for females to play should be that of "dutiful wives and loving mothers", "good family helpers" or "humble wives". All these make females dependent. So they always limit their behavior to attending to their husbands and raising their children, shifting their potential strength that should have contributed to society to their families. In this confined space, they while away their time, waste their intelligence and spirit for the household affairs. Besides, the heavy burden of thousands of years of feudalism in China has established unfair requirements to females both by the society and by males. All these compounded factors extremely confine the space for women's activities and their development, and endangers women's psychological and ideological development. When this psychologically innate hindrance and prejudice of people (including women themselves and the proper society) towards library work collide with each other, various non-amplified modes of thinking, logic and behavior can be seen in the acts of some of the female librarians.

In addition, over the few decades after the founding of the People's Republic of China, the government didn't have sufficiently money and strength to pay attention to library work due to poor national strength. During the Cultural Revolution, library work was swamped, lots of precious historical documents and literature were treated as the heritage of feudalism, capitalism and revisionism and were all destroyed. The library became a "temporary home" for the old, weak, sick and disabled people. Libraries were regarded as "leisurely palaces" or "comfort nests" for some people to entertain their friends and relatives. All these social and historical influences have given rise to the unsatisfactory quality of women librarians. Although this extreme situation has gone forever, its remaining "scars" and "sequels" can not be healed in a short period.

This is the deduced dialectics o the Chinese female librarians: they have been "propping up half of the sky" and taking good care of China's library work on the one hand, and on the other hand, the "half of the sky" bears unconsciously a negative influence which arouses anxiety in some people.

Such is the reality that is independent of the human will. Bearing the "foetal mark" or "brand" of history, tradition, ideology, society, male... China's female librarians cannot climb up to the top of the value of life in one move, but they must treasure and exploit their possibilities today, and they are looking forward to a tomorrow which will be created by themselves together with the society.

Ushering in A New Era: for Tomorrow's Great Female Librarians Joining Efforts with the Whole Society

The key lies in the improvement of the overall quality of libraries, if we want to develop human resources for female librarians and bring up an excellent female contigent. Dispersing the "fog" and clearing up the "dust", the "half of the sky" in China's library will be brighter than ever and more colourful and attractive.

In order to enhance overall quality of female librarians we are required to do the following: First of all, we must focus on education. Here I would like to present two groups of statistics which contrast sharply. The 1990 census shows that, among

the 180 million illiterates of age of fifteen and above, females make up 70.1 per cent on the one hand. On the other hand, among the total number of Chinese science and technology workers, females make up 40 per cent, a ratio much higher than that of the advanced countries: in the U.S. 12.2 per cent (1992) and in Japan 12.5 per cent (1982). As for engineers, British females make up 5 per cent, and American females 6.7 per cent of their total number, while in China the female ratio is 19 per cent. The sharp contrast between Chinese illiterates and professional females mirrors the inequity in women's education rights. Therefore, the Chinese government has solemnly declared its commitment to wipe out illiteracy of 300,000 women a year; to give on-the-spot training or vocational training to 70 per cent of women in towns, and to offer practical and technical training to 50 per cent of countryside women by the end of the year 2,000.

What would it mean to us? It would mean that all the libraries, whether big or small, should have their own measures in concert with the solemn commitment of the government. In fact, all the libraries, from national libraries and the China

Library Society, to libraries of provincial, municipal, and autonomous regional levels, and their corresponding libraries and societies, have adopted measures to improve the professional quality of female librarians through educational programs, and have made some achievements.

In regard of the library at the Guangzhou Institute of Foreign Trade (now part of the Guangdong University of Foreign Studies) where I am working, among the 40 staff members, 23 females have received various kinds of professional training, making up 72 per cent of the total of females. Female librarians under the age of 40 are able to operate computers. In recent years, 14 female librarians have published academic papers, winning 5 scientific research awards of the college level, 2 awards of the municipal level, 5 awards of the provincial level, and 4 awards of the national level. In an assessment and evaluation for libraries at colleges and universities in Guangdong in 1995, my library was graded "excellent" for two areas, Information Service and Document Retrieval, among the appraisal of three areas. These two areas had been developed by female librarians who started working from scratch and were joined by almost 90 per cent of the women in the library.

Generally speaking, educational programs aiming at improving the overall quality of females librarians in China are yet to be increased and expanded, so that females, including female directors, may have opportunities to refresh their knowledge and achieve a higher administrative level.

Secondly, to improve their professional quality by means of executive measures and academic activities while protecting their status. According to a reliable source, China is going to establish a national monitoring system for women's status and a database for women. China is also planning to establish coordinating organizations at various governmental levels to raise the status of women and to include women's development into the overall social development. In 1990, the Ministry of Personnel issued "The Circular Concerning Retirement of Senior Experts", which stipulates that the retirement age of senior female experts can be moved to 60 if they are healthy and willing to work. It shows the concern of the authorities towards women and facilitates the development of female human resources.

This brings us to the following questions: What can we do to help our female librarians? Can we keep personal files for female librarians so that we can have a good command of their basic conditions? Can we raise a fund or set aside some money from the budget to sponsor activities for female librarians? Or to subsidize their scientific research and advanced learning, and reward their achievements? Can we write a special column in our library journal publishing their papers, and discussing questions they are concerned about? Can we set up "societies", "salons", or organize get-togethers and seminars for them to discuss topics beneficial for their health and mind and convenient for them to exchange notes?

A stern answer to these questions is "Yes, we can if we want" Nothing is difficult to a willing mind. Female directors and librarians should strive for its realization; parties concerned should give support as much as possible. However, what really matters is "me" or myself. The improvement of the overall quality of female librarians starts from "me": daring to dissect "me", daring to face the individual "me", daring to bid farewell to the old "me", to turn self-abasement into self-respect, ignorance into self-confidence, dependence into self-reliance,and indolence into self-improvement. In one word, female

librarians should stand at the entrance to the new era, brushing aside the traditional definition of women's role and throwing themselves into the grandeur of change at the turn of the century.

The 21st century is an epoch of intelligence being the uppermost factor. Once the Chinese government realizes its commitment and offers women the necessary educational rights, China's women will soar with their wings of wisdom.

Similarly, having thrown off the shacks of reins of the old regime, the clan, the divine and the husband's rights, China's female librarians who have been "propping up half of the sky" can certainly shed much more glory to the new era.

III. LIBRARY MANAGERS AND GENDER

WOMEN AS MANAGERS OF LIBRARIES:
A DEVELOPMENTAL PROCESS IN INDIA

Kalpana Dasgupta
Director
Central Secretariat Library, Department of Culture
Ministry of Human Resource Development
New Delhi, India (1997)

Abstract

The paper deals with the status of women in Indian libraries under the broad concept that librarianship is a woman oriented vocation. The dichotomy of the Indian situation has been analyzed from the modern management point of view. The author suggests developments within the professional field to prepare women for the responsibility of senior positions in the libraries of tomorrow.

1. Introduction

The status of women has to be measured by the actual position occupied by women in the society, family, place of work and within the economic power structure. Since status is synonymous to power, prestige and privileges, the measurement of actual status of women in any society will obviously mean the power enjoyed, followed by the prestige and privileges attached to the seat of power.

In the Indian context, the power enjoyed by a woman till very recently was basically dependent on the hierarchical position within the family and motherhood specifically of male children. The economic status of an Indian woman was dependent on the family occupation and the position enjoyed by the father, husband or son. Selection of profession was not common for women within the economic system of the middle and upper echelons of Indian society. The educated working woman is a new concept mainly of the late 19th and the early 20th century in the world and the process is slower in the Indian context.

The freedom movement and the partition of the Indian sub-continent have been vital in the emergence of economic role of the Indian woman in the educated Indian society. Women's participation in white-collar employment other than teaching, nursing and the medical profession is a 20th century phenomenon in India.

2. Librarianship as a Profession for Women

Librarianship as a profession in India was for the scholar librarians till the early part of the 20th century. Mostly men of letters only were custodians of libraries and the written cultural heritage. However, the first woman credited with occupying and key-post in India was Anandibai Prabhudesai who was the superintendent at the Children's library in Baroda in the 1930s.

The social stereotype is clearly reflected in the division of professions, which need specific training and higher education. Academia, Scientific profession, Research, Law etc. are male oriented and male dominated professions whereas teaching, social work and later librarianship have been considered as service professions which are suitable for women. It has always been mentioned in both the developed and the developing countries that women by nature and upbringing can support the service professions better. The main dichotomy of the situation is that when it comes to the higher positions there is a hierarchical discrimination because the decision makers allege that the women bearing poor health, lack of business and decision making ability justified their second rate status within the profession.

Through various surveys it has been seen that in more developed countries women still accounted for more than 80% of the library profession. But in most countries there is a dual career structure for men and women. In the Indian context the situation is slightly different. Women were admitted in the professional arena mainly during the first half of the 20th century. In 1940 the first group of students were admitted to a training course conducted by the Bengal Library Association, Calcutta and in 1942 the first qualified female librarian took a job at the Bengal Legislative Assembly. Till 1975 the number of women in the field of librarianship in India was not very significant. Though it was felt that this profession would be very right for women in India because nature has bestowed women with qualities of patience, sympathy and perseverance, the enrolment statistics now available show that librarianship is still not a female intensive profession in India. The average ratio of male female enrolment in the Bachelor of Library and Information Science and Master of Library and Information Science is 3:2, 3:1 respectively. Teaching remained the main occupation for women in India till the early 1970s.

3. Why Women in India Select Librarianship as a Profession?

Though women of the middle class families have started working outside the family structure, the social pressures on educated women to accept those jobs, which will fit into the stereotype of Indian womanhood still persist. Teaching, social work and the medical profession were acceptable because these professions were needed not only for the compartmentalization of the sexes, but also to restrict Indian womanhood within the four walls of approved diktat. Librarianship as a profession developed in the early 1940s and by the 1960s the major universities had training courses in librarianship. Education being the main thrust of independent India the need for setting up libraries became inevitable. Employment in libraries came within the purview of the government, universities, academic institutions, research organisations, etc.

Women opted to take up librarianship as a career often due to the following reasons:

(i) Women who wanted employment but were not particularly prepared to teach, considered librarianship a good alternative, because the environment would be academic whereas the work will not have the requirement of teaching on a regular basis.

(ii) Security of women is a major factor in an Indian family. Indian society being totally compartmentalized between the sexes which is reflected in the upbringing of boys and girls, the work place which ensures security has a very important role in women's employment.

(iii) The qualities expected in an Indian woman are suited to activities in a library.

(iv) Librarianship generally does not demand mobility in service, and women in India are not expected to be mobile outside the family structure.

(v) Jobs in a library allow women to remain unattached to colleagues and the public, especially males.

4. Status and Hierarchical Position of Women in Librarianship in India

The Indian Library system can be divided into five major areas of work.

(i)   National Library System

(ii) Academic Library System

(iii) Special Library System

(iv) Public Library System, and

(v)   Informatics.

Within these systems of librarianship, women now work in various capacities and positions. However, the age-old stereotype of regarding women's roles as teacher, and child bearer and child rearer is reflected in the staff structure of these systems also. Within these systems there is a major difference between the types of libraries that absorb the maximum number of women. Very much like in the Western world, children's libraries, school libraries and to a certain extent college libraries employ women as librarians in larger numbers in contrast to scientific and specialized libraries. Women are also in demand in girls' schools and women's colleges, which exist in significant numbers in India. But within the hierarchy of the library system the prevalence of women in these types of libraries does not make them eligible to occupy top positions in major libraries. In the government library sector the maximum number of women are seen in a cadre which is above the paraprofessionals but below the decision making level.

The percentage of women librarians in different categories in the three large libraries under the Government of India, namely, the National Library, the Central Secretariat Library and the Delhi Public Library, clearly shows that most women hold posts up to the sectional head only. The highest positions are still held by males in general.

The reasons for this situation are manifold.

(i)   Women professionals are often satisfied with the qualifications, which will place them at a convenient level in the professional ladder.

(ii) Since mobility of women is not an acceptable feature in an Indian family, especially for married women, women in libraries have to wait for their chance for promotion on seniority basis as and when such vacancies arise.

(iii) Most families consider women's income as a supplementary input, which caters to the additional necessities of a household in general. Therefore, women are satisfied to hold a convenient position, which will enable them to pay more attention to their family responsibilities.

(iv) The male ego often works as a deterrent for women of substance to aspire for higher positions in service.

(v) It is still true that women are brought up to be more concerned about personal and familial relationships in contrast to men whose personal achievements reflect the achievements of the family as a whole.

(vi) The qualities that are expected and accepted in men are not acceptable in women. A man who is career oriented is lauded, whereas a woman who is equally concerned about her capabilities and career is branded as careerist in a negative sense.

(vii) Women lack training to cope with new developments in the profession.

5. Redeeming Features in the Indian Situation

There are two major factors to be observed:

(i) Unlike the developed countries most Indian libraries, which are under the Government or under the institutions supported by the Government, do not have disparity in the pay structure of men and women librarians for holding similar posts and responsibilities.

(ii) Since the promotional channels are the same within the different institutions, there is less possibility of discrimination in promotion when such vacancies arise.

In spite of these two major issues there are just a handful of women who have reached higher positions within the library system in India. Out of these women many have served in the American libraries and the British Council Libraries in India.

Since most women especially those who are married cannot attend training programmes organised outside the city of work, the women lag behind their male colleagues. Therefore, when promotions are considered by seniority cum fitness, the assessment reports do not reflect any additional qualification or achievement. This condition becomes a deterrent in the case of women. Moreover, since librarianship does not have an organised cadre as yet, most vacancies are advertised through various media channels. These posts are to be filled through direct recruitment and interviews. Such posts comprise a certain percentage of the total posts available in an institution.

Women, while facing the interviews, often do not satisfy the expectations of selectors in a new environment for the following reasons:

(i) They are generally shy and not out-going enough to face the interview board

(ii) The interview boards which mainly consist of men in high positions, have in-built bias against women candidates if the post to be filled is of managerial rank.

(iii) Due to lack of proper training women candidates are not informed enough to be able to face the board with confidence.

6. Present and Future Trends in Management of Libraries

The libraries of tomorrow will be information centres of a new type relying on information technology for almost every aspect of library activities. The skills needed to handle the future library services will be different from what they are at present. In this new world of information technology the woman librarians of tomorrow will also have to be equally skilled to reach the status which they deserve. However, at present the indications are that women will have less opportunities to develop the skills needed for running the libraries of tomorrow due to the factors mentioned earlier. Special motivating facilities will have to be created to provide equal opportunities to women professionals at all levels. The future managerial models will also change with the changing concept of librarianship.

6.1 Influences of Gender in Librarianship

For centuries it has been accepted that leadership comes automatically to men, while women being dependent and submissive lack in leadership qualities. However, research from the points of view of both psychology and management has been done in developed countries on this issue. Though women were expected to accept the male behavioural stereotype when they held high position in the past, the recent concept emphasises that in a democratic and humane management the old male-oriented, autocratic and directive style may not be accepted in the future. Interpersonal relationship and participative style of administration often leads to better task accomplishment. In the information age the old hierarchical system of administration may appear too bureaucratic, and the future system may rely more in communication flow within the system. In this new environment, the women's understanding, patience and sincerity might prove better and more fruitful than the male-oriented competitive, tough and decisive administration. Women will help in interacting with subordinates and encourage participation rather than issue directives to subordinates from the top.

6.2 Acceptance of Women as Leaders

Although the scenario throughout the world, and in India as well, is developing towards acceptance of women in high places, in the field of librarianship the notion of women as leaders is still foreign to both men and women. Usually women who reach the top positions have to be extremely well qualified, must have proven records of accomplishment and have to be well prepared for the position they aspire for. Once these positions are attained, women have to balance between their accepted behavioural pattern and the role expected of a professional in that particular position.

7. The Prospects for Women in Indian Managerial Context

Though I am a woman librarian, I have had the opportunity to hold some of the highest positions in the library system of India. In spite of the fact that this is an exception rather than the rule, I have felt that there are some problems which the Indian woman faces if given higher positions; but at the same time the qualities available in the psyche of the Indian woman often make it easier for her to work as a successful administrator in a democratic setup.

In the Indian context, it is seen that once a woman proves her ability as a professional and acquires a high status within the profession, the situation permits her to develop in the right direction and she is given her due respect and importance by her male colleagues as well as by her superiors. Strangely enough, she often finds women subordinates facing problems if she believes in equality between her subordinates. Women employees often take undue privileges citing their social and familial responsibilities, while male bosses usually do not interfere in this situation. A woman superior who is well aware of such behaviour may become unpopular if she does not believe in granting privileges at the cost of duties and expects equality in responsibility between male and female professionals. This situation, however, may be just a passing phase, because women are also becoming more aware of their responsibilities in their place of work and the social attitudes in the Indian society are simultaneously undergoing alteration. There is displayed a new wave of anti-discriminatory attitude, and there are less patriarchal and dictatorial males. All this development will help in changing the attitude of women as professionals also.

7.1 The Changing Role of Women in Indian Librarianship

Though librarianship has been stereotyped as a woman-oriented profession in the developed countries, the Indian situation cannot be stereotyped in that direction. As mentioned earlier, it is seen that, even at the university level, the number of female students is still less than that of their male counterparts. There is also the dropout factor. However, the reasons in discontinuance are different for males and females. Whereas the male student often discontinues studying to join more lucrative avenues, women often have to discontinue due to marriage and to suit the family convenience.

But in the past twenty years, it is seen that the number of women managers in libraries has increased. The International Year of the Women 1975 did not see more than ten senior professionals in this field, whereas at present eight libraries are being headed by women librarians in the city of Mumbai alone. Of course, the situation in Mumbai is not representative of the country as a whole and does not necessarily indicate the trend, however, many specialised libraries in larger cities are also being headed by women.

Yet there are certain developments that should take place within this field in order to allow women to become good managers. While gauging women's management capabilities it may be said, that there are natural abilities in Indian women that will help them to become good managers. To elaborate this point one can state that the psyche of Indian woman is a product of familial and social situation. The expectations of both family and society from an Indian woman include sincerity, patience and understanding. All these three qualities help in making a person a successful administrator in new environment.

The library system as a whole should emphasize the following aspects in order to allow women to perform well at higher levels.

(i) Women should be able to select their placement so that they can utilize their capability to the maximum. Since employment is no longer available on a platter, they have to take jobs for which they are neither competent nor have interest to perform. Such situations lead to placement of women in libraries and institutions where their actual capabilities are not recognised. Therefore, the vicious circle of non-performance and thereby non-selection for higher decision-making positions starts.

(ii) Women should be encouraged to take up jobs in new and challenging fields of work. Libraries and information systems which cater to the needs relating to women's development, may be taken up as a new challenge by women librarians. Dissemination of relevant information for women's development is the need of the hour in the Indian Society.

(iii) Suitable training facilities relevant to women's special needs should be organised so that they are equipped to handle the new environment in libraries.

(iv) There should be developed a support system to help women cope with the responsibilities of family and career. This facility, of course, is a part of the larger social responsibility of institutions as a whole and not that of the library in particular.

(v) That women are not suitable for managerial positions because they cannot handle a large staff is a myth which has to be suitably exploded through seminars, discussion groups, etc., to ensure women's development in the field of librarianship.

(vi) More research on the status of women in libraries should be conducted to collect and analyse data that is not available so far. This would help to better the present situation within the library system.

8. Conclusion

Women's role in all aspects of Indian political, social and economic fields is undergoing positive changes. India has national and state level commissions that are responsible for dealing with women's issues arising in different situations. The constitution of the democratically elected urban and village level local administrative bodies with not less than one third of the seats occupied by women has provided tremendous boost to the empowerment of women in India. When women start playing a major role at these levels, the status of women in all fields will automatically change. As a consequence, women will then become capable of coping with positions at higher levels also in all professional fields, and librarianship will not be an exception.

References

Becker, Cheryl.(1989) "Librarianship". In Women's Studies Encyclopedia. v.1 Westport, CT: Greenwood. pp. 208-209.

Biskup, Peter. (August 1994) "Gender and Status in Australian Librarianship: Some Issues". Australian Library Journal 43:164 -179

Carmichael, James V.(March 1994) "Gender Issues in the Workplace: Male Librarians Tell Their Side". American Libraries 25: 227-230.

Kumar, P.S.G.(1975) "Women and librarianship". Herald of Library Science 14 (4): 221-224

Maack, Mary Niles. (1994) "Gender Issues in Librarianship". In Encyclopedia of Library History edited by Wayne A. Weigaud and Donald G. Davis Jr. New York: Garland Publishing. pp. 227-232.

Moran, Barbara B.(1992) "Gender Differences in Leadership". Library Trends 40 (Winter): 475-491.

Schiller, Anita R. (1974) "Women in Librarianship". In Advances in Librarianship, edited by Melvin J. Voigt. London: Academic Press. pp.103-141.

Somerville, Mary R. (April 1995) "Yin Management in a Yang World". Wilson Library Bulletin 69 : 30-32.

Varalakshmi, N. (October 1992) The Problems and Prospects of Women Librarians Working in Indian University Libraries: a Survey . Unpublished dissertation. Gulbarga University.

MOTIVATION TO MANAGE:

A comparative study of male and female library & information science students in the United States of America, India, Singapore, and Japan

Sarla R. Murgai

Professor

University of Tennessee at Chattanooga,

Chattanooga, Tennessee, USA (1999)

Abstract

This study compared the managerial motivations of library and information science (LIS) students in the United States of America with LIS students in India. The students responded to a questionnaire containing 41 statements on managerial motivation. These statements were divided into 10 categories: task orientation, fear of success, perseverance, reaction to success/failure, future orientation, competitiveness, independence, rigidity, social needs and acceptance of women as managers. Demographic factors such as educational attainment, age, marital status, mobility etc. were also included and compared. Respondents consisted of 665 students from 11 southeastern universities in the United States, 814 students from 23 universities in India, 73 from Singapore, and three from Japan. Fifty percent of Indian and Singaporean students were males; only 20% of the USA respondents were males; and from Japan there were one male and two females. A majority of the Indian, American, Singaporean and Japanese LIS students were motivated to achieve the objectives they set for themselves and were future oriented. They were aggressive in setting their goals and expected that task orientation and perseverance would enable them to accomplish those objectives.

The agreement percentages were close on "task orientation", "perseverance", "future orientation", and "competitiveness", between countries and by sexes. The differences between the sexes were found on factors like "women as managers", "reaction to success or failure", "fear of failure", and "social acceptance". Prevalent culture determines the gender roles in an organization. Theories of management & motivation work best when they are modified according to the social norms.

Introduction

Women's under-representation in management is a common finding all over the world, even though the degree may vary from country to country (Adler and Izraeli, 1994; Chen, Yu and Miner, 1997). This under-representation of women in management has been attributed to women's motivation to enter and succeed in managerial positions (Powell, 1993). Economic conditions, a sense of devaluation of the domestic, and a desire to find self-fulfillment drove women into the job market. The female experience of lower pays glass ceiling (U.S Dept. of Labor, 1991), slower promotions, and organizational discrimination, that keep the women at the lower levels of management, have over the last thirty years prompted many scholars to search for empirical evidence regarding the validity of such attributes (Acker, 1990; Chumer, 1988; Nieva & Gutek, 1981; Wendy, 1992). This is another attempt to compare the managerial motivations of males and females in the Library/Information Science (LIS) profession. Assessing the impact of managerial motivation of women in the Library and Information Science (henceforth LIS) is of particular importance because fifty to eighty per cent of the workforce in the LIS consists of women, in the countries under study, and only zero to six per cent of them are in higher administration. Librarians can use these findings to enhance their motivation to acquire management skills. Human resource policy makers could address the problem of under-utilizing the talents of women (Miner, 1980; Oliver, 1982; Mintzberg, 1983; Weber, 1968)

The concept of achievement-motivation draws on four basic theories: 1. Need fulfillment, 2. Social learning, 3. Personality, and 4. Development.

Need Fulfillment

According to the need fulfillment theories, job motivation is determined by the biological, psychological, and social needs of the individual (Astin, 1984; Atkinson, 1957; Murray, 1938). These needs influence the behavior of the individual. These needs are largely unconscious, and one of these needs is the need to achieve.

Social Learning Theory

Social Learning Theory emphasizes environmental factors as opposed to individual factors in the development of personality. Elements beyond the control of the individual exert a major influence on career choice. The principal task confronting a person is the development of techniques to cope effectively with the environment (Osipow, 1983, p.10; Singhal and Misra, 1994). As Maehr (1974) pointed out:

> Achievement is a function of more or less ephemeral social expectations that are embodied in what we call norms. In a very real sense, a social group tells a person what to strive for as well as how to attain this end. The effect of such norms is clearly an important variable in an achievement situation. (P.66).

Girls have been taught not to aspire to prestigious occupations (Fottler, 1980). Sex role socialization leads women to focus on marriage rather than career, and from this early experience comes the notion that one survives by marrying and taking care of the man, who must earn the living. Girls learn to satisfy their pleasure needs and their contribution needs by direct service to others.

Social values, however, are changing in the US and in the rest of the world. Worsening economic conditions, the need for two incomes per family, rising divorce rates, and insecurity in marriage have prompted women to plan and prepare for a career. Women realize that they are more likely to satisfy their survival needs directly through their own earnings, rather than indirectly through the income of their spouses.

Medical and technological advances such as amniocentesis, artificial insemination, in-vitro fertilization and surrogate motherhood provide women a greater control over their lives and bodies. Of benefit to women, too, is the social acceptance of the smaller family as well as general increase in life expectancy. All these factors give women more freedom to prepare for and plan their futures.

Nations and Cultures

Different nations have different cultural heritages which are values collectively held by a majority of the population (possibly differentiated by social classes), and these values are transferred from generation to generation through education, early childhood experiences in the family, schools, and through socialization in organizations and institutions. These values become social norms for that society. It is hard to see this process in one's own culture. A deep and painfully acquired empathy for other cultures is required before one becomes sensitive to the range of social norms, for truths in one society may be falsehoods in another (Hofstede, 1980). P.373-374).

63

Hofstede (1980), after analyzing research data from forty different modern nations, has come up with a scale of characteristics that can be used to distinguish the prevailing cultures in various countries of the world. Hofstede's definition of these concepts is elaborated below.

Individualism

It is the relationship of individualism and collectivism in a human society. The prevalence of the value of individualism or collectivism expected from members of a society or an organization will strongly affect the nature of the relationship between person and the organization to which he or she belongs.

Power Distance

In an organization the inequality in power between workers and their bosses, and the level at which a society maintains that equilibrium. Power distance is a measure of the interpersonal power or influence between a boss and subordinates as perceived by the least powerful of the two, the subordinate.

Uncertainty Avoidance

The concept of uncertainty is often linked to the environment and includes everything that is not under direct control of the organization and is a source of uncertainty. The organization tries to compensate for it through technology, rules, and rituals to reduce the stress caused by it. Factors like the economy, demographics, political system, legislation, religion, etc., can be the cause of uncertainty. In his studies sex differences in uncertainty avoidance were negligible.

Masculinity: The duality of sexes masculinity and femininity

In organizations, there is a relationship between perceived goals of the organization and the career possibilities for men and women. Some business organizations have "masculine" goals and tend to promote men; others try to maintain a balance between the sexes.

Hofstede's Criteria	USA	INDIA	SINGAPORE	JAPAN
Individualism	91	48	20	46
Power Distance	40	77	74	54
Uncertainty avoidance	46	40	8	92
Masculinity	62	56	48	95

Based on that scale Americans would be characterized as high in individualism, low in power distance, low on uncertainty avoidance, and average on masculinity. Indians (middle class) would be average on individualism (relative to their wealth), high on power distance, low on uncertainty avoidance, and average on masculinity. Singaporeans would be characterized as low on individualism, high on power distance, very low on uncertainty avoidance and average on masculinity. Japanese would be average on individualism, average on power distance, very high on uncertainty avoidance and high on masculinity. A combination of these characteristics plays a major role in management motivation according to Hofstede.

The commonality of achievement motivation values between the USA and India prompted McClelland (1965) to suggest that achievement training would be a solution to the problems in underdeveloped countries. He went to India to teach the managers the theories of achievement motivation. This resulted in exportation of the theories of achievement motivation to the rest of the world. Later research shows that only those managers who could fit these theories into their own culture have been able to use these management concepts profitably (Hofstede, 1980)

Personality Theory

Through their careers women engage in productive work, develop skills and talents, and get a sense of self-fulfillment (Lott, 1991). The challenge of work that is valued by their peers gives them a sense of achievement, and a realization of self-worth. This gaining of self-esteem in large part is instrumental in satisfying their pleasure and contributory needs Astin, 1984; Hacket & Betz, 1981). Recent studies of females in professional employment show that men and women do not differ in self-ratings, self-confidence and work values (Adler and Izraeli, 1994; Florentine, 1988; Fottler and Trevor, 1980; Kolberg and Chumir, 1991). Also, with the development of better measuring instruments of job evaluation there is a narrowing of the differences in the styles of management, motivation and leadership between males and females. Information and knowledge-based society of today, and people-oriented leadership style render women more qualified than men in management.

Developmental Theories

Developmental theories emphasize lifetime development, adaptation to change, and making the best use of opportunities (Ginsberg, 1972; Super, 1957, 1980). To prepare for management and to develop self-confidence women in every country have sought higher education, and training to promote themselves in professional and managerial fields. Today, there is a dramatic increase in the number of women pursuing graduate and professional education. In the U.S., 54% of college students are women. Thirty six percent of the students enrolled in business are women, 33% in law, and 13% in engineering. Just like the U.S. an increasing number of Indian women are preparing to take up professional careers. Of the total number of students enrolled in the colleges 43% females are enrolled in medicine, 77% in higher education, 61% in graduate programs (Bachelor, Masters, Masters of Science, etc.) (Kumar, 1989). Singaporean women workers in general are better educated than their male counterparts (Report of the Labor force survey of Singapore, 1991). Labor statistics have consistently shown that woman's labor force participation increases with education (National University of Singapore, 1980-81 - 1983-84). Japan has the highest rate of high school graduation at 94% (Steinoff and Tanaka, p.79).

High achieving women have high expectations in both career and home areas (Astin, 1984; Diamond, 1984; Glass-Ceiling, 1991). Young men and women are striving to be financially independent, prepare for a career, and obtain recognition from colleagues (Florentine, 1988; Katz, 1988).

When girls become economically independent through education, job, and position, they want to be respected as equal members of the society. Women with more education however show greater desire for independence and for the opportunity to perform managerial roles (Brenner, 1989), and when such opportunities are denied to them, the results are low self-esteem, low self-confidence, and curtailed achievement levels (Basow & Metcalf, 1988; U.S. Department of Labor, ...Glass-Ceiling, 1991). A recent report showed that our education system even today leaves women with lower self-esteem than men (Daley, 1991). There has to be a motivational synergy towards new conceptualization of intrinsic and extrinsic motivation at workplace (Amiable, 1993).

Library and Information Science and Women

In the Library and Information Science field in the U.S., more women than men have been earning their masters (69%to 80%) and doctorates (69% to 72%) since the 1980s (U.S. Statistical Abstracts, 1996, pp.192-3). Women are undertaking in-service training and continuing education courses, to improve their skills and to stay abreast of the career needs and innovations in the field. Such exposure makes women aware of their strengths and boosts their self-confidence (Hiatt, 1983).

Personality studies of LIS students and specialists in the U.S.A., do not show any significant difference in motivation to manage scores between males and females. In fact the scores of female respondents in three recent studies were even higher than the males (Martin, J.K.; 1988; Murgai, 1987,1991; Swisher, DuMont, and Boyer, 1985). Computerization and automation are having a profound effect on the occupational structure in Librarianship. Technical and managerial jobs like systems engineers, information specialists, or knowledge brokers etc. are on the increase in the profession. Unfortunately however, most managers are men, and women are left to carry on the routine services. Top positions in the field are being filled with non-librarians (Harris, 1993).

Since literature research did not show any studies done comparing the motivation of males and females in LIS, in other countries, the general condition of females in India, Singapore Japan, and U.S.A. is described below in order to build a comparative understanding of the status of women in these countries.

Status of Women in India

India presents a very interesting study of how the class system of the West is no more egalitarian than the caste system of the East. The British colonialism created a middle class in India, which allowed some women to break free of the structures by taking advantage of opportunities in the professions. At the beginning of this century Indian women began to move into professions like medicine and teaching. This happened as a response to the demand for education and healthcare among the female relatives of middle class men, and also because of sexual segregation. Female seclusion demanded that other women provide these services. When India became independent (1947) the Indian women's movement also succeeded in raising women's legal position to a level comparable with many rich countries of the West. The Indian constitution conferred equal rights and status to all citizens forbidding any discrimination on the grounds of caste, creed, religion or sex. A bill has recently been introduced in the Indian parliament to reserve 25% of the seats for women in the state and national assemblies (Times of India, 1996, p.1). After independence government service and administrative jobs were opened to women (Ashana, P. 1974; Desuza, V. 1980 Liddle and Joshi, 1990). Educated elite women who had played an active role during the independence movement took up leadership positions. By 1988 ten per cent of members of parliament were women, and eighteen percent of women who ran for office in the state legislative assemblies in 1983 won, while only seventeen percent of the men who sought such offices won (Bumiller, 1990, p.152).

A majority of women in India as in the United States however are in feminist professions. Both societies place low status on such women's professions and pay them less than men. Educational attainment and employment does bring status to individual women. It improves their chances of marrying in a higher caste or status family. It gives them economic independence. The freedom that women win from their constraints in the change from caste to class society does not constitute emancipation, only a different type of control (Liddle and Joshi, 1989).

The Indian professional women experience job segregation, as well as discrimination in selection, promotion, training and assessment just like the American women. In employment, restrictions are imposed on their physical mobility and their social interaction with males by sexual harassment at work, and by gossip affecting all aspects of their lives (Liddle and Joshi, 1989). Employment may not release women from subordination, but it does provide the psychological basis for women to exert and exercise power. As Eli Bhatt said:

> Self-employed workers are realizing their self worth. They are overcoming the barriers of caste and class. They are getting rid of the guilt feeling associated with neglecting the family as a result of employment and are collaborating with each other for the common good . (Bumiller, 1990, p.139).

Their teachers, employers, fathers and husbands who steer them into careers associated with domestic roles, control the lives of Indian women. Men gain greater share of the scarce resources spent on education. Added to this is the notion that a woman's education should not exceed her husband's education. Thus male superiority is enforced in the family (DeSuza, 1990; Asna, Pritima, 1974; Liddle and Joshi, 1989). In the family women's lives are controlled through the male authority figure by imposing the entire burden of domestic work upon them in addition to the paid work outside the home. By defining women as primary domestic workers and the sexual and reproductive property of men, and by assigning priority to man's paid employment, the society devalues educational attainment, and economic and social contributions of women. One of the major locations of women's subordination rests on the personal relations of the family. The personal arena is the place where women have to negotiate the conditions of their lives on an individual basis. Men resist conceding their privilege. They do not want to forego their domination of women. During the debates on the Hindu Code Bill, Pandit Nehru remarked:

> When it came to implementing the principle of sexual equality in the domestic arena many nationalist men were forced to admit that whilst they were determined to resist national subordination they did not want to forego their domination of women (Sarkar, 1976; p.355; Nanda, p.87; Mazumdar, p. xvi)

Indian women, who travel to western countries for education and later seek employment, often find that ideas of gender and race inferiority augment the discrimination they encounter in those supposedly enlightened countries. The context of western domination imports not only the idea of women's inferiority in relation to men, but also a notion of Indian women's inferiority in relation to western women. The myth of the third world's inferiority helps justify continued western exploitation of India and its resources. This exploitation hurts women's chances of education and employment and enforces the notion that women are less capable than men. As a result multinational companies in India and abroad use this to limit the opportunities for women in employment (Liddle and Joshi, 1990).

Status of Women in Singapore

In 1991 Singaporean women were ahead in their earnings capacity than the rest of the world. In non-agricultural activities women earned 75% of what men earned as against 71% of the USA, and 50% of the Japan. (ILO 1991; SLFS 1991; U.S. Bureau of Census 1991). The World Competitive Report (1990) ranked Singapore as the most competitive country in a group of ten newly industrialized economies. Singapore earned the highest scores in productivity, company support for education and training, quality of trained workforce, workforce organization and practice (Chan and Lee, p.129).

Women represent 51% of the workforce. The proportion of women among the technical and professional workers is 40%. Of these 16% are administrators and managerial workers. Though no comparable data is available, the percentage of women executives would be about the same as in the U.S.

Women are still under-represented in the sciences and technical fields. Many continue to avoid technical areas of study in favor of feminist occupations such as nursing, teaching and administrative work. In 1990 women comprised almost 21% of the total group of research scientist and engineers. More mothers pursue their careers, not only for personal fulfillment, but also to meet the higher family expenses and to provide for better education of the children. Husbands do not share the work at home, except for some of the younger men. In 1988 the Prime Minister spoke of the urgent need for young women to get married and have children because of the declining birth rate. The government gives financial help in the form of stipends to the family who begets a third child. But the rate of unmarried women in the workforce is many times higher than that of men. The women feel they cannot handle the pressure of work and home (SCWO Survey, 1989; Voices and Choices, 1993).

Working women turn down promotions because of the burden of trying to balance work and family. Eighty two per cent of the women who quit work cited childcare and household duties to be the reason for doing so.

From time to time women in parliament have added to the discussions of national policies, the issues that effect women and the family. As a result of their efforts childcare has improved, flexible work hours have been introduced, and corporations and government have provided special work incentives, and training and retraining programs. Official endorsement of women participation in the workforce has brought a change in the social attitude towards working women. The growing trend of dual career families in Singapore has helped to improve the condition of women in Singapore. A lot of men, however, have not learnt to deal with women as equals or superiors or in ways that are not sexual. Some male bosses and coworkers still discriminate, husbands hinder their wives' careers by not doing their fair share at home, and working women are beset with guilt, and stress from combining work and motherhood.

The following gender barriers exist in the Singaporean society towards women: Women, who graduate in the same year as men receive lower pay, and have to wait longer to secure their first job. Social attitudes and structures do not welcome women managers (1984 Graduate Employment Survey, 1985; 1990 NUS and NTI Graduate Employment Survey, 1991). They are excluded from real power networks. Women seldom see their job as a step stone to advancement and power. "The status, perks and power are not worth the sacrifices and hassle", (Arasu and Ooi, 1984).

Status of Women in Japan

Japan has a higher rate of high school completion than even the United States of America. Ninety four per cent of the people complete high school and one third of them go on for higher education. Although women appear to be equal to men in overall rate of high school education, in 1990 about 60% of the women receiving higher education went to two-year institutes as compared to less than 5% of men (Ministry of Education, 1991). In 1990, women constituted 41% of the labor force and 69% of all the non-agricultural part-time workers.

Traditionally, large corporations hire workers straight from colleges and keep them for their whole life, till retirement. Their consensus-oriented decision making style of management requires leaders to be attuned to the sensitivities of the co-workers with whom they grow up and become sensitive to each others feelings. This style enables them to avoid conflicts, once the decision is made. Relatively few women remain on the career track long enough to attain management level position in those large corporations. Japanese culture mixes work with play. A married woman cannot socialize after hours. Since the companies must groom young women for future internal positions, it will be very long time before women will be well represented in Japanese corporate management.

However, the number of such highly qualified women who stay longer is increasing in small privately owned corporations, and in public sector enterprises, because of the Equal Employment Opportunity Law 1986. From 1986 to 1990 there was an increase of more than 50% of women presidents of such small companies (Teiku Data Bank, 1986; 1990). Equal Employment Opportunity Law has also prompted some research on actual status of women in large organizations.

Women schoolteachers work till retirement age even if they marry and have children. At the elementary school level the principals are primarily women, whereas at the prestigious at the high school level the principals are predominantly men. At the national government level only 1.1% of women are managers at the bucho (division head) level, and .6% are at the kacho (section head) level. At the city level the percentages are higher (Steinhoff and Tanaka, 1994).

Women managers in small and medium sized enterprises are more likely to be married and have children. They appear to come from families that encourage women to study and work. A substantial minority has working mothers as the role models.

Women achieve managerial positions by working around the male career patterns, rather than competing within it (Lebra, 1992; Nohata, 1986). American studies have also found that women take different routes than men to reach the same management positions. JAWE study found that 90 % of women had decided to keep working even if they got married and had children (Takaji and Nakamura, 1986). These findings suggest that the women achieved managerial status, because of special ability and circumstances unlike most Japanese males, who are directed towards such careers from childhood on. There is no difference in ability between female and male managers. Being able to handle the male-female relationship effectively is an essential skill for Japanese women managers. In Japanese context this skill includes avoiding status confrontations with men: adopting deferential, non-aggressive posture; using maternal managerial style. However, women in position of authority in government feel freer to adopt an authoritarian style that transcends gender roles (Lebra, 1992).

Even though larger companies in Japan profess support for promotion of qualified women, only six percent of the companies found the trend desirable (Japan Manpower Administration Research Institute, 1986). Labor shortage and broadening competitive economy will increase women's opportunities.

Status of Women in the United States of America

Since a mention has been made to the comparative status of the American women while discussing every other country, I will only present below some of the comparative statistics in this regard.

In 1990 women comprised 45% of the US labor force. A majority of these women are secretaries (99%) nurses (67%) and sales workers (60%) (U.S. Department of Labor, 1992). In 1992 women managers were 42% of the managerial labor force. U. S Department of Labor estimates that women fill only one to two percent of senior executive positions (U.S. Department of Labor, 1989). Women's participation in management is growing, though slowly. Women managers are highly concentrated in medical/health, personnel/labor relations, and education/administration areas. In the management categories women earned 62% of the amount that men earned.

An increasing number of women are securing advanced degrees, e.g., Bachelors (46%), Masters (34%), and doctoral degrees (24.4%). Although women are obtaining college degrees and securing management jobs, they are having difficulty securing upper level jobs.

Compared to male colleagues, executive women are thirteen times more likely to be single, separated, divorced or widowed (Parasuraman and Greenhaus, 1993). Moreover, executive women are significantly more likely to be childless (60%) than the executive men (3%) (Powell, 1988).

A great deal of research in management literature exists to show that men and women have similar traits, motivations, leadership styles, and skills and that women perform equally or better than men. During the decade 1970-80 most female managers tried to copy the style of male managers to succeed in their newly acquired roles. Aound the end of 1980s the women realized that in today's information technology environment, where personal skills are more useful, the female ways of management are better suited than those of males (Greenhaus and Parasuraman, 1990; Offermann and Armitage, 1993).

Yet, there is a perception that women and men as managers are different. Women managers are believed to be less likely than their male counterparts to possess the attributes of a successful manager. Stereotyping and prejudice seem to be the primary reason impeding women's ability to rise to the top of their corporations.

Purpose of the Study

This study was undertaken to compare the managerial motivations of male and female library and information science (LIS) students in America with LIS students in India, Singapore and Japan. Students are generally used for such studies because their values are as important to the researcher as those of the practitioners. An additional advantage of surveying students is an immediate feedback (Campbell, 1986; Greenberg, 1987). The LIS students are adults when they enroll for professional education. They have well-developed personalities and attitudes towards sex roles. A survey of the literature did not show any cross-cultural studies that have been done on this subject, in the LIS field. McClelland felt that there are enough commonalities between the American management value systems and those of from colonial rule recently freed Asian countries. He suggested that teaching achievement motivation theories could help the managers in developing countries, and he went overseas to India to teach them those theories (1961). Hofstede's studies show that the prevalent cultural values have a great influence on the management styles, and only those managers who are able to change and adopt the theories of achievement motivation according to the local climate are able to implement them successfully. This is an attempt to find out if there is a difference among the LIS professionals (males and females) in the US and India, Singapore and Japan, as far as achievement motivation is concerned.

Methodology

Instrument

A simplified version of the Ory and Poggio Measure of Achievement Motivation (1976) was selected for this study. Also, six questions from the Women in Management questionnaire by Terborg (1977) were used. The content of each item was related to one of several achievement motivation constructs. The questionnaire consisted of two parts, the first section consisted of 41 statements requiring students to indicate relative agreement or disagreement, according to a forced choice Likert-type format, with four response alternatives labeled "Strongly Agree", "Agree", "Disagree", and "Strongly Disagree". Number four represents the maximum agreement and number one represents least agreement. The second part consisted of 16 short answers to multiple choice statements that provided personal data (Appendix).

The survey was conducted at the 11 Southeastern library schools in the United States of America, twenty three universities in India, one in Singapore and one in Japan. The data were collected by mail and/or by visiting the campuses. The 41 statements in the questionnaire were divided into 10 scales. The SPSS Reliability Procedure was used to compute Cronbach's alpha for each scale. Items whose inclusion would have resulted in a lowering of alpha were deleted from each scale. For each scale a two-way factorial analysis of variance on mean agreement with items within the scale was conducted. In each analysis, main effects of Sex and Country and the Interaction of Sex and Country were assessed. Analogous two-way analyses of variances were performed on those few individual items that were dropped from the scales. On the average 1550 cases were analyzed.

Demographic analysis

The respondents consisted of 665 students from the USA, 814 from India, 73 from Singapore and three from Japan. Fifty percent of the Indian students, 46% percent of Singaporean students, 20% of the American students, and one Japanese student, were males. A majority of the Indians were younger, unmarried and full-time students, with very little work experience. A majority of the American and Singaporean students were older, had more library experience and were part-time students. Many more Americans, and all three of Japanese students were holding scholarships and/or work study assistantships as compared to the Indians and the Singaporeans. Fifty percent of the Indian students graduated from a coeducational institute, which marks a change in terms of segregation of sexes. A majority of Singaporeans and Japanese graduated from large co-educational colleges. Parents of American and Japanese students were better educated than the Indians and Singaporeans. Also, 60% of the American mothers, 19% of the Indian mothers, 37% of Singaporean mothers, and one of the Japanese (male) student's mother, work outside their home.

Since there were only three respondents from Japan (not a viable sample), except for percentage responses no further analysis of the data were performed.

Table 1. Task Orientation Questions - Percent of Respondents Who Agreed by Gender

(Table is not available here. Please contact the author.)

1. Task Orientation: Statements 01, 11, 20, 31 were used to analyze this characteristic. The female and male percentages were similar for the USA and India for statement #1. Though a majority of all respondents agreed with the statements #1, the level of agreement was lower for Singapore respondents, when compared to other two countries. There was a big difference between males to females responses on statement #1 (68% vs. 51%); on statement #11 (20 % Vs 34%); and on statement 20 (35 % Vs 21%) from Singapore. Within the USA male and female percentage response to all four questions were similar. Percentage response from Indian students, males and females to questions 1, 20, and 31 were similar. On question #11 more females than males prefer to choose moderately difficult tasks rather than very difficult ones. McClelland did indicate that successful managers choose moderately difficult problems that they can solve, rather than very difficult ones. Male and female percentages were lower for Singapore than the USA and India. Statement 1 was significant by country ($p < .003$), and not by sex. Statements 11, 20 and 31 showed a significant relationship by country and by sex ($p < .000$).

1. Future Orientation: Statements 06, 16, 25, 37 were used to test this scale. Statement 25 was deleted leaving items 6, 16, 37. Alpha for these 3-items was .71. Response percentages were well matched between all the three countries with agreement ranging from 77% to 96% on statements 6, 16, and 37. Within the three countries the female and male responses were also close. Major difference was noticed in responses to statement #25. A majority of the USA and Indian respondents disagreed with the statement, where as 100 percent of Singaporeans agreed with the statement, "I am not as much concerned about the present as I am the future".

Statement #25 showed a significant relationship by country and by sex ($p < .000$). Statement #37 showed a significant relationship by country ($p < .000$), but not significant by sex. Analysis of variance showed a significant difference by country and sex ($p < .028$, $df = 2$, $F = 3.602$).

Table 2. Future Orientation. Percentage of Respondents Who Agreed by Gender

(Table is not available. Please contact the author.)

72

Table 3. Perseverance. Percentage of Respondents Who Agreed by Gender

(Table is not available. Please contact the author.)

3. Perseverance. Statements 02, 12, 27, 34 were included in the analysis of Perseverance. Percentage agreement for all the statements was high among the respondents from the three countries. Between the countries the response percentages were similar on question 2, 12 and 27. On statement # 34 the agreement was lower for Indian males. On statement 12 the percentage agreement was lower for the USA females, and for Singapore males. Within the countries the responses from males and females were fairly close.

Statement # 2 showed a significant relationship by country ($p < .001$) and by sex ($p < .000$). Statement #12 was significant by country ($p < 002$) and not by sex.

Table 4. Social Acceptance. Percentage of Respondents Who Agreed by Gender

(Table is not available. Please contact the author.)

4. Social Acceptance. Statements 04, 22, 33, 35 were used to analyze this scale. The alpha was .74, so none of the items were deleted. A majority of respondents from the USA disagreed on all the statements. On Statement #4 the respondents from India and Singapore were close in their thinking. A lesser percentage of females agreed with the statements 4, 22, 33, and 35 than the males, from each country. On statement #33 a higher percentage of Indian students, males and females (70 % to 78%) agreed with the statement "social recognition is the primary goal of any undertaking". On Statement #35 Indian and Singaporean males were closer in their opinion. All four questions showed a significant difference both by country and by sex ($p < .000$). All the four questions showed a significant difference both by country and by sex ($p < .000$).

5. Competitiveness. Statements 07, 26, 38 were included in the analysis of Competitiveness. Statement #38 was deleted. The resulting alpha was .50. Responses from Singapore and the USA students were close to each other for statement #7. A majority of respondents from the USA and Singapore do not enjoy competing against the clock. A majority of Indian students however, agreed with that statement. A majority of males and females from all the three countries agreed with statement #26. On statement #38 the percentage responses were considerably different between sexes, and between countries.

Statement # 38 showed a significant difference by country ($p < .000$) and by sex ($p < .005$).

Table 5. Percentage of Respondents Who Agreed by Gender and Competitiveness

Table 6. Percentage of Respondents Who Agreed by Gender and Reaction to Success or Failure Questions

(Tables are not available. Please contact the author.)

6. Reaction to Success/Failure. Statements 15, 19, 24, 36 were used to analyze this scale. The alpha was .61. Statements 15 and 36 were deleted. The resulting alpha was equal to .74. Response percentages were very similar for all the four questions. A majority of respondents agreed with all the statements. Statement #24 showed a significant relationship by country ($p < .003$) and by sex ($p < .000$). Statement # 36 showed a significant relationship by country ($p < .000$). Analysis of variance by sex and country showed a significant relationship ($p < .01$, $df = 2$ and $F = 4.489$).

Table 7. Percentage of Respondents Who Agreed by Gender and Their Reaction to Fear of Success Questions

(Table is not available. Please contact the author.)

7. Fear of Success. Statements 03, 13, 21, 32 were used for the analysis of fear of success. Statement 21 was deleted. The resultant alpha was .48. Response percentages to questions 3, 13, and 32 were similar with the majority agreeing with these statements. A majority of LIS students from all the three countries disagreed with statement #21. Statement # 13 showed a significant relationship by country ($p < .004$) and by sex ($p < .000$). Statement #21 showed a significant relationship by country ($p < .008$). An analysis of statement #21 revealed a significant main effect ($p < .001$) of Sex and Country.

8. Rigidity. Statements 09, 18, 29, 41 were used to analyze this scale. The alpha was .70. A high majority of respondents from the USA disagreed with all of the four statements. A majority of respondents from Singapore also disagreed with statements 9, 18, and 41. A majority of Singaporean and Indian students agreed with the statement # 29.

All the four statements had a significant relationship both by sex and by country. The analysis corresponded to the USA respondents. Agreement among Indian respondents was higher than others on other three statements, also, variance by country and sex showed a significant relationship ($p < .015$; $df = 2$; $F = 4.215$).

Table 8. Percentage of Respondents Who Agreed by Gender and Rigidity Questions

(Table is not available. Please contact the author.)

9. Independence. Statements 8, 17, 28 and 39 dealt with independence. The percentage agreement for Indians was higher than for Singapore and the USA on statements 8,17, 28. The percentages were similar for males and females from the USA and Singapore on statement number 8. For statement 17, 28 and 39 the female percentage agreement was much lower for Singapore and the USA. The chi-square showed significant relationship with country and sex for statements 8, 17 and 28. Statement 39 showed a significant difference by country only.

Table 9. Percentage of Respondents Who Agreed by Gender and Independence Questions

(Table is not available. Please contact the author.)

10. Women as Manager Scale. Statements 05, 23, 10, 40, 14, 30 were used to analyze this scale. The alpha was equal to .65. A very high majority from all three countries disagreed with statements number 5, 23, and 30. A majority of respondents from the three countries agreed with statement number 40, and the percentage agreement from the USA were higher than from India and Singapore. The difference among the males and females was also significant. On statement 14 the percentages were comparable among countries and sexes, with the majority still disagreeing with the statement.

Statements 5, 23, 40 and 30 showed a significant difference by sex ($p < .000$) and country ($p < .000$). Analysis of variance showed a significant difference by sex and country ($p < .010$; $df = 2$; $F = 4.654$).

Table 10. Percentage of Respondents Who Agreed by Gender and Women as Managers Questions

(Table is not available. Please contact the author.)

Summary and Remarks

In this study a majority of the American, Indian and Singaporean LIS students were highly educated, achievement oriented, future oriented, persevering and competitive. The response percentages of the majority of respondents from all the three countries show that the majority of them were motivated to work hard, devote their energies to the task at hand, plan for the future and be competitive professionally. Significant relationships were found in the following categories: "task orientation", "future orientation", "perseverance", "social acceptance", "competitiveness", "reaction to success/ failure", "fear of success", "independence", "rigidity", and "women as managers scale". Looking broadly at the percentages, responses from the USA and India were closer to each other on "task Orientation", "future orientation", "perseverance", and "competitiveness". Responses from Indian and Singaporean LIS students were closer on "social acceptance", and "fear of success". Responses from Singapore and the USA were closer on "rigidity", "independence", and "women as managers".

Task Orientation. The percentage agreement of Singaporean students was lower then the USA and Indian students on the statement, "I am highly motivated when I know that a task is difficult". There was a vast difference in the percentages on the statement, "I often choose moderately difficult tasks rather than very difficult ones". A majority of Singaporean students disagreed, whereas a majority of both males and females from India and the USA agreed. McClelland did suggest that high achievers choose moderately difficult tasks that they could accomplish rather than very difficult ones. A higher percentage of Indians, however, felt that very difficult problems were more motivating than moderately difficult ones, compared to the Americans or Singaporean students. Again, a higher percentage of Indians liked finishing many easy tasks rather than a few difficult ones. Question one showed significant relationship by country, whereas questions 11, 20 and 31 were significant by country and by sex. The percentage of responses from the USA and the Indian students was closer than that of Singapore students. A higher percentage of females agreed with all the four questions than the males.

Future Orientation. The response percentages were well matched between all the three countries, on three of the four questions. A major difference was on question number 25. A majority of the respondents from the USA and India disagreed with the statement "I am not as much concerned about the present as I am of the future". One hundred percent of Singaporean students, male and female, agreed with the statement. Evidently Singaporean students think the future is much more important than the present. Singaporeans are very competitive. There is a lot of emphasis on education, training and retraining by the government. They have made a great deal of progress as a nation since independence. Indians and Americans think that the present is as important as the future. The percentages from Singapore and India were closer. The percentage agreement among males was higher than among females.

Perseverance. Percentage agreement on all questions was high among the respondents from the three countries. Within the countries the responses from males and females were fairly close. The percentage agreement was comparable between India and the USA, rather than with Singapore. Agreement among the females was higher than the males.

Social Acceptance. A majority of respondents from America disagreed with all the four questions. On the question "social acceptance is more important than personal success" the percentage agreement from Indian students was very high compared to the other two countries. A majority of respondents also agreed with statement number 4. Evidently for the American students personal success is more important than social acceptance or social recognition. This attitude on the personal level translates into self-development and independent achievement at the individual level. On the other hand the value of social acceptance and social recognition translates into putting the goals of the society or the organization first and the achievement of the personal goals second. This coincides with Hofstede's (1980) criterion of differences in the cultures. According to Hofstede, even though Americans are high on individualism, for them individualism translates into every individual striving to gain wealth, recognition, self-direction and self-actualization. For Indians wealth is less important and conflict-ridden. For Indians and Singaporeans group solidarity and family are more important than the individual himself. For them self-actualization is more of the meditative type. More Indian students were willing to change their opinion in order to build a consensus in a group than the American students. Indians also wanted more friendly relations with the coworkers, rather than flexibility at work.

Although Indian and Singaporean administrations follow an open-door policy, there is still a greater distance between the superior and the subordinate than compared to American organizations. Hofstede refers to it as respective high or low "distance from the power". Indians are more likely to look to their superiors for approval and guidance than the Americans. In a bureaucratic organization American managers learn to respect authority. Both men and women need the desire to exercise power to climb up the corporate ladder. It is consistent with the findings in the USA in the studies on the hierarchical motivation theory (Miner, 1993), the need for power theory (McClelland and Boyatzis, 1982) and Hofstede's (1980) power distance (Chan, Yu, and Miner, 1997, p.170).

Indians are poorer than Americans and in need of the job, thus they are afraid to disagree with their employer. Such fear is evident in the following remark by a senior Indian executive, with a Ph.D. from a prestigious American University:

> What is most important for my department and me is not what I do or achieve
> for the company, but whether the Master's (i.e., the owner of the firm) favor is
> bestowed on me. This I have achieved by saying "yes" to everything the
> Master says or does. [T]o contradict him is to look for another job. I left my
> freedom of thought in Boston (Hofstede, p.128).

Percentage of responses from India and Singapore were closer than the USA. Agreement among the males was higher than the females.

Competitiveness. A majority of the USA and Singaporean students disagreed on the statement, "I enjoy competing against the clock", whereas a majority of the Indian students enjoy competing against the clock. Mild competition keeps the excitement of achievement high and competing against the clock builds speed (White, 1957). There is a lot to be said in favor of progressing at your own pace as most of the Americans like to do, however, competition leads to innovation and adds spice to achievement motivation. In this study both sexes in India and in the USA were quite competitive.

More American and Indian students wanted to work in "libraries that pay well rather than those that pay less, but allow flexibility". A smaller percentage of respondents from Singapore, and a smaller percentage of females than males from the USA and India, agreed with this question. A higher percentage of Singaporean females agreed with the question compared to Singaporean males. The percentage of USA respondents who agreed was closer to Indian students than to Singaporean students. Male percentages were higher than the female.

Reaction to Success or Failure and Fear of success. Response percentages were similar for all four questions. Female percentages were higher than males.

Rigidity. On question number 9, "A true challenge is one that is practically impossible to achieve", a majority of the American and Singaporean students disagreed, but a majority of Indians agreed. On question number 18 "I would rather have my superior set deadlines than set them myself", a majority of Americans and Singaporeans disagreed, but a higher percentage wanted the superior to set the deadlines. This tendency could be prompted by a "dependence motivation" as pointed out by Pareek (1988). It could lead to a tendency to avoid responsibility. Management research shows that people who set their own goals are more motivated and committed to achieve them, and they are also more likely to take responsibility for the consequences of their actions. On the other two questions responses from Indian and Singaporean students were closer to one another than the Americans. On question 29, "It is more important to have friendly co-workers than flexibility on the job", Americans prefer flexibility on the job and Indians and Singaporeans prefer friendly relationship with the coworkers. Also, the Indians and Singaporeans were more willing to change their opinions to build a consensus in the group than were the American students. It again could be a reflection of the culture. American students are more individualistic and Indian and Singaporeans are more group-oriented in their thinking. Percentage responses of sexes were the same.

Women as Managers Scale. A majority of the respondents felt that challenging work is as important to men as for women. It is as desirable for women to have jobs that require responsibility as for men. Many more Indians than USA and Singaporean students felt that women have the objectivity to evaluate library situations properly. A higher percentage of American students agreed with the statement number 40, "Women would no more allow their emotions to influence their managerial behavior than would men". A majority of Indian and Singaporean students also agreed. All respondents disagreed with the statement number 14 that "Women cannot be aggressive in managerial situations that demand it". A majority felt that women are ambitious enough to be successful in challenging and responsible managerial positions.

On the category acceptance of Women as Managers more Indian males than the American and the Singaporean males, look at women in a stereotypical light. Forty percent of the Indian males versus two percent of the American males and 16% of the Singaporean males agreed with the statement #23 - "It is less desirable for women than men to have a job that requires responsibility". Also, about 30% Indian males versus three percent of the American males and 10% of the Singaporean males felt that (Question number 30) women are not ambitious enough to be successful in managerial position. In the business world, in all the countries, the majority of men perceive women as lacking in competitiveness, ambition and leadership abilities. Fifty two percent of the Indian women themselves felt that they do not have the objectivity required to evaluate library situations properly. In this study Indians were more conservative than the Americans and the Singaporeans in accepting women as managers.

Conclusion

In this study a majority of both men and women from the three countries surveyed were highly educated and motivated. The agreement percentages were similar on "task orientation", "perseverance", "future orientation", and "competitiveness", between countries and sexes. These are the categories that matter most as far as the work environment is concerned. The differences between the sexes and countries were found on factors like "women as managers", "reaction to success or failure", "fear of failure, " and "social acceptance".

Social acceptance showed the highest difference between the respondents from the three countries. A majority of the Americans respondents disagreed with all the four questions. For Americans personal success is more important than social acceptance or social recognition. This attitude at the personal level translates into self-development and independent achievement at the individual level. On the other hand the need for social acceptance and social recognition for the Indians, Singaporeans, and Japanese translates into putting the goals of the society or the organization first and the achievement of individual or personal goals second. This coincides with Hofstede's criterion of the differences between the cultures. According to him for Indians, Singaporeans and Japanese, the concept of self as a separate entity from society and culture does not exist. It includes the person himself, and his intimate societal and cultural environment, which makes existence meaningful. As this study also indicates they would modify their views more easily in favor of their friends to keep harmony in their environment than the Americans. These countries score low on individualism. Society in turn plays a supportive role and thus the dimensions of "reaction to success or failure", and the "fear of success", also gets minimized.

The United States of America is a major exporter of modern organizational and management theories abroad. But the position of extreme individualism of the Americans in comparison to collectivism of most other countries calls for major modification of these theories to suit the environment of those countries and cultures. Most managers who were able to modify the theories have had success in implementing them in their own context.

Another difference was found on the factor "women as manager". A higher percentage of Indian males look at women in a stereotypical light than of the Americans. The American and Singaporeans were more positive about accepting women in management. Even 52% of the Indian women themselves felt that they do not have the objectivity required to evaluate library situations properly. However a majority of them agreed that women are ambitious enough to be successful as managers in challenging and responsible positions. They also felt that women would not let their emotions influence their managerial behavior any more than men would. This indicates that even though women feel they can handle most managerial situation, they get doubtful of the abstract values attached to those roles by the organizations or societies.

This survey shows that a majority of American and Singaporean men and women are ready to concede, at least at the conceptual level, that women can successfully take up managerial roles. A majority of the young Americans and Singaporeans have realized the need for two incomes for the family and are gradually adapting to the changed economic conditions. The Indian economic conditions also demand a similar adaptation. The American women have worked hard to get to this level. They are still struggling to achieve equality in work place and in the domestic arena. There is a big gap still between the conception and the reality, however.

Our opinions are influenced and shaped by the societal forces and personal characteristics. Prevalent culture determines the gender roles in a society. In most countries, societies expect women to be subservient towards men and, therefore, assume that men will exercise authority over other people. These perceived behaviors have been attributed to childhood socialization or an innate psychological or biological disposition. Societal and organizational messages conveyed to women, in most countries, have been that women themselves have the primary responsibility to rectify the situation. As a response to this challenge women turned to business and professional schools, earned higher degrees, and gained managerial experience at whatever level they were allowed. Women entrepreneurs and professional women organized networks for mutual support. They lobbied for laws to be changed. They also undertook research to determine the causes of their slow progress and low salaries. After some thirty years, at about the end of the 1980s women had started questioning this image of a typical male-dominated society. Entrepreneurial women who excelled in their own business, when compared to their equally qualified colleagues, who stayed with the corporations, and were not promoted to executive levels, clearly demonstrated institutional and organizational discrimination. Most of the research studies also indicated that there are negligible differences between sexes as far as managerial motivation is concerned. By focusing on individual characteristics the organizational factors like discrimination and stereotypical social values affecting the careers of women were ignored or camouflaged. Even in professions where a large number of qualified women are at the middle level, like LIS, men dominate the top level of management. Women advocate that organizations should eliminate discrimination and adopt objective methods of selecting, promoting and rewarding. Organizations can gain by sharing executive ranks with some of the more talented women and thus maximize their human resources. For success such a change is needed at the individual, organizational and social levels.

Economic independence, self-confidence and personal achievement motivation are the only tools that serve women well in negotiating their status in the family with their husbands and other family members. Women's employment in particular marks a significant rejection of male control. In all countries and cultures, men resist conceding their privileges in personal, domestic, sexual and family relations. The resistance experienced by women comes in personal areas of marriage, inheritance and the guarantee of domestic equality. This resistance demonstrates just how political the personal arena is in gender relations. Legal reforms do not work well in this arena. This is especially evident in the increasing rate of family violence, divorce rates and child abuse and neglect in both countries.

This study, like most personality studies did not find substantial differences between the personalities of the male and female respondents in the performance categories of "task orientation", "perseverance", "future orientation", and "competitiveness". There seems to be a need to bring about an attitudinal change towards accepting women as managers based on such empirical studies. Both males and females have similar career aspirations and both want to be leaders and/or managers. While the basic theories of management can be taught in all the countries, the difference lies in the implementation of these theories. Management motivation theories work well if the managers are sensitive to, and can modify them, to suit the prevalent culture of the organization or the country.

References

Acker, Joan (1990) "Hierarchies, jobs, bodies: A theory of gendered organizations", Gender and Society 4(2):139-158. Adler, Nancy J. and Defna N. Izraeli (eds.) (1988) Women in management worldwide. Armonk, N.Y.: M.E Sharpe

Amiable, Teresa M.(1993) Motivational synergy: Toward new conceptualizations of intrinsic and extrinsic motivation in the work place. Human Resources Management Review 3 No. 3: 185-301.

Arfken, Deborah E., Stephanie L., Bellar, and Marylyn M. Helms. (Fall 1998) "Ultimate glass ceiling: Women on corporate boards". A Leadership Journal: Women in Leadership-sharing vision. 38(1): 95-105.

Arasu, Siva and Ooi, Suzanne (1984). "Women who have risen high", The Sunday Times, November 4, p.19.

Ashna, Pratima (1974). Women's movement in India. Delhi: Vikas. p.23.

Astin, H. S (1984) "The meaning of work in women's lives: A sociological model of career choice and work behavior". The Counseling Psychologist, 12: 117-126.

Atkinson, J.W. (1957) " Motivational determinants of risk-taking behavior". Psychological Review, 64, 359-372.

Atkinson, J.W. (1964) An introduction to motivation. Princeton, N.J.: Van Nostrand.

Auluck-Wilson, C. A. (1995). When all the Women left. Signs, 20: 1030-1038.

Baig, Tara Ali (1976). India's women power. New Delhi, S. Chand.

Basow, A.S. and Medcalf, K.L. (1988) Academic achievement and attributions among college students: Effects of gender and sex typing. Sex-Roles, 19, 555-567

Bem, S. L. (1974) "The measurement of psychological androgyny". Journal of Consulting Psychology, 42: 155-62.

Brenner, O.C. (1989) Relations of age and education to managers' work values. Psychological Reports, 63: 639-642.

Bumiller, Elisabeth (1990) May you be the mother of a hundred sons: A journey among the women of India. New York: Random House.

Campbell, J.P. (1986) "Labs, field and straw issues". In Lock, E.A. Generalizing from Laboratory to Field Settings. Lexington, Mass. Lexington Books: 269-279.

Chan, Audrey and Lee, Jean (1994) "Singapore women executives in a newly industrialized economy: The Singapore scenario". In Competitive frontiers: Women managers in a global economy, edited by Nancy J. Adler and Dafna N. Izraeli. Cambridge, MA: Blackwell. pp: 127-142.

Chen, Chao C., Yu, K C, Miner, J B. (June 1997) "Motivation to manage: A study of women in Chinese state-owned enterprises". The Journal of Behavioral Science: Arlington, 32(2) 160-173.

Chumir, L.H. and Kolberg, C. S. (1991) Sex role conflict in sex-atypical jobs: A study of female male differences. Journal of Organizational Behavior, 12: 461-465.

Cook, E. P. (1985) Psychological androgyny. New York, Pergamon Press.

Coopersmith, S. (1960) Self-esteem and need for achievement as determinants of selective recall and repetition. Journal of Abnormal and Social Psychology, 60: 310-317.

Daley, S. (1991) Something causes girls to lose self-esteem. The Chattanooga Times, c2, p.1-2.

Deci, E.L. and Ryan, R.M. (1985). Intrinsic motivation and self determination in human behavior. New York: Plenum.

Diamond, E.E. (1984). Theories of career development and the reality of women at work. In B.A. Gutek and L. Larwood (eds). Women's career development. Newbury Park, CA: Sage.

D'Souza, Victor S. (1980). " Family status and female work participation", In Alfred de Souza (ed), Women in contemporary India and South Asia. New Delhi: Manohar, p. 129.

Fagenson, Ellen A. and Jackson, Janice J. (1994). "United States of America: The status of women managers in the United States". In Competitive frontiers: Women managers in a global economy, edited by Nancy J. Adler and Dafna N. Izraeli. Cambridge, MA: Blackwell, pp. 127-142.

Feld, S.C. (1967). "Longitudinal study of the origins of achievement strivings". Journal of Personality and Social Psychology, 7: 408-414.

Florentine, K. (1988). Increasing similarity in values and life plans of male and female college students? Evidence and implications. Sex Roles, 18: 143-158.

Fottler, M.D. and Trevor, B. (1980). Managerial aspirations of high school seniors: A comparison of males and females. Journal of Vocational Behavior, 16: 83-95.

Fullerton, H. N. Jr. (1990) "New labor force projections, spanning 1988 to 2000", In U. S. Department of Labor, Bureau of Labor Statistics, Outlook 2000, Bulletin No. 2352, pp. 1-11. Washington, D. C.: U. S. Government Printing Office.

Gilligan, C. (1986) Reply to Carol Gilligan. Signs, 11: 324-333.

Ginzberg, E. (1972) Toward a theory of occupational choice: A restatement. The Vocational Guidance Quarterly, 20: 169-176.

Greenberg, J. (1987) The college sophomore as guinea pig: Setting the record straight. Academy of Management Review 12:153-159.

Greenhaus, J., Parasuraman, S., and Wormley, W. (1990) "Effects of race on organizational experiences, job performance evaluations and career outcomes". Academy of Management Journal 33:64-86.

Hacket T, G. and Betz, (1981) A self-efficiency approach to the career development of women. Journal of Vocational Behavior, 18: 326-339.Chapters 19 and 20: 486-548.

Handbook of personality: Theory and research ed by Lawrence A. Pervin, (1990). New York, Guilford.

Harris, Roma M. (1992) Librarianship: The erosion of a women's profession. Norwood: Ablex.

Heidrick and Struggles (1986) The corporate women officer. Chicago: Heidrick and Struggles.

Hiatt, P. (1983) Management skills: Key to better service delivery. Journal of Library Administration, 4: 21-39.

Hiatt, P. (1983). Should professionals be managers? Journal of Library Administration, 4: 21-39.

Hofstede, Geert. (1980) Culture's consequences international differences in work-related values. London: Sage.

Hong, Gui-Young. (1991) Gender as a joint construct by individual agents and socio-cultural contexts. Paper presented at the 1991 Southern Humanities Counsel Conference, Chattanooga, TN.

Horner, M.S. (1988). Sex differences in achievement motivation and performance in competitive and non-competitive situations. Unpublished doctoral dissertation, University of Michigan, Ann Arbor, MI.

Jacob, Jerry A. (1992) Women's entry into management: Trends in earnings, authority and values among salaried managers. Administrative Science Quarterly, 37(2):282-301

Japan Manpower Administration Research Institute (1986) Shprai Arubeki Jinji ... [1985 research consideration of desirable manpower management of the future]. Tokyo, Japan Manpower Administration Research Institute.

Katz, J. (1988) Career values for men and women, Paper presented at HRMOB. Association for Human Resources Management and Organizational Behavior.

Kolhberg, C.S.; Chumir, L.H. (1991). Sex role conflict in sex-atypical jobs: A study of female male differences. Journal of 0rganizational-Behavior, 12: 461-465.

Koesner, R., Ryan, R.M., Bernieri,F. and Holt, K. (1984) Setting limits in children's behavior: The differential effects of controlling versus informational styles on intrinsic motivation and creativity. Journal of Personality, 52: 233-248.

Lebra, Takie Sugiyama (1992) "Gender and culture in Japanese political economy: Self portrayals of prominent business women", In Shumpei Kuon and Henry Rosovsky (Eds.), The political economy of Japan, volume 3, Cultural and Social Dynamics, pp. 364-419. Stanford, CA: Stanford University Press.

Liddle J. and Joshi, R. (1989). Daughters of Independence: Gender, caste and classes in India. Princeton, N.J.: Rutgers University Press.

Lott, B.E. (1987) Women's Lives: Themes and variations in gender learning. Monterey, CA: Brooks/Cole, 1987.

Maehr, M. L. (1974) Culture and achievement motivation. American Psychologist, 29: 887-896.

Maehr, M.L. (1984). Meaning and motivation: Toward a theory of personal investment. In R. Ames and C. Ames (Eds.), Research in motivation in education: student motivation 1, 115-144. New York: Academic Press.

Maehr, M.L. (1987) Motivation and school achievement. In Current Topics in Early Childhood Education, 7: 87-107.

Martin, J. K. (1988). Factors related to the representation of women in library management. Master's thesis, University of Georgia.

MaZumdar, Vina (1976) The social reform movement in India. In B.R. Nanda (Ed.) Indian women from purdah to modernity. New Delhi: Vikas

McClelland, D.C. (1961) The Achieving Society. Princeton, NJ: Van Nostrand.

McClelland, D.C. (1984) Motives, personality and society: Selected papers. New York: Praeger.

McClelland, D. C. (1987) Characteristics of successful entrepreneurs. Journal of Creative Behavior, 3: 219-233.

McClelland. D.C. and Boyatzis, R.E. (1982) "Leadership motive pattern and long time success in management". Journal of Applied Psychology, 67 : 737-743.

Mehta, Sushila (1993) Revolution and the status of women in India. New Delhi: Metropolitan.

Mernissi, Fatima. (1975) Beyond the veil. New York: Wiley.

Miner, J. B. (1993) Role motivation theories. New York: Routledge.

Ministry of Education (1991) Gakko Kihon Chosa [Basic Research on Education). Tokyo: Printing Office, Ministry of Finance.

Murgai, S.R. (1987) Managerial motivation and career aspirations of library/information science students. (Ed.D. dissertation, University of Tennessee, Knoxville, TN.). Dissertation Abstracts International. Murgai, S.R. (1991) Attitudes towards women as managers in library and information science. Sex Roles, 24: 681-700.

Murgai, S. R. (1996). Motivation to manage: A comparative study between male and female Library and Information Science students in the United States of America and India. Presented at The 62nd IFLA Conference at Beijing, China, August 25-31, Booklet No. 6:16-39

Murray, H. A. (1938) Explorations in personality. New York: Oxford University Press.

Nanda, B.R.(Ed)(1976) Indian women from purdah to modernity. New Delhi: Vikas.

Nieva, Veronica F. and Gutek, Barbara A. (1981). Women and work: A Psychological Perspective. New York: Praeger.

Nohata, M. (1986) ... [Factors and process of career formation of managerial women]. Shakaigaiku Hyron 34: 458-456.

(Nineteen...)1990 NUS and NTI Graduate Employment Survey (1991) Singapore: National University of Singapore University Press.

Offermann, L. and Armitage, M. (1993) "The stress and health of the woman manager", In E.A. Fagenson (Ed.) Women in management: trends, issues and challenges in managerial diversity, pp. 131-161. Newberry Park, CA: Sage Publications.

Ory, J.C. and Poggio, J.P.(1976) The development and empirical validation of a measure of achievement motivation. Bethesda, MD: [ERIC Document Reproduction Service ED 124 567].

Osipow, S.H. (1983) Theories of career development. Princeton, N.J., Prentice-Hall.

Pareek, . U. (1988) "A motivation paradigm of development". Journal of Social Issues, 24: 115-122.

Parasuraman, S. & Greenhaus, J. (1993) "Personal portrait: The lifestyle of the woman manager". In E.A. Fagenson (ed) Women in management: trends, issues and challenges in managerial diversity, pp. 86-211. Newberry Park, CA: Sage Publications.

Pittman, R. S.; Davey, M. E.; Alafat, K. A. ; Wetherukkm K. V. and Kramer, N. A.. (1980) Informational versus controlling verbal rewards. Personality and Social Psychology Bulletin, 6:228-233.

Powell, G. (1988) Women and men in management. Newberry Park, CA: Sage Publications.

Powell, G. (1993) Women and men in management. Newberry Park, CA: Sage Publications.

Prichard, S.H. (1993) Feminist thinking and Librarianship in the 1990's: Issues and challenges. A paper presented at the annual conference of the Michigan Library Association.

Regins, Belle Rose (1991). "Gender effects in subordinate evaluations of leaders :Real or artifact?" Journal of Organizational Behavior, 12: 259-268.

Report of the Labor Force Survey of Singapore (1991) Singapore: Research and Statistics Division, Ministry of Labour.

Ryan, R.M. (1982) Control and information in the interpersonal sphere: An extension of cognitive evaluation theory. Journal of personality and social psychology, 43: 450-461.

Ryan, R. M., Mims, V. and Koesner, R. (1983). Relation of reward, contingency and interpersonal context to intrinsic motivation: A review and test using cognitive evaluation theory. Journal of Personality and Social Psychology, 45: 736-750. Sarkar, Lotika (1976) Jawaharlal Nehru and the Hindu Code Bill. In B.R. Nanda (ed.) Indian women from purdah to modernity,. Delhi: Vikas.

Sarkar, Lotika and Mazumdar (1974) " Note of Dissent", in Department of Social Welfare, Towards Equality: Report of the Commission on the Status of Women in India. New Delhi, Government of India, p.355.

SCWO salutes Singapore Women 1980-1990 (1991) Singapore: The Singapore Council of Women Organizations (SCWO) publication.

Singhal, R. and Misra.G. Achievement goals: A situational-contextual analysis. International Journal of Intercultural Relations, 18: 239-258.

Spence, J.T. and Helmreich, R.L. (1983) Achievement related motives and behaviors in achievement and achievement motives. Austin,TX: University of Texas Press.

Spence, J.T. and Sawin, L.L. (1985) Images of masculinity and femininity: A re-conceptualization. In V. Oleary, R. Unger and B.Wallston (Eds.), Sex, gender and social psychology (pp. 35-66). Hillsdale, NJ: Erlbaum.

Steinhoff, Parricia and Tanaka, Kazuko (1994) "Women Managers in Japan". Chapter 5 In Competitive frontiers: Women managers in a global economy. Cambridge, MA: Blackwell. pp.79-100.

Swisher, R., Du Mont, R. R., and Boyer, C. J. (1985). The motivation to manage: A study of academic libraries and library science students. Library Trends, 34:219-234.

Super, D. E. (1980). A life span approach to career development. Journal of Vocational Behavior, 16 (3): 282-298.

Teikoku Data Bank (1986 and 1990) Josei Shacho no Rankingu 100sha [The 100 top ranking companies with women Presidents]. Tokyo, Tikoku Data Bank.

Terborg, J R. (1977) Women in Management. Journal of Applied Psychology, 62: 647-664.

U.S. Department of Commerce. (1995-96). Statistical Abstract of the United States. Washington, D.C. GPO.

U.S. Department of Labor: Office of Federal Compliance Programs (1990-91). A Report on Glass-Ceiling Initiative, edited by Lynn Martin. Washington D.C., GPO.

U.S. Department of Labor (1989a) "Women in management", Facts on working women, No. 89-4. Washington, D.C. : U.S. Government Printing Office.

U.S. Department of Labor (1992) Employment and earnings. Washington, D.C.: U.S Government Printing Office.

Vanucci, T and Kliener, B.H. (1989) "Understanding and coping with fear of success". A paper presented at the annual conference of the American Management Association.

Victor S. (1980) "Family status and female work participation", In Alfred de Souza (ed), Women in Contemporary India and South Asia. New Delhi: Manohar, p.129.

White, R.W. (1959). Motivation reconsidered: The concept of competence. Psychological Review, 66: 297-333.

APPENDIX

Survey of Library/Information Science Students.

We want to know how you feel about the following statements. Some of the statements may depend on the situation, but we want your choice to be the one which best reflects your opinion in general. Your participation is voluntary — you may quit at any time. Data from the survey will be used in aggregate form and no single individual will be identified from the responses. Please circle the letters to the right of each statement to indicate relative agreement or disagreement with the statement. There are no right or wrong answers. Please answer all statements.

(Survey is not available here. Please contact the author.)

SETTING-UP A WOMEN'S STUDIES LIBRARY

Marie Jacquelyn

Librarian,
University of California-Santa Cruz,
Santa Cruz, CA, USA (1994)

Abstract

This paper details questions on access, use, collection policies, cataloguing and classification, staffing, weeding, preservation and funding for women's studies collections at women's centers or libraries.

Introduction

In this era of growing interest in and enthusiasm about women's issues, women's studies (sometimes called gender or feminist studies) are of primary importance in higher education. Women's Studies scholars often lobby for the development of a center to disseminate information on women's studies courses or in fact to encourage professors to teach such courses.

The fledgling center often needs a board or committee to discuss the options for this center. Perhaps it will be a women's center at a university, which will be open as well as to scholars also to community women to fulfill their needs. Perhaps it will be a center affiliated with a women's studies or gender studies program and open only to scholars. However, soon after such a center is opened, whether academic or community or a combination of both, people start bringing in books and materials from their personal libraries, faculty bring in papers, reports, and journal articles, others bring in bibliographies, flyers and announcements of events of interest to women appear in the mail. Unfortunately the center is often unprepared. It may have been set up with no intentions of having a library.

Perhaps there is already an excellent library on the campus and no one wishes to duplicate efforts. On the other hand a gender or women's studies center may wish to have a library attached to it. Or perhaps there is a need for just a reading room with a bulletin board for flyers and other such material. In all these cases some thought should be given to a policy for such a library.

Starting Library Collections

These are some questions to be asked:

1. Should there be a library?

2. Who would use this library?

3. Will people be able to check out these materials or just use them in local? Will there be copying facilities?

4. What type of materials should be collected? Books? Journals? (popular, women related, academic) Newsletters? Student papers, bibliographies? Ephemeral materials such as articles, letters, leaflets from organizations or demonstrations? Audio or visual tapes? Films?

5. Will there be periodical indexes available such as Women's Studies Abstracts or Studies on Women Abstracts? Will these indexes be in paper or on computer?

6. Should there be funding for materials and where should such funding come from?

7. How should these materials be arranged? Should the books be catalogued? By author, title, subject? Will a numbering scheme be used? Will a subject classification scheme be used? Will it be the Library of Congress classification or another library classification system or one made up for this particular collection? Will there be handwritten or typed cards or will there be a computerized catalog?

8. How long will materials be kept? Where will older materials be housed? Will there be any attempt to preserve materials?

9. Who will be available to help users? Will a librarian be hired? With library training?

10. Who will do the collecting? the classifying? the weeding?

11. Who will make the decisions about this library, its focus, its parameters?

All these questions may seem overwhelming but need to be thought out, hopefully, before a single book is put on the shelf or a single article is filed away in a drawer.

Although there have been innumerable books published in practically every country and in many, many languages on women's issues and the women's movement, these topics have also generated many pamphlets, oral history tapes, videos, films, and articles in alternative magazines as well as academic journals. There are also unpublished reports, bibliographies and guides. Materials on women's issues are proliferating.

The rule seems to be that when a women's center has empty shelves they will be filled almost immediately with much of these materials. Women are very generous in donating their books and other materials. Sometimes there are materials that are not relevant for the center and therefore have to be rejected. This is the case when the center's criteria for inclusion of materials will come in handy. Women's studies are interdisciplinary covering many fields of knowledge. It will be impossible to collect and preserve all these areas, so a focus on particular areas of special interest to the scholars using the library will be beneficial. Duplication of materials, particularly journals and books available in other nearby libraries, may not be necessary.

Ephemeral materials such as newsletters and flyers are very useful and not usually collected in university libraries. However, they should be weeded regularly unless this will be a historical collection and these materials will be preserved.

Cataloguing and Classification

Another area that is very important for discussion is the classification of all the materials in order to make them easily accessible to the users. The language of women's studies changes as new topics come up for discussion, new terms are invented or old terms are changed to reflect a new awareness of cultural, racial and sexual differences. For example, in the United States the terms used by and for a person of African heritage residing in the United States have changed from "Negro" to "Colored" to "Afro" to "Afro-American" to "Black" to "African American". Therefore, the words used to define a subject and to assign various materials under them should no be offensive to anybody. These words should also come to mind as readily as possible, when a scholar researches a particular topic.

Often traditional subject headings are inappropriate for women's collections. Therefore, the National Council for Research on Women in the United States developed a list of terms in English used for various women's issues, including those of international women, after close consultation with librarians, scholars, and women in women's community organizations. As they state in the foreword of their excellent book, "A Women's Thesaurus sets national standards for terms to use in writing, cataloging, and research and is an up to date reference guide for non-sexist use of language". This thesaurus can be used as a start to developing subject headings for files and even for books. Then the needs for that particular library and its clientele should be analyzed and other headings could be developed to fit those needs. A broad heading such as health probably needs to be broken down into narrower headings such as abortion, birth control, nutrition and pregnancy but probably not into more narrow headings such as ectopic pregnancy, types of birth control and so on. The priority for subject headings or any kind of classification system is their ease of use so that people may find materials as quickly as possible and that others will be able to file or shelve them in a timely manner.

Librarian's Reference List

The following list includes useful books and articles to help in classifying books and other materials on women's issues as well as building a women's studies collection. These titles are in English and primarily contain English language materials; however, some also list materials in other languages.

Chapman, Anne. Feminist Resources for Schools and Colleges. A Guide to Curricular Materials. Old Westbury, NY: Feminist Press, 1986.

Ariel, Joan, (Ed.) Building Women's Studies Collections: A Resource Guide. Middletown, CT: Choice, 1987.

Ballou, Patricia K. Women. A Bibliography of Bibliographies. Boston: G.K. Hall, 1986.

Capek, Mary Ellen, (Ed.) Women's Thesaurus. An Index of Language Used to Describe and Locate Information by and about Women. New York: Harper & Row, 1987.

Dickstein, Ruth. Women in LC's Terms: A Thesaurus of Library of Congress Subject Headings Relaton to Women. Phoenix, AZ: Oryx, 1988.

Feminist Bookstore News. P.O. Box 8822554 San Francisco, CA 94188, USA. A newsletter of women's bookstores, publishers, book reviews from an international perspective.

Feminist Collections: A Quarterly of Women's Studies Resources. V. 1, No. 1, 1980 to present. Madison, WI: Women's Studies Librarian, University of Wisconsin Library System.

Loeb, Catherine, Susan Searing and Esther Stineman. Women's Studies: A Recommended Bibliography. Littleton, Colorado: Libraries Unlimited, 1987.

Marshall, Joan K. On Equal Terms: A Thesaurus for Non-Sexist Indexing and Cataloging. New York: Neal Schuman, 1977.

Women's Collections: Libraries, Archives and Consciousness. New York: Haworth, 1986.

This collection of essays includes information on collections of international women's materials, reference works for the study of minority and third world women, feminist library services and issues of non-sexist language.

Women's Organizations

All libraries in women's centers whether affiliated with a community or women's organization or a university program should be aware of and collecting in international women's issues. There are many resources available. The various agencies of the United Nations, the Commission of the European Communities and other women's agencies around the world produce pamphlets, bibliographies, newsletters and other kinds of materials. The most useful directory is Women's Movements of the World, which lists the principal official and unofficial organizations for each country. Many of these organizations publish materials in a variety of languages. In the following is a list of organizations, books and journals with international information on women.

African Training and Research Centre for Women (ATRCW), ECA, P.O. Box 3001, Addis Ababa, Ethiopia. Publishes various reports, bibliographies and ATRCW Update.

Asian and Pacific Centre for Women and Development (APCWD), APCD, P.O. Box 2224, Kuala Lumpur, Malaysia.

Boulding, Elise. Handbook of International Data on Women. New York: Wiley, 1976.

Carter, Sarah and Maureen Ritchie. Women's Studies: A Guide to Information Sources. London: Mansell Publishing, 1990. An excellent source of English language reference works and annotated listings of many international journals and organizations.

Change International Reports. P.O. Box 824, London, SE24 9JS. England. Publishes reports on the condition and status of women in the world.

Connexions: An International Women's Quarterly. 4228 Telegraph Ave., Oakland, California, 94609, USA. A journal which publishes articles from around the world translated into English.

Fenton, Thomas and Mary Heffron. Women in the Third World: A Directory of Resources. Maryknoll, New York: Orbis Books, 1987.

International Center for Research on Women. 1717 Massachusetts Ave. NW, Suite 501, Washington, DC, 20036, USA.

Women in Economic Activity: A Global Statistical Survey (1950-2000). International Labour Organization INSTRAW, Santo Domingo, Dominican Republic, 1985.

International Women's Tribune Center. 777 United Nations Plaza, New York 10017, USA. Publishes a journal, THE TRIBUNE, and various reports.

ISIS International. Via San Saba 5, 00153 Rome, Italy; Casilla 2067, Correo Central, Santiago, Chile. Publishes two journals, The ISIS International Women's Journal, and Women in Action. Also has published Powerful Images: A Women's Guide to Audiovisual Resources, 1986.

Nordic Association for Feminist Research, Centre for Feminist Research and Women's Studies, University of Copenhagen Amager, Njalsgade 106, 2300 Copenhagen S, Denmark. Published a guide to women's studies in the Nordic countries in 1988.

Richter, Werner, Liisa Husu and Arnaud Marks. The Changing Role of Women in Society: A Documentation of Current Research. Berlin, Germany: Akademie Verlag, 1989. A major source on Eastern Europe including the USSR. It lists sponsoring institutions and researchers.

Seager, Joni and Ann Olson. Women in the World: An International Atlas. London: Pluro, 1986.

Shreir, Sally. Women's Movements of the World. London: Longman, 1988.

Third World Women's Review. Third World Communications, Kwame Nkrumah House, 173 Old St., London EClV 9NJ, England. A journal published since 1986 focusing on third world women.

United Nations, Statistical Office. Women's Indicator and Statistics Database (WISTAT), United Nations, New York 10017, USA. Microcomputer spreadsheet files covering 178 countries on a variety of topics.

Women's International Democratic Federation, Unter den Linden 13, 1080, Berlin, Germany. Publishes, a journal in six languages.

Women's International Network (WIN), 187 Grant St., Lexington, Mass. 02173, USA. Publishes WIN News, a journal on women's health internationally.

World Feminist Commission, Ave.des Scarabees, 1050 Brussels, Belgium.

IV. INFORMATION SERVICES FOR WOMEN: ACCESS AND HINDRANCES

WOMEN AND CONSUMER HEALTH INFORMATION:
ISSUES FOR THE 21ST CENTURY

Claudia J. Gollop

School of Information and Library Science

University of North Carolina

Chapel Hill, North Carolina, USA (1997)

Abstract

Today, women, like much of the general population, have begun to take more responsibility for their health than had previous generations. While the physician or other primary health care provide remains the dominant source of treatment and consultation, increasingly, women are very interested as well as involved in acquiring health information. In many parts of the world women are living longer than ever before and continue to outlive men by several years. This increase in the number of women living longer has also seen more women exposed to disease and illness. Exploring the availability and acquisition of consumer health information (CHI) is an important component of life-long learning that could have positive effects on the physical well being of women almost immediately and improve their level of health maintenance in the future. Libraries and other information disseminating organizations are beginning to play a larger part in providing consumer health information. This paper will focus on issues related to health information for women. Specifically, it will examine the following areas:

- Historical background on the consumer health information (CHI) movement, primarily in the United States
- Review of women's health issues
- Consumer health information services for the 21st century, and
- Implications for libraries and future trends for health information for women.

Introduction

No matter where in the world we look, regardless of the differences in language, customs, religion, or education, one of the most important factors relative to survival and advancement of any population is the level of health enjoyed by that society. Clearly, the physical and mental well being of any population as well as its life expectancy have figure heavily in its endurance and development.

At around the turn of the century it was assumed that life expectancy of the average individual was less than 50 years in the United States and many other "modern" countries, while it was significantly shorter in much of the rest of the world. It was also assumed that large numbers of people would die at even earlier ages, particularly between infancy and adolescence from out of the many as yet incurable or untreatable childhood diseases. Added to high mortality rates was the common occurrence of women who died due to complications as a result of childbirth.

It was not until the 20th century, which brought with it great advances in science and technology, that we saw the treatment and near eradication of several deadly diseases such as scarlet fever. The routine use of insulin to control life-threatening diabetes did not occur until 1937. And it was not until the 1940s that the powerful antibiotic, penicillin, was regularly administered in the treatment of illnesses such as pneumonia and syphilis. Diseases such as malaria and poliomyelitis were beyond our control before medical science discovered effective vaccines and therapies with which to combat them in the 1950 and 1960s. Over time, advancements in medicine, health care and sanitation have provided for the development of healthier, stronger, longer-living societies that, as a whole, have contributed to the growth and stability of their respective nations and to the world.

Having prospered and conquered many of the threats to survival, society now finds itself at the fairly comfortable stage in human development where it feels free to exercise options for achieving further advancement – both personally and professionally. This stage of human development corresponds to what Maslow called "self-actualization", which rests at the top of his "hierarchy of needs" paradigm. According to Msslow, after basic human needs are met (e.g., water, food and security), people are motivated to further progress in order to satisfy other desires – what he called "growth needs". Among growth needs are love and belonging, achievement, knowledge and self-actualization which is the highest of all the needs that humans attempt to fulfill (Madsen, 1974).

Consumer Health Information Movement

Over the last fifty years, the United States, as is the case for many countries in the world, has evolved into a largerly consumer society. Manufacturing fewer goods than in previous decades, importing more and raising the personal consumption of non-essential goods and services to an art, the force that most predominantly drives the economy is that of the service industries. In general, consumers have also evolved into sophisticated, assertive information seekers. As a by-product of heightened levels of purchasing and understanding their power and their relative impact on the economy, a consumer consciousness was born. Influenced by and characteristic of the seemingly tireless consumer crusader, Ralph Nadar, consumers now investigate the quality, authenticity, pricing practices and product safety of everything from the food we eat to the clothes we wear to the cars we drive. Purchasers not only want to know more about what they are buying but also about the companies providing the products or services. They have become very active and in some instances got organized enough to demand to be involved in the design, production and delivery of goods and services and, thus, sometimes in their success or failure.

Gartner (1982) said of the United States: "This society is characterized by enormous expansion in the production and consumption of human services, both paid and unpaid, with the most significant expansion occurring in health, education, and welfare services". By extension, it comes as no surprise that the growing interest and involvement in matters of health maintenance and improvement te public has occurred on the part of the general and is causing health care providers and policymakers to reevaluate their relationships with patients and laypersons.

While the CHI movement is clearly a byproduct of the larger consumer movement, it in itself has grown and has spawned diversification within health information acquisition and services along the way. For example, entire collections as well as individual publications (both print and electronic) have been developed to address a specific medical area, such as cancer, or the health concerns ofa particular segment of the population. For example, Duke University recently opened a library especially to serve the information needs of cancer patients and their families.

Of the increased interest and activity, Alan Rees (1994, p. vii), library and information science professor emeritus and an well-known authority on CHI and libraries, said:

In 1981, — the dissemination of health information to the public was considered to be a fringe activity of dubious value and legitimacy. By 1994, a vast industry of publishers, database producers, journalists, TV reporters, librarians, and information specialists has evolved with the explicit purpose of supplying authoritative and current medical information to patients and consumers.

The consumer health movement has grown since it began to take hold in the early 1970s. This can be seen by the demands by the general public for:

1. Accountability of health care providers and the health care system

2. Greater participation of the health care decision-making process

3. Disclosure of information regarding practices and procedures

4. Dietary and nutritional information including food labeling

5. More health promotion and disease prevention information

6. Information on alternative and complementary therapies

7. Increased government support of consumer health issues

This movement has also generated and increased the number of information seekers interested in products and services designed to assist, for a fee, in the health and wellness efforts of a large, maturing population, commonly referred to as the baby boom generation. Estimated at 75 million people, in the United States alone, this huge group is in search of ways to stay well as they grow old youthfully. Industry and government are paying close attention to the needs and demands of "boomers" and their legendary trend-setting tendencies. The mass media has steadily increased coverage of CHI topics. This becomes evident when one observes the intensity with which the media continues to create channels for information dissemination – channels by which, it is their hope, a larger audience will be won.

It is not uncommon to find television news programs as well as general interest newspapers and managizes that regularly feature segments dedicated to consumer health issues. In addition, entire publications as well as television and radio programs devoted to issues of consumer health are on the rise. This is, in no way, meant to criticize but rather to emphasize the dramatic focus being placed on this topic of CHI.

Many people now believe that greater awareness of health related issues and taking more responsibility for their own physical wellbeing are the best ways to ensure that proper treatment, maintenance, and methods for an enhanced state health are available to them. This is understandable when one considers that the people of many nations are facing major policy shifts that have prompted increased efforts by employers to reduce health care spending and to restrict health insurance benefits. This is compounded by the uncertainty of health care reform outcomes and a global growing, aging population of unprecedented proportions which is living longer than any generation n the world history.

Women's Health Issues

Just a few decades ago, as a result of unsanitary conditions and common deadly diseases, the high rates of morbidity and mortality plagued the general population, particularly infants and young children. Those rates increased for women who had to contend with the added health dangers that often accompanied pregnancy and childbirth. Women today typically outlive men – by approximately seven years in the United States. The blessings of increased longevity for women has also witnessed an increase in the number of women exposed to disease and debilitating illnesses that occur most often at mid to later life. Older women, those of sixty-five years of age and above, are predicted to make up a significant proportion of health care recipients as the population of aging adults grows. According to Schneider & Beckett (1992, p. 349):

Furthermore, there are gender differences in the incidence and severity of illness. Older women experience higher rates of potentially disabling illness, such as arthritis, osteoporosis, hypertension, and diabetes. Women are more likely than men to have mobility problems, to be bedfast, and to be unable to perform essential self-care tasks. Because of the longer life expectancy, women often have to cope longer with chronic illness than do men.

In addition, while it is true that issues of health are of concern to bnoth men and women, the literature suggests that historically, in many parts of the world, women have played the part of caregiver. Today, because they are living longer, older women are continuing in that role. "Caregiving of elderly people in modern society is almost exclusively a task carried out by women, many of them elderly themselves" (Manheimer, p. 57).

The incidence of stroke, heart attack, hypertension and cancer have also increased in many parts of the world where previously morbidity rates for such illnesses were below those of the North American. Using breast cancer, primarily a women's disease, as an example, it is not difficult to grasp the impact on the lives of women who do contract the disease and the important need to provide health promotion and disease prevention information, particularly among those in the world who are less aware of them. While the United States has the highest incidence of breast cancer, countries such as China and Japan, which still maintain very low rates comparatively, have seen an increase in recent years.

Therefore, it is not surprising to find that women have become involved with the movement toward the acquisition and promotion of consumer health information. Today women like much of the world's population have begun to take more responsibility for their personal health than had previous generations. While the physician or other primary health care provider remains the dominant source for treatment and consultation, women increasingly are becoming very active in issues of consumer health.

Until recently, in many parts of the world and including the Western world and the North America, limited means existed for women to advance themselves within their respective societies. Women were not afforded the opportunities to attain basic education, not to mention secondary or higher education and/or any of the benefits of gaining such knowledge. It is common knowledge that numerous economic barriers existed and many persist today in areas of education and employment for women around the globe. Certainly, since most of the doors to acquiring an education, which lead to career advancement for men, were closed, positions requiring professional education were closed too. However, even when the knowledge and skills were secured, women were still not always welcome. These facts are not recounted merely as tales of woe. Viewed in a more positive way, it can be said that women throughout the world and throughout history have persevered and advanced in the process, usually finding their own ways and creating opportunities for themselves. In some ways, it can be said that women have always been "lifelong learners".

Consumer Health Information Services for the 21st Century

The availability and distribution of information to assist people in making informed decisions about their health is not a new concept or practice. While CHI services are conducted differently in various locations, health information for the layperson has been disseminated for some time. In addition, women traditionally have been seekers of health information, since they were the primary caregivers for the entire family. Gann (1996, p. 244) invites information professionals to improve on the provision of health information to meet the challenges of the future by going beyond the tendency to provide "complacent". "passive", and "superficial" levels of service. He adds:

If we are fully to realize the potential of health information services for consumers we must now grasp the nettle of providing information about quality and outcomes of treatment. It will not be easy to present this information in an understandably way but that is our challenge as information providers – not a problem for consumers.

First of all, it is important to remember that in many cases facilities for dispensing CHI are already in place. There is no need to form new organizations, agencies, or to build libraries in order to provide this important service. Public libraries have been collecting and housing CHI for many years. However, other public service agencies and organizations also distribute health-related information. More than ever, it is time that those involved with CHI delivery build stronger, more proactive cooperative relationships. It is no secret that collaborative efforts among libraries and information service organizations can increase the strength of any one program while it simultaneously decreases the fiscal and material responsibility for all parties concerned, by sharing the tasks of information acquisition and dissemination.

The information explosion has yet to peak and there are few libraries or information centers that can afford or even want to own everything. It would be far too costly to provide the necessary resources required to build an adequate CHI collection from the ground up. Thus, sharing resources and exchanging information benefits the agencies and the consumers alike. Most library and information science professionals understand the issues of access vs. ownership. Here, access and the timeliness with which the information is provided are the key when it comes to CHI, because the information sought may assist a user making a decision about an important health issue.

Reliable, useful CHI that is both available and accessible (*) to the average person worldwide is not yet a reality. Nonetheless, developments in computer technology, especially with regards to Internet and the World Wide Web, have made it possible for the existing gap in access to be narrowed significantly. Some database producers already provide CHI as part of their product line. For example, IAC's (Information Access Corporation) InfoTrac SearchBank system contains the popular Health Reference Center that includes, in addition to bibliographic citations to medical and CHI literature, abstracts and full-text articles for many of the sources indexed. OCLC's First Search includes medical and health files as part of its database system. Both the Health Reference Center and First Search are usable by the average lay person. In addition, several reliable and worthwhile sources of CHI are accessible primarily via the World Wide Web. It should be said that in some cases no print equivalent to the Web version exists. It is easy to see how such circumstances could cause other concerns for information seekers and providers. That is a topic for another discussion.

(* The author considers that there is a difference, as fine as it may seem to some, between information that is available and information that is accessible. An example of this is the fcat that there is much health information which is available on the World Wide Web that is not accessible to those not able to log onto to the Net because they lack the proper infrastructure and/or equipment to do so.)

In the United States, the Department of Health and Human Services launched the Healthfinder gateway website in the spring 1997. Healthfinder serves as the door to a multitude of links to consumer health information web pages such as the National Library of Medicine which offers further access to health information, including free MEDLINE (its biomedical database) searches, and to coverage of health issues specific to women (e.g., breast cancer) monitored by the Office of Women's Health.

Commercial producers such as HealthGate allow users free limited access to CHI. In addition, Doc in the Box offers consumers access to medical and other health professionals via their web page where health related questions are guaranteed to be answered within forty-eight hours. To attain full access to these services, of course, users must pay a subscription fee. However, it is very likely that in the future commercial health care services like those just mentioned will be even more common than they are currently.

Several examples of cooperative arrangements among libraries illustrate the response to the demands of the public for more access to CHI as well as what can be accomplished when there is mutual interest and resources are shared in an effort to meet those demands. For example, NOAH, the health information databank on the Web that combines the resources of the New York Public Library and other interested agencies and which provides CHI in both English and Spanish. The introduction to the page reads:

NOAH (New York Online Access to Health) is a guide in English and Spanish to the latest health information and resources from volunteer and local governmental agencies, and from other health sites on the Internet. NOAH currently focuses on thirteen main health topics: aging, AIDS, alternative medicine, cancer, diabetes, healthy living, heart disease and stroke, mental health, nutrition, personal health, pregnancy, sexuality, sexually transmitted diseases, and tuberculosis.

NOAH is a pilot project funded by the U.S, Department of Commerce's National Telecommunications and Information Administration (NTIA) and matching grants. Partners in this project are the City University of New York, the New York Metropolitan Reference and Research Library Agency, The New York Academy of Medicine, and the New York Public Library.

CHI on the Internet is gaining lots of attention, primarily because it is instantaneously accessible, easily readable and, ideally, available to anyone. However, CHI has been available in public libraries and health sciences and hospital libraries for decades. An example of this is the well-known Planetree Health Resource Center in San Francisco. The Center that originated as part of the California Pacific Medical Center (Cosgrove, 1994) and was established for patients and their families who were in search of health information, is now open to the public.

CHI services currently exist in several locations as well as in various combinations of print, non-print, and electronic formats with more and enhanced applications on the horizon. If the proliferation of books, journals, articles and World Wide Web sites is any indication, the general public, particularly women, will request more from the producers and distributors of health information. The point that should be emphasized here is that more attention must be given and greater efforts are needed in terms of international advocacy and funding of CHI programs. Resources and services that allow consumers around the world to make appropriate informed decisions will be beneficial to all concerned and must become more easily available.

Lifelong Learning

I would be amiss if I did not discuss issues of lifelong learning, given the theme of this conference. Of course, exploring the availability and acquisition of CHI is an important component in life-long learning that could have positive effects on the physical well-being of women almost immediately and improve their level of health maintenane for the future.

Lifelong learning is not a new or a recently developed concept. There has always been individuals who have pursued learning throughout their lives either formally or informally. Occasionally, the media will cite an older person for some notable achievement or other, such as graduating from college or successfully completing some exceptional physical feat at 70, 80, 90 or even 100 years of age. However, almost nothing, let alone great achievements, occur in a vacuum. Rather, most accomplishments are the result of thought, hard work and persistence and that can be true for persons of any age.

The regular pursuit and gathering of information and the action taken as a result is the mark of lifelong learning. What are the avenues of lifelong learning? Although the literature discusses variations in learning styles and numerous methods of acquiring information, it is also clear that these have not necessarily replaced older, traditional methods, such as merely asking questions of health professionals and peers and then critically evaluating the responses received – instead of accepting them as pure truth – in order to make a decision. The literature tells us that sizeable segments of the world's population actively pursue various forms of continued learning in such forms as formal education programs, reading groups, library literacy programs, community college courses, etc. Thus, it is probably less important to focus on the ways by which people continue to learn throughout their lives but to promote education, inquiry and information seeking and to respond as advocates with the best, most applicable resources and services at our disposal.

What can we envision as future trends in the area of health information for the female population? Says Douglas Weiss (Lumsdon, 1993), at Employee Managed Care: "We find that people are not prepared to think about their values and preferences in specific health care situations. They need the tools to educate and empower themselves to weigh risks, benefits and the bottom line". Clearly, the more women investigate ways to improve and preserve their health and that of their families, the more they will demand of the health care system to conduct research reflective of their unique health concerns and to provide adequate information relative to those concerns.

It is quite possible and remains the hope of the author that the library and information profession will witness a trend in which several world wide collaborative efforts will emerge that will work toward providing CHI for women, particularly in those locations where it is most needed.

The physical wellbeing of individuals and their families has been the focus of every group of people since the beginning of time, if not, they would certainly overexpose themselves to illness or danger and ultimately cease to exist. That is, individuals have always demonstrated an interest in improving and preserving their health. Today, the emergence, followed by the expansion of access to valuable, useful CHI supports the lay persons in their efforts to participate in their health care.

As librarians and information workers continue to advance the cause of CHI acquisition and dissemination by joining with others who share in understanding the importance of such efforts, the words of Heiberg (1996, p. 94), a physician at University of Oslo, also lend their support:

There is still much to investigate. There is much more we need to know, and there is an urgent need to have access to the new knowledge to attain a world that promotes the fundamental rights of health for all people, men and women alike. Librarians have a key role in this process.

In the future, various forms of cooperation and collaborative efforts will exist to provide health information to lay persons. Furthermore, the understanding that libraries and information organizations of different types around the world will operate, increasingly, as agents of access, hopefully will encourage those agencies to create powerful, international information partnerships.

References

American Library Association/ Reference and Adult Services Division/ Standards and Guidelines Committee. (1992) Guidelines for medical, legal, and business responses at general reference desks. RQ, 31, Summer, 554-555.

Beckett, J.O. & Schneider, R.L. (1992). Older women. In R.L. Schneider & N.P. Kropf (Eds.) Gerontological social work: knowledge, service settings and special populations, pp. 323-358. Chicago: Nelson-Hall Publishers.

Brandon, A.N. & Hill, D.R. (1994). Selected list of books and journals in allied health. Bulletin of the Medical Library Association. 82, (3) Jul, 247-264.

Cosgrove, T.L. (1994) Planetree health information services: public access to the health information people want. Bulletin of the Medical Library Association, 82, (1) Jan, 57-63.

Gann, B. (1996) Consumer health information in the year 2000. Aslib Proceedings, 48 (10), Oct, 241-245.

Heiberg, A.N. (1996) Access to the world's resources: women's health. Bulletin of the Medical Library Association, 84, (1), Jan, 91-96.

Humphries, A.W. & Kochi, J.K. (1994) Providing consumer health information through institutional collaboration. Bulletin of the Medical Library Association, 82, (1), Jan, 52-56.

La Rocco, A. (1994) The role of the medical school-based consumer information service. Bulletin of the Medical Library Association, 82, (1), Jan, 46-51.

Lumsdon, K. (1993). Baby boomers grow up. Hospitals and Health Networks, 67 (18), Sept, 24-30.

Manheimer, R. (1995) The Second Middle Age: Looking Differently at Life Beyond 50. Detroit: Visible Ink Press.

Rees, A.M. (1997) Consumer health U.S.A. (2nd ed.) Phoenix, AZ: Oryx Press.

—. (1994) The consumer health information source book (4th ed.) Phoenix, AZ: Oryx Press.

—. (1982) Developing consumer health information services. New York: R.R. Bowker.

SERVICES PROVIDED FOR WOMEN BY THE LIBRARIES OF THE RYAZAN REGION

Lyudmilla Pronina

Director

Ryazan Gorky Regional Library

Russia (1996)

Introduction

The feminist movement in Russia has deep rooted traditions. In the 19th century this movement was democratic. At the beginning of the 20th century it was connected with mandatory public education.

The feminist movement has rejuvenated itself recently. It is a coalition of a great number of national associations and clubs. Women of different professions and religious beliefs take an active part in the political and social life of Russia. All of us would like to live in peace, be well off, and see economic, cultural and educational progress in Russia. We stand for a strong and prosperous country, the country where old people and children must be happy. We believe in future social stability.

Change Towards Democracy

Russia's huge move from a totalitarian state towards a functioning democracy is not expected to be uncloudy. Russia is at a turning point. So the reason for the prevalence of problems is part and parcel of the immense chaos that exists when a system experiences changes that Russia now is undergoing. In the rampant economic and financial crisis of the past two or three years, the social position of women in Russia leaves much to be desired. We are witnessing deterioration of the living conditions, impending unemployment, scant family budgets, poverty, prices growing higher several times quicker than the average public income, low birth rate and many other problems. The opportunity for women to realize their dreams, hopes and ambitions is diminishing.

Chechnya has become a symbol of the cruelty and senselessness of a military conflict. It is another painful problem. Women of Russia are yearning for trust and peace to be established in Chechnya. They demand concrete projects and actions which would favour, through dialogue, the change from war to peace. Citizens should no longer sacrifice their lives in a bloody senseless war, but rather live them. Women are not deprived of the right to express their views. Peace in the minds of women! Violence never again! During this difficult stage in Russian history women unite and work together. Without their participation in the political life there would not be moral balance and social stability in Russia.

Women's Increasing Need for Information

As women are acknowledged to be an influential force in society they need information as never before, and they come to the libraries. Within the last two years the number of women asking for information in the libraries has increased significantly. The libraries in the Ryazan Region cooperate with many social movements at the local, regional, national as well as international level". The Union of Women of Russia" is one of them, and the libraries ensure access to information about their activities. Russian librarians are more active than ever. They are displaying miracles of inventiveness in their activity. They do their best to understand the needs of library users and to fulfill their requests. The librarians in the Ryazan region work in conjunction with the local womens' organizations and provide adequate information services to local enterprises, associations and interest groups. The publication of a manual providing recommendations to librarians in their work with womens' organizations belongs to the achievement of the Gorky Regional Scientific Library.

In some local public libraries, librarians are at the head of the feminist movement in the Ryazan Region. The Central Public Library of the town of Rybnoye is significant in this field of activity. Having protested the Chechen War, the librarians, mostly women, collected about 5,000 signatures. They gave unaminous support to the candidates for the State Duma from "The Union of Women of Russia". (December 17, 1995)

Women Librarians and Women Library Users

Over 1,500 librarians, 99 per cent women, are working in the libraries of the Ryazan Region. The Gorky Regional Scientific Library serves as an all-region, universal research and information centre. Within the last two years there has been a constant increase in the number of its users. According to recent statistics the users come to the library for the purpose of preparing for classes (50%), improving their professional skills (20%), and changing trades and professions (20%). 5 percent of the readers come to the library to listen to taped reviews of new publications, to see regular exhibitions or to take part in literary discussions and parties arranged by librarians; 80 per cent of participants are women. The library provides 3 per cent of its users with fiction for leisure reading. The remaining 2 percent visit the library in search of reference material. Among the library users are students (50%), teachers and teacher trainers (30%), economists, lawyers, doctors (15%), and housewives and pensioners (5%). 45 percent have received higher education.

More than 65 per cent of the library users are women. Irrespective of age and religous beliefs, readers come to the library because it is the only place now to offer free access to self-education and a pleasant pastime with cultural and intellectual treasures. Today our libraries inform unemployed women about job opportunities, family problems, and give practical pieces of advice on a wide range of related subjects. Men's reading tends to be more pragmatic. Women read books both for education, including self- education, and for pleasure. The library has a wide selection of books about family, children and domestic science. All the libraries subscribe to many periodicals for women. One can count over 40 titles of such periodicals in the Gorky Regional Library. The most popular among them are the magazines "Verena", "Burda Modern", "Sandra", and "Italian Fashion". The magazine "The World of Women" has been in great demand lately.

Library Services for Families

The Year of 1994 was known as the International Year of the Family and it was celebrated in many libraries. On the occasion in September 1994, the Gorky Regional Library, in collaboration with the Russian State Library for Youth and the publishing house of the magazine "The World of Women", organized a round table on the theme "Books, Libraries and Family". A number of experienced librarians from the local libraries as well as those from the city of St. Petersburg and the Vladimir region were invited to take part in the event. They were debating the questions of information services for women, the education of the children and their future, and the painful problems of the family. Also discussed was the law on librarianship drafted by the Ministry of Culture.

The Children's Central Library in the city of Ryazan has analysed the reading circle of our women within the last two years. The results are as follows: Pensioners (women age 55 or older) like to read both Russian and foreign classics as well as detective stories. The reading circle of young women includes reading guides for helping young mothers, books about children and how to care for them. Well educated women prefer to read fiction, literary magazines, memoirs, literary criticism, historical novels and books on the history of Russia and foreign countries. (The U.S., Great Britain, France, Germany, Italy, Spain, Australia, Japan, China) Recently we have seen a public love for the Bible, books by A. Solzhenitsyn, V. Nabokov, M. Bulgakov, I. Bunin, V. Pikul, V. Solovyov, Z. Bentsomi, L. Ron Hubbard, D. Carnegie, E. Hemingway, S. Maugham, O. Wilde, T. Dreiser, J. London, A. Hailey, F. Archer, S. Sheldon, E. M. Remarque, A. Camus, J.R. Tolkien, M. Mitchell, C. McCullough, and D. du Maurier. Detective stories by A. Christie, D. Hammett, E. Gardner, E. McBain, R. Chandler, S. Chase, and J. Le Carre are very popular among the library users and also in great demand. All women love to read books on needlework.

Women's Cultural Heritage

The 8th of March, International Women's Day, is annually celebrated in all libraries of the Ryazan region. Last year they organized interesting literary and family parties for women: "Reading in My Family", "Family Thursdays", "On Saturday Evenings" and others; debates and competitions: "Charovnitsa" (A Girl Who Makes Miracles), "Dochki Materi" (Daughters Mothers), "SuperBabushka" (Super Grandmother) and others; topical exhibitions such as "A Woman's Theme in Foreign Literature" and "Russian Women", as well as displays of photographs of the most prominent women.

Since ancient times women have been the glory of the Ryazan Land. We can find their names in the chronicles: Fevroniya, a peasant woman doctor, later the Murom Duchess; Ardotya Ryazanochka, who came to the rescue and released the Ryazanovites (the Ryazan "polon") from Mongol Tatars' captivity; Natalya Naryshkina, Peter the Great's Mother; Nadezhda Khvoschinskaya, a writer; Anna Golubkina, a famous sculptor ; and the tractor driver, Darya Garmash, who organized the first tractor brigade of women during the Great Patriotic War (World War II). In 1995, in the village library of Bagramovo, eight surviving women who worked in this tractor brigade, gathered together to reminisce and to remember those years. The attendants sang songs, recited poems and listened to stories of the accomplishments of the Russian people during the Great Patriotic War.

In the region more than 20 women's clubs and interest groups gather in the libraries, such as "Frontovichka", "Nezabudka", "Prochanka", (Women War Veterans), "Bereginya" (Preserving the Family and House and Home), "Rukodelnitsa", "Khozyaushka", and "Umelye Ruki" (Women who are clever with their hands). The librarians arrange meetings with cultural activists (teachers, doctors, lawyers, artists, actors) and often invite mothers to these meetings. They help single mothers, senior citizens, invalids, and unemployed women of all ages.

Research on Library Usage

The Gorky Regional Library is involved in library science research. In 1992-93 it participated in the research work on "Reading of Librarians in Russia" conducted by the Russian National Library. The librarians from almost all the libraries were asked to give answers to the following questions: "How do they spend their leisure time? What books do they read? How do they plan their reading? What books do they recommend to their library users for reading?"

The results showed that 95 per cent of librarians spent their leisure time reading books, 62per cent working in the garden, 49 per cent doing needlework, and 40 per cent going to the cinema or theatre, to concerts or exhibitions. In recent years 73 per cent of librarians have shown an increased interest in new books and periodicals and planned their reading themselves; 67 per cent have found the information about new books in the newspaper "Knizhnoye Obozreniye", 89 per cent from talks with colleagues, and 46 per cent from conversations with library users. For development of their professional skills the librarians are reading such periodicals as "Biblioteka", (The Library), "Bibliotekovedeniye" (Library Science), "Kultura" (Culture), "Literaturnoye Obozreniye" (Literary Review), "Knizhnoye Obozreniye" (Book Review), "Scientific and Technical Libraries", "Literature at School", "Voprosy Literatury" (Questions of Literature), and "Slovo" (Word).

Professional Improvement

In the libraries of our region much attention is paid to the improvement of professional skills. Experienced librarians transfer their knowledge to the young personnel. They gain knowledge through lectures and conferences, seminars and workshops, debates and contests, business games and competitions, and exhibitions and presentations. Within the city of Ryazan, some libraries have begun to recognize exemplary librarians through the activities of "Benefis Bibliotekaya" and "Benefis Biblioteki".

For many years the Gorky Regional Library has compiled and published methodological manuals to assist librarians. Some examples include: "Information about Literature on Librarianship and Professional Reading of Librarians" and "Extension of Knowledge about the Profession of Librarians". Quarterly lists of new books for librarians, teachers, and agricultural workers are sent to the local libraries.

Conclusion

The public library is the local centre of information, making all kinds of knowledge and information readily available to its users. The library services are adapted to the different needs of the communities in urban and rural areas. Professional and continuing education of librarians is indispensable to ensure adequate services. In the world of unlimited information, knowledge must include the intellectual skills necessary to find, screen, analyse, and synthesize information.

WOMEN'S DEVELOPMENT AND INFORMATION ON WOMEN IN KOREA

Young-Joo Paik

Korean Women's Development Institute

Seoul, Korea (1998)

Abstract

In the traditional Korean society, women were largely confined to the home. But women's social participation has become active in the contemporary Korean society, and the social recognition of women's rights and roles has changed. As recognition of women's issues has grown, both domestically and world-wide, the need for comprehensive and reliable information on women and their concerns has increased.

This paper will review women's development in Korea over the past 50 years. Its focus is on legal issues of concern to Korean women, and the activities on women's information management and networking initiated by the Korean Women's Development Institute. It will stress the importance of cooperation between women's groups or organizations to collect, process and disseminate information in developing an information exchange system.

1. Women's Development in Korea over the Past 50 Years

A. Introduction

In traditional Korean society, women were largely confined to the home. From a young age, women were required to learn the Confucian virtues of subordination and endurance to prepare themselves for their future roles as wife and mother, while being denied any opportunity to participate in activities outside the home. Their role was limited to managing a large extended family and to producing a male heir so that the family line might continue unbroken. And the discrimination between the sexes in favor of the male – based, as it was, on feudal Confucianism – dominated all aspects of women's lives. As a result, women had to live subordinated to men.

At the end of 18th century, the emergence of Practical Science introduced the issue of equal human rights and, in a limited way, provided positive views on the women's social participation. The introduction of Western Learning became the prime motivating factor in stressing the equality of humanity and in treating women as human beings. At the end of 19th century, the opening of Korea to the outside world accelerated women's social participation.

Under the influence of the introduction of Practical Science and modern civilization from the Western World into the country, the necessity of education became intensified and educational opportunities increased, which raised women's consciousness about the discrimination they had experienced under the Korean patriarchal society.

Women's social participation, then, became active in the Korean society and the social recognition of women's rights and roles changed. These developmental changes were due to the increase of women's roles on the basis of social change, the elevation of educational education, and the familial change, but most of all the change happened due to the strong demands by women seeking development for themselves.

"Women's development" means increase in their economic participation, and equal opportunity and equal treatment in the work force, as well as the discarding of the discriminatory perception of women in society. It also means that women, as members of society, should take equal responsibility and share equal burdens in the society where the legal and social system support equally women and men.

The problems and barriers that women have faced should be recognized as social problems and should be resolved through national concern and policies. This would lead to the development of women and, therefore, of the society and of the country.

B. The 1950s – after the Liberation in 1945

The 15 August, 1945 was not only a day of national liberation but also a day of liberation for Korean women. The suppression and discrimination suffered under the Japanese occupation gave way to a Western democratic system which provided women with opportunities to enjoy a more active and wider social participation. Women, who had been until this moment for hundreds of years of history confined to the extended family, began to realize their own rights and some women leaders worked to construct various organizations. New women's groups were formed and previously existing ones were reorganized and invigorated to contribute to a variety of fields, such as politics, social affairs, religion, education, and social service.

In 1946, the Women's Affairs Bureau of the Ministry of Health and Social Affairs was opened as the first governmental office to deal with the growing needs and problems of women. The Constitution of the Republic of Korea, established in 1948 following the liberation, declared gender equality and the equal right of women to vote. It stated that men and women are equal and that women are equally entitled to receive education, are able to work and participate in the society. These seminal constitutional changes marked women's entry into equal participation with men in many aspects of their life in a newly developing society. A woman was elected in a by-election to the first National Assembly. In 1951 another woman successfully passed the national judicial examination and became the first woman lawyer.

The Korean War (1950-1953) proved how strong and self-reliant women could be under the most adverse conditions. Many women had to support their families and themselves while their husbands or sons were away fighting the communists. Many even lost husbands and sons in the war. As a result of their war experiences women realized the importance of developing their own capabilities, not only to be able to survive but also to prosper economically. They also cared for war orphans, widows, and wounded soldiers and made truly remarkable contributions to the reconstruction of Korea after the tragic war. Following the signing of the armistice, the government returned to Seoul in 1953, and women's social participation expanded remarkably in scope and nature. The new government began to formulate specific women's policies such as for supporting war widows and for prevention of prostitution.

The Labor Standard Act was enacted in 1953, which guarantees basic equality between men and women in employment and special protection for women during pregnancy and maternity. The National Council of Women was organized in 1959 and implemented a core role in women's activities.

C. Toward the Industrial Society in the 1960s: Changes in Women's Roles

In the 1960s Korean society was faced with a period of great change from an agricultural society to an industrial society with national policies stressing economic growth. The industrialization process was initiated by export-oriented manufacturing industries. These labor-intensive industries flourished exploiting low-wage labor of young and unmarried women. In 1963 there were 2,835,000 economically active women among a total female population of 7,670,000 aged 15 years and older, i.e., 37.0 per cent.

The changes in household types toward nuclear families and the decline in the birth rate resulting from family planning urged by the government had a profound effect on women's lives. Since the inauguration of a compulsory education system in 1953, the educational opportunities for women had greatly expanded that were accompanied by an increase in female enrollment at the elementary, secondary and higher levels of education. In 1962 The Prevention of Prostitution Act was enacted and the first revision of the Family Law was passed.

D. The 1970s: Increase in Women's Employment

Although women were strongly participating in economic activities, as part of the driving force to maintain economic growth, the employment conditions and wage levels for women were considerably inferior to those for men. The International Women's Year of 1975 and the subsequent United Nations Decade for Women (1976-1985) brought about significant advancement for Korean women. During the International Year of Women in 1975, the Year of Women in Korea was proclaimed thus linking the women's movement in Korea to the worldwide women's movement. Korean women's organizations dispatched representatives to various international conferences held in connection with the UN Decade for Women to solidify cooperative relations and to exchange information with foreign counterpart organizations. The adoption of the Convention of Elimination of All Forms of Discrimination Against Women by the United Nations General Assembly in 1979, with its worldwide impact on further improving and enhancing of the status of women, has greatly changed public attitude in Korea towards sexual equality and the concept of women's advancement.

Starting with Ewha Womans University in Seoul in 1977, women's studies has been introduced into various universities. This has provided the theoretical basis for helping to solve women's problems and has contributed to raising women's consciousness. Aiming at improving women's status, the activities of women's groups covered diverse fields such as the improvement of labor conditions for female workers, the extension of women's social education, the opposing campaign on Kisaeng-sightseeing or prostitute-sightseeing.

E. The 1980s: The Establishment of Women's Policies Organizations

With joint efforts for the advancement of women by women's organizations and the government, three National Machineries dealing with women's affairs were established in the 1980s: the Korean Women's Development Institute (KWDI) in 1983, to make a comprehensive study on women's issues and to link its findings with actual policies; the National Committee on Women's Policies in 1983, with representatives of the concerned government ministries, and the Ministry of Political Affairs, in 1988. The Ministry of

Political Affairs, which had been in charge of formulating and implementing women's policies, was dissolved and the Special Committee on Women's Affairs directly under the office of the President formed in February 1998.

In 1985, the National Committee on Women's Policies adopted the "Master Plan for Women's Development" and the "Guidelines for the Elimination of Discrimination Against Women" as government policies.

The central administrative system dealing with women's affairs is composed of the Ministry of Political Affairs (2) and the Women's Welfare Division of the Family Welfare Bureau of the Ministry of Health and Social Welfare. The Women's Welfare Division sets up general plans for women's welfare, administers women's guidance and educational programs, and supervises shelters for disadvantaged women. Fifteen Bureaus of Family Welfare headed by women were established in fifteen major cities and provinces in 1988. These Bureaus work for women's welfare in their respective areas and have close ties with the central Women's Welfare Division.

The Korean Constitution was amended in 1987, introducing a new clause on the duty of the State to promote women's welfare and equality. The Equal Employment Opportunity Law, drafted by the Government in 1987, went into effect in 1988. A section on equal pay for equal work was inserted into the law in 1989. With a view to safeguard the security and welfare of single-mother households, the Government enacted the Mother-Child Welfare Law in 1989. A drastically revised Family Law was also passed in 1989. This revision was a direct result of the struggle by women's organizations which had fought to remove the discriminatory patriarchal elements in the earlier Law passed in 1958.

Feminism had begun to advance in the artistic fields of literature, painting, drama, film, and dancing in the 1980s. Women artists described the objective reality of women's oppression and featured these realities from a variety of feminist perspectives.

F. The 1990s: Continuing Women's Protection

In 1994, as the erstwhile result of having become a formal member of the United Nations in 1991, Korea was elected as a member state of the UN Commission on the Status of Women, which is expected to open a new phase in dealing with women's issues on an international level. Regarding legal rights, the Infant Care Act was promulgated in 1991 for the promotion of home welfare by bringing up infants and pre-schoolers whose guardians have difficulty protecting them; and the Act Relating to Punishment of Sexual Violence and Protection of Victims was enacted in 1993. The Prevention of Prostitution Act was revised in 1995.

In 1991, according to a regulation concerning the commission and regulation of administrative authority, the authority to coordinate the tasks of the KWDI was transferred from the Ministry of Health and Welfare to the Ministry of Political Affairs (2), which resulted in rearranging the administrative systems way of dealing with women's policies. In the same year, 274 Family Welfare Divisions, under the Ministry of Health and Welfare, with women heads in towns, counties and wards were also founded to deal with women's welfare issues. With the introduction of local government, the increase of women's political participation is expected.

The Special Committee on Women at the National Assembly was established as a permanent body in 1994, which could serve as a channel to support the enactment and revision of the laws relating to women.

The Seventh Five Year Economic and Social Development Plan includes a new women's development plan for the period 1992-1996 with special emphasis on education, employment, cultural and social activities, welfare and international cooperation.

The Ministry of Labor has prepared "The Basic Plan to Promote Working Women's Welfare" (1994-1997) which aims to contribute to improving the status of working women and their welfare by implementing a policy of equal opportunity, expanding maternity protection, and developing human resources through women's work capabilities.

2. Women's Status

During the last three decades, Korea has achieved remarkable economic growth. However, despite a number of significant changes in the economic, political and social fields (as have been briefly described above) the progress in improving the status of women has been less impressive.

Until the creation of the Republic of Korea in 1948, sexual discrimination against women, which was due to the acceptance of Confucian social rules dominated all aspects of women's lives.

The Constitution of the Republic of Korea, promulgated in 1948, guaranteed respect for the dignity of individuals and equality between men and women as a guiding principle under the initiative of democratic legislative measures. Based on this principle, various legislative reforms have been implemented and the status of women in Korea has undergone enormous changes. Accordingly, discrimination against women in political, economic, social, cultural, and other fields has lessened.

A series of successful economic development plans has helped Korea achieve remarkable economic growth and social transformation. Women have had increasingly greater opportunities to take part in economic activities. As of 1996, there were 8.4 million working women who accounted for 40.6 percent of the total work force. Despite this increase, the number of women holding policy-making positions in administration and management is still very small.

Korean women today, however, are actively engaged in a wide variety of fields including education, medicine, science, engineering, scholarship, arts, literature and sports. There are female lawmakers, business executives and university presidents. Though only a handful in number, some women have proved their excellent abilities and leadership as cabinet ministers. These changes all attest to the fact that Korean women, given opportunities, can develop their potential and make significant contributions to society.

The increasing presence of women and the changes in Korean society have brought the government to the realization that it must develop new policies for women. By a presidential decree, the National Committee on Women's Policies was formed in 1983. The KWDI was established in the same year. In compliance with the changing social environment, the government established the Ministry of Political Affairs to handle women's matters in 1988. The government named a woman minister to lead this ministry. In the same year, 15 Family Welfare Bureaus with women directors were also established at the provincial government level.

Also, development and changes in the economy and society in the last thirty years have resulted in significant changes in the lifestyles of women. Some of these are: a longer life expectancy for women, a drop in the birth rate, an improved standard of education, more nuclear families, changes in family life resulting from a raised consciousness, less of a burden from household responsibilities due to the availability of electrical appliances, etc. All these factors combined have brought about a steady increase in the number of women engaging in various social activities and the number of those wishing to do so.

In spite of the above-mentioned advances and changes, the unemployment rate of women in higher academic careers still remains high. Most women workers are still engaged in low-wage jobs where they are subject to employment or wage discrimination. Although the participation of married women in economic activities is continuously increasing, the supply of public childcare facilities for children of low-income women workers falls short of the sharply growing demand. These problems have continued to increase despite the Government's implementation of economic and social development plans. Improvement of women-related laws and social systems have failed to yield substantial results or to enhance the position of women. Though it is difficult and thus time-consuming to completely eliminate entrenched traditions of discrimination against women, and to fully realize their equal participation in every field, the Government must work to promote the conditions under which women can improve their status. This must be done not only at the de jure level but also at the de facto level. Only in this way can women fully demonstrate their capabilities and contribute to society on an equal footing with men. Specifically, the Government must work to eliminate persistent, stereotyped concepts based on traditional sex roles and provide a climate conducive to women's full participation in society.

In the future, various efforts should be exerted to implement the plans in the Long-Term Perspective on National Development Toward the Year 2000. This would be in accordance with the guidelines suggested by the United Nations in the Nairobi Forward Looking Strategies for the Advancement of Women, which aims to promote the development of women's capacity, the utilization of women's resources, and a more healthy family life.

3. Introduction of Women's Studies

Women's studies as an academic teaching subject came into being in Korea in the middle of the 1970s. The introduction of feminist-oriented Women's Studies into universities was sensational and created a debate concerning the relevance of the Western-born scholarship of Women's Studies to Korean society. The main point was that Korean society is culturally different from Western societies, so that Western theories of feminism could not be applied to Korean women.

Women's Studies has been one of the fastest developing academic fields in Korea. Women's Studies courses have been introduced into and taught at many universities and colleges even though - as yet - no college or university has instituted Women's Studies as a major or minor discipline at the under graduate level.

As of 1996 most of the more than one hundred universities and colleges in Korea have come to include various Women's Studies courses in their general curriculum. A survey conducted by Seoul Women's University in 1996 revealed that 77 courses related to Women's Studies were offered in Korea.

4. Information on Women

A. Systemization of Women's Information

As recognition of women's issues has grown, both domestically and worldwide, so has the need for comprehensive and reliable data on women and their concerns. Unfortunately, accessing well-organized information on women has not been easy. Although the volume of information about women in such fields as politics, business, education, labor and industry has been growing rapidly, information is still widely scattered and badly organized and remedying these problems has not been easy. The value of collecting information specifically about women is still not widely recognized in many countries and the process of collecting, classifying, analyzing and managing women's information is difficult when organizations and government agencies lack the necessary technical resources and expertise. Also many countries lack an efficient system for distributing women's information to women's groups and government agencies.

B. Definition of Women's Information

Information concerning the establishment of a welfare society based on equality between men and women is presented as the following:

- research into and survey of women's problems
- consciousness raising aimed at equality
- revision of laws and reform of social systems to promote the legal status of women
- increase in women's social and political participation
- advancement of women's lives and the development of women's capabilities

C. Information Flow

An information flow includes the production, dissemination, collection, storage, retrieval, and utilization of information. Regarding information phenomena. we can categorize three groups: producers, managers and the users of information.

1. Producers

Information on women emanates from three major sources:

- Government channels, which produce policy documents, reports, white papers, statistical data, etc.
- Institutional channels such as research institutes oriented social science with a focus on women's issues, women's studies research centers, universities, women's groups or organizations, and media groups, which produce research reports, working papers, proceedings, etc.
- Personal channels such as individuals interested in women's issues, who produce reports, literature writings, etc.

2. Users

Information is produced and processed to improve its availability and accessibility for target groups, namely the users. And sometimes the users are the producers of the information at the same time. The several categories of the users are:

- government policymakers, program implementers, and evaluators
- women's groups or organizations such as non-government organizations(NGOs) and their regional counterparts, women's welfare centers
- academic and research groups such as research institutes focused on women's issues, women's research centers at the universities, and professors and students not only involved in the women's studies programs but also in cognate subject-related departments such as social sciences, family, welfare, education, economics, politics, humanities, etc.
- mass media groups
- the general public interested in women's issues.

The information requirements of these different categories vary and need to be met by making information available in different formats and through a variety of channels

D. Women's Information Center and Networking

1. The Women's Information Center of the KWDI

The KWDI, a government supported organization, was established to promote women's social participation and welfare by carrying out research and studies on women, by providing education and training for women, and by assisting women's activities

The Division of Information and Publication of the KWDI has collected women-related materials home and abroad, systematized them and provided information services to researchers and activists on women's issues since the establishment of the Institute in 1983. The Division was enlarged into the Women's Information Center (WIC) in 1996 to try and meet the country's critical need for data on women. Since the Center was founded, it has been working with a wide range of government agencies and women's organizations both to improve the collection of data on women and improve its distribution.

The WIC's goals are to facilitate government policy-making and women's research and activities by systematically gathering data on women from various fields, organizing it, packaging it and distributing it to national, regional and world-wide audiences. To facilitate its work, the WIC plans to operate an information network which links women's organizations within the country to each other, to ESCAP's regional Women's Information Network for the Asia and Pacific (WINAP) and to women's information networks world-wide.

As part of its operations, WIC identifies users of information about women, assesses their needs, conducts studies on information management, and trains network members to set up and manage a women's information system. The WIC also raises awareness about the need for comprehensive data on women and how it can be used.

The WIC is organized into two divisions. The Information and Publication Division produces printed materials and operates a Women's Information Resource Center which gathers and maintains materials and other sources of information related to women. It also distributes KWDI's publications. The Information System Division develops, installs and operates computer software, hardware and network systems and creates and manages women's information databases.

2. Activities undertaken by the WIC

Since 1995, the WIC has developed a number of Korean-language databases which are now available online. These summarize the research and activities of the KWDI since the organization was first established in 1983. Individual databases include ones on laws and legal issues of concern to women in Korea; indexes and abstracts of the holdings of the KWDI Women's Information Resource Center; indexes to journal articles and newspaper clippings on women's issues; the full text of research reports, educational materials produced by the KWDI, and all issues of KWDI's journal, "Women's Studies" (1990~); and news and policies concerning women. English-language databases include laws which affect Korean women; status of Korean women; research articles on women's issues; and a summary of the KWDI's work.

In 1997 the WIC has established a networked women's information system, "The Integrated Women's Information System", supervised by the Ministry of Political Affairs. This network will systematize the collection of data nationwide, compile them into databases and disseminate these. To achieve this, the system will link women's local points in local government offices in 15 areas of the country. These local points will be responsible for collecting data and sharing them with other network users. This system is available through the Internet, and it will be used by government agencies, women's organizations, and researchers as well as the general public, and will be connected with WINAP and other women's networks outside Korea.

Databases of the Integrated System include:

- a directory of women's groups and organizations such as the women's divisions of government agencies, women's centers, women's groups, and women's research institutes

- a directory of women's resources which includes women experts, job seekers, and volunteers

- statistics on women, FAQ (Frequently Asked Questions) on women's issues, and

- the full text of proceedings of meetings and seminars.

As a national women's information center, the WIC will provide advisory services to help network focal points to develop their own local women's information systems. The WIC will continue to extend the databases and provide an English translation service to exchange information with women in other countries via the Internet.

In the course of its pioneering work in Korea, the WIC has identified a number of obstacles. These include the high cost of translating material from Korean to English for inclusion in databases, the lack of human resources to update databases and modify the system in response to user demand, differences in computer and communications hardware and software which make it difficult for network members to share data, and network members' lack of knowledge about how to use computers and communications systems.

3. WINAP as a regional network

Liason with WINAP is another important aspect of the WIC's work. As the regional focal point, WINAP provides a critical communications link among women in the Asia and the Pacific region. Important services which WINAP provides to Korea and other countries include technical guidance and advisory services to countries to strengthen their national women's information network; provision of a number of regional databases; the creation of region-wide statistics on women and region-wide bibliographic databases.

Some of the benefits of regional networking include improvements in the flow of data and information within and between countries and the sharing of resources. Networking not only allows the exchange of information, technology and know-how related to collection, processing, and dissemination techniques but also fosters cooperation between countries. By fostering cooperation between countries, networking helps reduce the duplication of efforts in the collection, compilation, retrieval and dissemination of information.

Conclusion

In undertaking its challenging task, WIC is committed to increasing the role of Korean women in developing the national women's information network through computer networking. To achieve this, the Women's Information Centre hopes to encourage in Korea the participation of women in social development and political affairs by providing them with high-quality information on issues of concern to them, as well as opportunities to exchange information and collaborate with women, both inside and outside the country.

A prerequisite for the implementation of policies for the advancement of women in the future is an easy access to reliable information. Such access will guarantee women opportunities in the global information society.

A CALL FOR A NEW DIALOG

Nira Shani

Librarian

AIPI - Lesley College extension

Natanya, Israel (2000)

Abstract

From my personal experience, as a woman, feminist, and professional librarian, I found that there is a deep gap between the UNESCO Manifesto for Public Libraries ideas and the reality in public libraries in Israel. With the new ways of thinking, feminism through its criticism can bring about changes in women's standing in Israeli society. Therefore it should be seen on the public library shelves to create a new awareness, as it is a trend that we can't ignore any more.

Introduction

Literature reflects the imagined reality of its writer. However, it also has the power to give its readers new perspectives to light up their lives. Books, through the stories they tell, are agents of knowledge, both formal and informal. The story itself is a literary or historical tool for transmitting and constructing the building blocks of cultural identity and even of national ethos. Even more so, story and narrative can be tools for constructing personal identities. Books can transport us to new regions, ideas, solutions and understanding of ourselves or of our fellow women. They can shed new light on various topics.

I can recall my experience of reading "The Women's Room". The experience of birth described there shook me up. It reminded me of the birth of my first son several months before. This book did what literature often has the power to do. It gives us a mirror of moments or experiences and forces us to look at them more closely, from inside out. New awareness rushes to consciousness and new insights are constructed.

Until then I had not understood just how painful the experience of birth and the attitudes of the staff in the delivery room had been for me. There had been moments when I'd felt neglected, moments when I'd been chastised for "unworthy" behavior. These moments resurfaced as I read with a great deal of difficulty. Yet it paved the way for my understanding that "I am not alone". Other women had been there and experienced their first birth in similar ways.

I was flooded with anger. When I understood that it is a universal feminine experience, I realized the need to hear about and become familiar with the experiences of other women, and from that point I came to the awareness of its importance for feminine literature.

Change in the Perception and Development of Women

I base my appeal on the following changes and theories:

The change in the "body of knowledge" on and about women and their world, better known as women's and feminist awareness, and "feminist epistemology".

115

The perception of women's knowledge and parallel personal development as presented in "Women's Ways of Knowing" (Belenky and others, 1986). The results of change in perception and development of women, as reflected on the bookshelves has led to the developing genre of women's literature from a feminist perspective in research, reportage and fiction.

Public Library's Social Function

My claims against the public library as it is currently reflected in Israel are based upon the gap that exists between what a library is called upon to do and how to fulfill its obligations:

- by professional perception and the social function of a public library as declare by professional associations, as opposed to, in my opinion to the situation that exists in reality

- by law: The library is a service of the local municipality on behalf of the community.

The UNESCO Manifesto for Public Libraries states "materials must reflect current trends and the evolution of society, as well as the memory of human endeavor and imagination" (UNESCO Public Library Manifesto, Nov. 1994).

- the library is called upon to serve its public impartially by highlighting various new streams of development in society and by paying attention to populations that have been defined by their special needs such as children, the elderly, the disabled, prisoners and so on.

To this list I would add women.

The current perception of the task of the library and of librarians as per the American Library Association (ALA) is defined as one of "social responsibility" whose importance lies in providing individuals and groups with information on their rights and liabilities as citizens. With this information they can assess their niche in society and act on their individual interests or promote social affairs that will surface from their new knowledge. Only in light of this familiarity with the prevailing organizations of state, religion and municipal offices can citizens act on behalf of the development of services suited to the needs of the community.

Some of the tasks of the library in democratic society, as they have been described by the Public Library Association - PLA (Sever, 1990) and have been adopted by the Israeli Library Organization are:

- The library must reflect a democratic vision of life. To do so, the library must promote groups from all sectors of the community

- The library must allow free approach to all library materials to the public, as per their interests. Librarians are forbidden to censure any material from the library on grounds of race, religion, or any pressure from the community

- The collected material must reflect all perspectives of contemporary dilemmas.

The Relevance in Israel

According to the Central Office of Statistics and the Woman's Lobby, in Israel there exists still a gap between men and women in many areas such as wages, work status, professions actually open to women, religious law enforced through Rabbinic courts that discriminate against women, the attitude towards women's health and so on (Kazin, 1999).

Israel, which is basically a society based on immigration, has absorbed people from 102 countries worldwide since its inception in 1948. These immigrants come from differing cultures and different social orders. Not all the immigrants have become socially absorbed. There are many who, even today, continue the customs of their ethnic group, even if these are opposed to the laws of the State, for example, forced marriage of minors.

It follows that even though the law may support women, often it is the social norm that prevails and its meeting up with the law is yet a long way off.

Seemingly women in Israel live in a country that endorses equal rights for women. Women vote for the Parliament and for the local municipalities and have made strides in education, in sports, etc. Their status by law is quite advanced, even as compared with other countries. For example: In Israel, a woman who has given birth is entitled to a paid vacation and the couple can choose whether the man or the woman will make use of this privilege. There are laws concerning women's representation (one-third) in government boards of directors, and forbidding sexual harassment and prejudice in the workplace based on gender.

However, many times the law in Israel has "no teeth" or even promotes the social norm that it was meant to replace. Norms change only after the public has discovered the benefit in the alternative or has been forced to agree with it. Often the norm develops from the altercation between society and the law.

Thus, so many women live in "normative" frameworks that act against them, and accept them. Such is often the case with violence in the family or prejudice in the workplace, etc.

Here are some statistics to strengthen my claim:

200,000 women in Israel are estimated to live with partners who beat them. The treatment of abusive men is relatively new on the Israeli scene. As of the 1970's this phenomenon has become to be recognized as illegal and it has started to meet with social opposition, however, the judicial system still retains its prejudice against women, as shown in the research of the Woman's Lobby in Israel (Kazin, 1999). The wage level of women, as per a review by the Central Bureau of Statistics (CBS), is 30% lower than of men in the same profession and for the same level of education. These statistics are true for 1997 (ibid).

Few women reach senior positions, such as in management, although they make up 62% of the workforce in governmental agencies with most of them in low status jobs. This naturally has an impact on their wage level. Women make up only 2.4% of management positions as opposed to 7.3% men (ibid).

Women are seen in society as those responsible for the household and the rearing of children. They are exposed to a double message. On one hand they are expected to go out to work, to develop a career and supplement the family finances. On the other hand they are not given the necessary tools or the financial remuneration to make this possible.

In light of the situation of women in Israeli society and the lack of awareness of many of them to their rights, I find that many women need information, practical or theoretical on their status, and their rights. They need to know about the possibilities open to them and the organizations that can help and support them. I find that in so many cases they are cut off from sources of information and support.

This then, is where the library can act as a mediator between women and the large pools of information that have become available. There is much professional and technical information aside literary material. There is information regarding links and referrals to women's organizations and volunteer organizations working on behalf of women in the community. As they link up with these sources they will discover new possibilities, awareness, acquaintance with worlds near and far that will empower their lives.

Feminist Epistemology

In this section I will present the "body of knowledge" on women (feminist epistemology), as a topic that can no longer be ignored. In this very short review, via some of the most important landmarks in the development of feminist thought, mostly I would like to stress the importance of this wealth of knowledge to women as individuals and as members of society.

Epistemology is the way in which mankind perceives and knows itself, its human identity and place in society.

Feminists claim that traditional methods of becoming familiar with knowledge distanced women from the ability to be knowledgeable, or the agents of knowledge. In their opinion, the voice of science is a male voice. History has been written from a sovereign or upper class male perspective. Such is the case with other sciences as psychology, sociology and so on.

Harding stated: "Feminists have argued that traditional epistemologies, whether intentionally or unintentionally, systematically exclude the possibility that women could be 'knower' or agent of knowledge" (Harding, 1986, p.3).

Simone de Beauvoir brought to our knowledge the recognition of the distorted situation of women. In the preface to her book "The Second Sex" she says, Thus humanity is male and man defined woman not in herself but as relative to him. She is not regarded as autonomous being. She is the incidental, the inessential as opposed to the essential. He is the subject. He is the Absolute. She is the Other (de Beauvoir, 1989, pp. xxii). This was the first time that the problem of woman's definition had been presented in a scholarly and well-documented way to readers, both male and female.

With the second wave of feminism in the 60's and 70's many investigators began to deal with the knowledge and experience of women. They turned to varied topics in the academic world and proceeded to investigate the physical, economic and psychological circumstances of women. They also examined their inner worlds, their creations and their lives over the centuries and in present times.

Gilligan exposed the problem of definition of psychological research that had become public knowledge in the twentieth century. She discovered that many famous scholars in the field of psychological research, such as Piaget, Erikson and particularly Kohlberg, had based their findings on observation of boys. There was usually no representation for women or girls (Gilligan, 1995). She explained her research of women by saying: "The goal I strive for is to reach a deeper and broader understanding of human development. This understanding is possible when the group, that until now has remained outside the theoretical framework of the pattern of human development, will be included and receive the attention that it has previously not received in the field of research" (Gilligan, 1995, p. 11).

Women's Ways of Knowing

The results of this study (by Belenky et. al.) stress five major stages of development that are outstanding in women's lives:

• "Silence". This stage is typical of women who have suffered sexual exploitation or have been neglected by family or society.

• Received Knowledge. This stage is very significant in a woman's development as it depends greatly on who her authority figure is. Often, by trust in an authority figure, a mistake in consciousness grows. When the authority figure disappoints or is seen to be unworthy, there is recognition and change from passivity to activity. The "self" begins to develop.

• Procedural Knowledge. This stage is characterized by receiving information from formal sources. Women at this stage want to learn more and more. They analyze the details of each event and try to learn and understand in maximum depth. An important part of this stage is understanding the complexity of thought and the differing voices of themselves and their environment.

• This stage divides into two. The first is the Separate Knowers and the other is the Connected Knowers. Those who are separate are defined as Anti-Subjective. They see each one's right to their own mistakes, as opposed to the Connected Knowers, who believe that any knowledge can be constructed from experience and be different from the experience of others. They refrain from judgment and they tend to hear other's experience with a great deal of empathy.

This is the highest developmental level in which women count on themselves and their own experience. Moreover, they dare to set out on a new path; they listen to their inner voice that calls upon them to act in accordance with their own consciousness and their own understanding. They are willing to listen to others and respect them and to respect themselves. At this stage women no longer need social recognition in order to pursue their "inner voice" and they dare to express it out loud.

In the closing chapter of this book a new way of teaching, in light of the findings on women, is presented. It is called Connected Teaching and represents a new way of thought in which the teacher distributes knowledge, as opposed to functioning as an authority figure who presents knowledge "as it is" that is irrefutable. It provides the place where she can bring her ideas and talk freely about them.

• Empowerment – is the ultimate aim where all the former comes to fruition and the society is able to reshape and process changes. To quote Sadan: "It is an important factor in the life of every person. Citizens who control their lives and are partners to decisions affecting their futures and their environment make an important contribution to democratic society as a whole" (Sadan, 1997, p.12).

It is well worth remembering that librarianship as a profession is only as good as the up-to-date service it renders. Staying abreast of development does not only refer to technological advances as is commonly thought. It also means renewing attitudes and approaches in keeping with social trends and the developments that stem from them (as stated in the UNESCO Manifesto).

Most of the feminist literature has been shoved aside into sub-topics within the major conventionally recognized ones.

Pritchard answers the challenge of changing attitudes by saying: "Inter-disciplinarily, in women's studies or other innovative areas, requires changes in traditional collection developing, cataloging, automation and preservation, to meet the needs of scholars and the patterns of public information seeking" (Pritchard, 1993, p. 5).

In some of the libraries I visited, in Israel, it was possible to find feminism by means of a search in keywords. However, from my experience as a librarian serving a largely female population (90%), I can testify on the gap between younger customers up to the age of 30, and those more mature who see the computer as being strange and threatening. In this situation, the use of keywords in the computer will be an inefficient tool and can even cause the seeker to back off from looking for the material she needs.

Many women no longer view themselves as they are viewed by library categorization and cataloging systems. It no longer authentically represents them as they are in real life outside the library. Presentation of the material in this way makes a significant statement about the status of woman in Israeli society.

A change of attitude of librarians towards feminism is needed. Whether it is in the scope of collections, the separate space awarded on the shelves or the creation of a unique feminist section, all of these and receptivity toward the learning models, presented under the title of Women's Ways of Knowing, can contribute to the furthering of feminist issues and awareness of women of their own issues in the public library.

References

1. Beauvoir, Simon de (1989) The Second Sex. N.Y. Vintage books.

2. Belenky, M., Clinchy, B., Goldberg, N., & Tarule, J. (1986) Women's Ways of Knowing. New York: Basic Books.

3. Gilligan, C. (1995) In a Different Voice. Tel-Aviv: Sifriay Poalim. [in Hebrew]

4. Harding, S. (1987) (Ed.) Feminism and Methodology. Bloomington, Indiana: Indiana University Press.

5. Kazin, O. (1999) Report on the Israeli Women. Ha'Aretz ; New York Times 31.12.99.

6. Pritchard, S. (1993) Feminist Thinking and Librarianship in the 1990s: Issues and Challenges [online].Available at http://www.libraries.wayne.edu/ftf/papers/femthink.html

7. Pritchard, S. (1994) Women's Studies Scholarship: Its Impact on the Information World [online]. Available at http://www.lib.wayne.edu/ftf/papers/wsscholar.html

8. Sadan, E. (1997) Empowerment and Community Planning. Tel-Aviv: Hakibbutz hameuchad Publishing House. [in Hebrew].

9. Sever, S. & I.(1990) The Library in the Society. Jerusalem: Merkaz Hahadracha [in Hebrew].

10. UNESCO Public Library Manifesto, Nov. 1994. [online]. Available http://www.ifla.org/documents/libraries/policies/unesco.htm

FREEING ACCESS TO WOMEN'S INFORMATION:
AN OVERVIEW

Beth Stafford

Women's Studies, University of Illinois Urbana-Champaign

Urbana-Champaign, Illinois, USA (2000)

Abstract

As major gatekeepers of knowledge and culture, libraries and their decisions regarding which materials to acquire, which to ignore, and on how to make their contents accessible through cataloging and classification, codify knowledge. By virtue of such decisions, libraries have essentially controlled access to, and imposed a structure and relational value system on, all forms of information.

A wide range of difficulties has hampered access to information about, by and of particular concern to females of all ages. In recent years, librarians all across the globe have organized to modify existing practices in libraries and documentation centers. They are working with national and international government and grassroots agencies to make information about women and girls more easily available so that public policies can be better informed on issues that disproportionately affect females.

Previously, many countries did not even compile statistics on social, political, and economic indicators on females. Any national statistics kept were not disaggregated by sex. As a result, public policy was crafted to coincide with beliefs rather than facts.

This paper gives an overview of activities undertaken by librarians and other information professionals worldwide over the past decade or so and currently. An impressive variety of agencies either specialize in women's information entirely or have specialized units within larger institutions that make information about women's and gender issues accessible, in paper and all electronic formats from the Internet to video and sound recordings to specialized discrete databases.

Introduction

The "Second Wave" women's movement that began in Western countries in the late 1960s spawned a generation of feminist scholars in institutions of higher education who challenged long-held assumptions about content and methods in traditional disciplines. These challenges continue in all parts of the world. Until the late 1960s most of the knowledge in contemporary civilizations had been produced by men, from a perspective that either excluded females or classified females as deviant. Called Women's Studies, the new field these scholars founded took as its purposes to enable women to become authorities on their own lives; to construct their own knowledge about women according to their criteria as women; and to empower themselves through knowledge making (Kramarae and Spender, 1992).

During the same time the new field was taking root, the United Nations declared 1975 to be The International Year of the Woman, with a convening conference in Mexico City. One of the major lessons women scholars and activists (frequently the same individuals) learned through the Mexico City experience and subsequent meetings was that the amount of government information on women was appallingly paltry. Some countries did not then keep many statistics on life indicators. Among those that did, very few statistics were disaggregated by sex. This meant that, for instance, examining crime statistics, it was not possible to distinguish between sex of perpetrators and the sex of victims.

While I realize that not all information about women is necessarily considered by some to be women's studies, for this paper I will use the terms "women's information" and "women's studies information" interchangeably.

Because, historically speaking, Women's Studies (WS) as a field is such a recent phenomenon that crosses nearly all disciplinary lines and refuses to separate the scholarly from personal experience, traditional libraries are still responding to the field in a variety of ways. Concomitant with the growth of WS is the increased general concern for gender issues due to the women's movement internationally. Libraries and women's groups the world over are attempting to provide both scholarly and "survival" information on women's and gender issues.

Access Issues

Although many materials that preserve women's history and accomplishments have been held in libraries and archives for many years, they have not necessarily been organized in ways that provide good access to them.

Libraries serve as major gatekeepers of knowledge and culture. As Sarah Pritchard observes, in effect, library decisions on which materials to acquire, which to ignore, and on how to make their contents accessible through cataloging and classification, codify knowledge. By virtue of such decisions, libraries essentially control access to, and impose a structure and relational value system on, all forms of information (Moseley, 1995).

Traditional cataloging and classification practices have been biased and judgmental. A majority of libraries organize their collections according to various classification schemes that assume a universality of experience that is male-centered. Terminology used in most library systems for finding information is usually also based on male-centered language as well. That is, too frequently sexist terms are still employed to express specific concepts.

Pioneering work by Joan Marshall and a group of feminist librarians in the United States in the 1970s led to many improvements in Library of Congress terminology, such as changing the heading from the generic "Woman" to "Women". In spite of these improvements and the continuing work of reformers such as Sanford Berman, the scheme continues to perpetuate the use of numerous indefensible headings concerning women, people of color, older persons, sexual minorities, poor people, and disabled people (Berman, 1993).

Many libraries use improved terminology for recent publications. However, the high cost of reassigning subject headings to older works cataloged before improvements were made still keeps a substantial portion of library materials by, about and of concern to women inaccessible.

In addition to these difficulties, traditional libraries too frequently do not make full use of improved terminology that is available and do not assign enough subject headings to books being cataloged. This practice renders important aspects of many books and other materials invisible.

In most traditional library collections, the use of approved controlled vocabularies in providing access to information about, by and of concern to women too frequently presents difficulties of primarily four types. One difficulty is subsuming terminology (i.e., using the heading "Man" to mean all human beings). A second problem is the modifier tactic (e.g., "Women as artists") as if women were not ordinarily capable or otherwise qualified to be artists. (This also strongly implies the stereotype that women's rightful place is in the home as nurturer.) (Berman, 1993).

Separate and unequal treatment of specific groups of people is a third problem that occurs through the use of words or constructions connoting inferiority or peculiarity. An example was the now defunct heading "Woman-Social and moral questions" while there was no parallel heading "Man-Social and moral questions". (Marshall, 1977)

The fourth and last major problem is complete omission of terminology particularly of interest or concern to those researching women and gender issues, such as "Gynocide", "Sex tourism", or "Feminist humor".

Clearly the problems of sexism in language and in subject terminology schemes are not limited to the English language, as demonstrated by the fact that feminist librarians and archivists in several countries have produced a number of thesauri to reflect the central concerns of those seeking information relevant to women and women's studies. The Women's Thesaurus was published in the United States in 1987. At approximately the same time the National Women's Education Centre in Japan published Thesaurus on Women and the Family. Women in Development Thesaurus, a joint project of the Indonesian Institute of Science and UNICEF, was published in 1991. The International Archives of the Women's Movement (IIAV) in Amsterdam published a thesaurus, Vrouwenthesaurus, in 1993. In Germany, FrauenMediaTurm published Feministischer Thesaurus in 1994. More recently, in 1998 a joint project between IIAV RoSa Documentioncentre in Brussels, the Nordic Institute for Women's Studies and Gender Research in Oslo, KVINFO (the National Danish Women's Library) in Copenhagen, and the National Italian Women's Library in Bologna culminated in publication of the European Women's Thesaurus, an English-language translation and adaptation of the earlier IIAV work. In addition, currently there are thesaurus projects in progress in at least Austria, Spain, Italy, and South Africa.

Some grass roots groups have not only compiled their own thesauri of terms but have also established their own classification schemes of call numbers for organizing their collections.

In addition to terminology and classification schemes that do not meet needs for information on women and gender issues effectively, library researchers are faced with the fact that very few reference works such as bibliographies, biographical directories or guides existed until approximately twenty-five years ago.

This means that, for the most part, until that time there was little guidance on which researchers or librarians could depend. What information there was on, for, or by women was scattered piecemeal throughout many individual resources generally based on the traditional disciplines.

Countries where libraries have existed the longest, such as India, Egypt, and China, began adopting Western models of organization and concepts of librarianship in the 19th and 20th centuries.

Libraries in some countries use adaptations of the Library of Congress Subject Headings scheme to provide subject access to their collections. Other countries, such as India and China, have their own national schemes of subject headings. In many countries, such as Japan, the use of subject headings is not a common practice at all.

Women's Information in Libraries

Currently, the best resources for women's information are found in a variety of libraries, documentation centres, and archives in different countries. In some countries, such as Japan, the strongest resources for women's information are not in university libraries but in special libraries in many women's centres funded by city governments. In other countries the national government or a supra-national organization affiliated with the United Nations (e.g., UNESCO) funds the best resources for women's information, again as special libraries or documentation centres, either in women's centres or as independent entities.

According to a survey by Marieke Kramer and Jytte Larsen (Kramer, 1995), in Europe, for the most part, three types of centres of information for the study of women and gender issues exist. The first group developed as a result of the first wave of twentieth-century feminism in the 1930s. They are professional, publicly funded, large general collections. These include the International Archives for the Women's Movement (IIAV in Amsterdam), Fawcett Library (London), and Bibliothèque Marguerite Durand (Paris).

Second is the group of centres that were established as a consequence of the "second wave" of feminism in the 1970s. These collections tend to specialize by subject and are well-suited for networking but usually depend on volunteers to maintain them because of funding scarcities.

Thirdly, there are those set up within public bodies and organizations (such as national organizations for equality policy) in the 1980s. These were planned from the start to have professional paid staff, are computerized, and function as national information centres.

Some centres, such as KVINFO (Copenhagen) and ARIADNE (Vienna), originated in their countries' national libraries. Others began by being affiliated with WS units of universities. The degree of professionalism in these centres is high, as is the degree of coverage of national publications.

Librarians in European Union countries and in non-member states such as Czechoslovakia are working hard to organize the collection and exchange of information on women and gender issues. One fairly recent development is the establishment of the Women's Library and Information Centre in Istanbul, Turkey, in 1990.

In Asia, India has the most WS programs and research facilities. Information on women and gender issues is found in special collections in academic libraries, collections in government agencies, and documentation centres in WS research centres and cells in women's organizations. Perhaps best known internationally is the Research Centre for Women's Studies Documentation Center at SNDT Women's University in Bombay.

More recently, a substantial number of online networks has been established throughout Southeast Asia. The largest women's research institute in the world is the Korean Women's Development Institute in Seoul, established by the Korean National Assembly in 1982. Among its divisions is an Information Centre that supports Institute research projects and action-oriented programs.

In the Middle East, the Institute for Women's Studies in the Arab World, founded in 1973, is housed at the Lebanese American University (formerly Beirut University College). The university library includes the Women's Documentation Centre, which has books and international periodicals.

Latin American women's groups have taken the lead in the use of electronic networks and communication systems to meet their information needs. (Women's groups in several countries in the Commonwealth of Independent States (CIS) have built information systems for themselves that are patterned after Latin American systems.) In Latin America, one of the best repositories of information on women is Isis Internacional in Santiago, Chile. Like many women's information centres in all parts of the world, Isis Internacional is a non-governmental organization (NGO) affiliated with the United Nations that seeks to provide needed information that is produced by or for women or is on topics of concern to women. Isis particularly serves women in Latin America and the Caribbean.

It appears that in most Latin American countries scholarly information for WS is best accessed through feminist groups such as the Centro de Investigación y Capacitación a La Mujer in Quito, Ecuador, or CIDHAL (Communication, Exchange, and Human Development in Latin America) Women's Centre in Cuernavaca, Mexico. In some countries, such as Brazil, scholarly productivity is very recent and resources scarce. Frequently the best access to information on women and gender issues is through private libraries.

In 1997, the African Gender Institute at the University of Cape Town, South Africa, hosted a pan-African workshop for librarians and documentalists with the aim of exploring ways to share gender information and resources throughout Africa. One result of that workshop is the Gender in Africa Information Network (GAIN),which has established an electronic network. The GAIN network enables libraries of many women's groups such as the African Centre for Women in Addis Ababa, Ethiopia, an NGO affiliated with the United Nations, to share resources and improve the flow of information with other entities such as the Women's Research and Documentation Project at the University of Dar Es Salaam in Tanzania.

Isis-Women's International Cross-Cultural Exchange (Isis-WICCE) in Kampala, Uganda, is an activist women's resource centre. One of its goals is to collect and disseminate information related to women and to facilitate communication and networking between individuals and women's groups from different parts of the world. Its documentation centre works with contacts in at least 154 countries.

Collection Development Issues

An inherent part of women's studies is the fact that many of the source materials are generated by activist groups. The standard practice in most libraries not to collect materials not easily available through the commercial trade effectively excludes books, journals, videotapes, etc. produced by small presses or enterprises unless someone in the library makes special efforts to acquire them. It is frequently the feminist presses, which are small by commercial standards, that publish the information most valuable to women's studies researchers. The same is true for videotapes, CD-ROMs, and information in other formats.

In most libraries, responsibility for selecting materials to add to the collection is divided up by traditional subjects. Most academic libraries do not have WS specialists per se. Because women's studies involves so many different disciplines, careful coordination of effort among various selectors is required in order to develop a good collection in WS. In recent years increasing numbers of academic libraries are designating one person to have formal responsibility for building the collection in this area (usually along with responsibility for other areas as well).

Women's Studies Librarianship

Women's studies courses began in the United States in the late 1960s and spread from there. WS librarianship began there also, in response to the new scholarship on women in both courses and research. The American Library Association has a Women's Studies Section that began meeting in 1979. One of its goals is to promote awareness of WS as a multi-disciplinary field of research and teaching that libraries must respond to.

Several projects initiated by the Section and its members have led to the publication of valuable resources in the form of directories, indexes, bibliographies and more. Another project has influenced producers of standard indexing services and databases to include more WS periodicals - thereby improving access to information vital to anyone interested in women and gender issues.

One aim of the International Federation of Library Associations Round Table on Women's Issues is to promote awareness of women's issues in libraries. This entails gathering and disseminating information about women in the profession of librarianship and surveying available information resources on women and their organization and use.

Progress and Prospects

In 1998 the International Information Centre and Archives for the Women's Movement (IIAV) in Amsterdam hosted an international conference for librarians and documentalists working with materials relevant to women and gender issues. The "Know How Conference" attracted approximately 300 information specialists and representatives of government agencies from over 80 countries. Presenters highlighted their projects and activities employing cyberspace as well as other means. Topics covered included, among others, indexing women's information on Internet; designing new online resources; cataloging and classification issues in handling women's information; and empowering women's information for women in rural, immigrant, and minority communities.

An impressive product that came from the above conference is an online guide to collections of women's information in all types of organizations everywhere, entitled "Mapping the World of Women's Information". This guide, a continuing service of IIAV, provides keyword and geographic access to collections literally worldwide.

Sarah Pritchard points out that librarianship is concerned with understanding the nature of information and recorded expression, the ways people seek and use it, and the best structures and processes for organizing, documenting, preserving, and sharing it. Feminist thought questions the nature of knowledge itself. Consequently it also questions the very structures and institutions built around our concepts of what knowledge is.

Libraries and librarians must continue to meet the challenges of WS as we decide what to make available (through print, electronic, or other formats), how to make it available, and what to preserve. Libraries need to mobilize resources to enable writers, librarians, publishers, faculty, students, policy-makers and women in the community to find information and to use it to create new services and structures in society. (Moseley, 1995). (Witness the increased public awareness and changed policies in many countries vis a vis issues such as women's legal rights or violence against women that have grown over the past 25 years, thanks in large part to the women's movement.)

We have touched on only a few of the current efforts to free access to women's information. Members of the global community of women's information specialists continue to make a difference through participation in local, national, and international activities such as the Beijing +5 meetings, progressing toward the goal Pritchard articulates.

References and further reading

Berman, Sanford (1993) Prejudices and Antipathies: a Tract on the LC Subject Headings on People. Jefferson, NC: McFarland & Company, p. 145.

Kramer, Marieke (1995) 'Getting It Together: Women's Information Services in the European Union' in Eva Steiner Moseley, Women, Information, and the Future: Collecting and Sharing Resources Worldwide. Ft. Atkinson, WI: Highsmith Press, pp. 101-102.

Kramarae, Cheris and Dale Spender (1992) The Knowledge Explosion: Generations of Feminist Scholarship, New York: Teachers College Press, p, 3. Marshall, Joan (1977) On Equal Terms: a Thesaurus for Nonsexist Indexing and Cataloging. New York: Neal-Schuman Publishers, pp. 7-9.

Pritchard, Sarah (1995) 'Women's Studies Scholarship: Its Impact on the Information World' in Eva Steiner Moseley, Women, Information, and the Future: Collecting and Sharing Resources Worldwide. Ft. Atkinson, WI: Highsmith Press, p. 16. Ibid., p. 15.

Addresses of Organizations

African Centre for Women

United Nations Economics Commission for Africa

Box 3001, Addis Ababa, Ethiopia

African Gender Institute

URL: http://www.uct.ac.za/org/agi ARIADNE

Kooperationsstelle Frauenspezifische Österreichische Nationalbibliothek

Josefsplatz 1, A-1015 Vienna, Austria

Tel: +43 222 53410/487

Fax: +43 222 53410/437

URL: http://onb.ac.at/ben/ariadfr.htm

Bibliothèque Marguerite Durand

79 rue National, F-75013, Paris, France

Tel: +33 1 447 08 030

Email: bnd75@club-internet.fr

Centro de Investigación y Capitación a La Mujer

Casilla Postal 0901-10201, Guayaquil, Ecuador

Fax: +593 4 408087

CIDHAL Communication, Exchange, and Human Development in Latin America)

Cuernavaca, Apartado Postal 579, Morelos, Mexico

Fawcett Library: The National Women's Library, London Guildhall University

Calcutta House, Old Castle Street, E1 7NT London, United Kingdom

URL: http://www.lgu.ac.uk/fawcett/main.htm

Institute for Women's Studies in the Arab World, Lebanese American University

P.O. Box 13, 5053 Beirut, Lebanon

Tel: 811968

URL: http://www.lau.edu.lb

International Information Centre and Archives for the Women's Movement (IIAV)

Obiplein 4, 1094 RB Amsterdam, Netherlands

Tel: +31 20 6651318

URL: http://iiav.nl

Isis Internacional Santiago

Esmeralda 636 2P, Santiago, Chile

Tel: +56 2 6334582

Fax: +56 2 6383142

Email: isis@reuna.cl

Isis-WICCE (Women's International Cross-Cultural Exchange)

Box 4934, Kampala, Uganda

Tel: +256 4 1543 953

Fax: +256 4 1543 954

Email: isis@starcom.co.ug

Korean Women's Development Institute (KWID)
1-363 Bulkwang-dong, Empyung-ku, 122-707 Seoul, Korea
Tel: +82 2 3560070
Fax: +82 2 384767
URL: http://kwominet.or.kr

KVINFO, Danish Centre for Information on Women & Gender
Christians Brygge 3, DK-1219 Copenhagen I, Denmark
Tel: +45 33135088
Fax: +45 33 4156
Email: kvinfo@kvinfo.dk
URL: http://www.kvinfo.dk

National Women's Education Centre
728 Ranzan-cho Oazo Sugaya, Hiki-gun, Saitama-ken 355-02, Japan
Tel +81 493 626711

Research Centre for Women's Studies Documentation Centre
SNDT Women's University
1 Nathibai Thackersey Rd, New Marine Lines, 400 020 Mumbai, India

Women's Library and Information Centre
Fener Mah, Fener P.T.T. yam (tarihi bina), Halic, 34220 Istanbul, Turkey
Tel: +90 212 5237408

Women's Research and Documentation Project, Women's Research and Documentation
Centre, Box 35108, University of Dar Es Salaam
Dar Es Salaam, Tanzania

WOMEN, DEMOCRACY AND PARTICIPATION IN THE INFORMATION SOCIETY

Louisa Mayer

General Manager of Educational Services

Tschwane Metropolitan Library and Information Services

Pretoria, South Africa (2002)

Abstract

South Africa can easily be one of the countries in the world with the largest percentage of abused and discriminated-against women. It is surely also one of the Countries with the bravest strong-hearted women:

- More than 60 per cent of the population is illiterate or semi-literate

- The average age at which a girl gives birth is sixteen

- The number of babies born with the HIV/Aids virus has increased with 65 per cent during the last ten years.

Community Library and Information Services in South Africa are playing a vital role in empowering especially women by ensuring that they are informed and able to take financial care of themselves.

This paper will attempt to outline the various ways in which this mammoth task is attempted and aims to give practical advice to achieve results with the minimum of financial and other resources.

Introduction

She was approximately seventeen years old and about seven months pregnant. A two-year-old toddler was peeping out behind her tattered dress. In a shy whisper she asked me: "Do you perhaps have books with pictures where I can see where babies are coming from". It was at this exact moment that I realised the intensity of the information and education task we as Librarians in post-apartheid South Africa are facing, especially towards the women of this wonderful Country.

This happened four years back. Margaret is currently employed as a councilor specializing in assisting abused women. She attended the Literacy, Sex education and HIV/Aids education classes offered by the Community Library and Information Services. She is a regular visitor to the nearby Municipal Clinic and receives free contraceptives. She was referred by the Library Services to an institution that provided Free Legal Aid to abused women and is currently receiving maintenance from the fathers of both her children. Both her children attend all the reading hours, educational activities and holiday programmes offered at their local Library. They are well cared for children, bright and eager to learn. Margaret told me later that it took all her courage to visit the Community Library and Information Service, as she perceived it as a place only to be visited by the literate and wealthy, but she was desperate to change her life of poverty and ignorance.

2. Women in South African Society

South Africa can easily be one of the countries in the world with the largest percentage of abused and discriminated against women. It is surely also one of the Countries with the bravest and strong-hearted women.

The following statistics speak for themselves:

- One adult woman out of every six in South Africa is currently assaulted by her partner
- Research carried out in Soweto in 1994 found that one in three women attending a clinic for any reason had been battered at some time by her husband or boyfriend
- At least one woman is killed by her partner every six days in South Africa
- One in three girl children will be sexually assaulted before the age of 18, and one in eight boys will be sexually assaulted
- An estimated million women are raped annually in South Africa – approximately one rape every 35 seconds
- More than 60% of the population is illiterate or semi-literate, the majority hereof being women
- The average age at which a girl gives birth is sixteen
- The number of babies born with the HIV/Aids virus has increased with 65% during the last ten years.
- More than 15 million adults are estimated to have HIV/AIDS on the African continent, 64% of the world's total positive population
- Close to 8 million African women are HIV positive, compared with 10 million women infected worldwide
- Female-headed households have 50% higher poverty rate than male-headed households.

Women are more vulnerable to abuse, HIV infection and subsequently poverty because of their status in South African Society. The birth of true Democracy in South Africa in 1994 did not mean total democracy for especially the African women. Because women in South Africa, and single mothers in particular, are often economically disadvantaged, their access to health care and information in general is compromised. Distribution points for free condoms such as clinics and schools are lacking in areas where poverty is rife, especially rural areas. Poor women have less access to information and resources that will help them make informed choices in life.

It is however not only economically and political disadvantaged women that are affected by the lack of status. Until recently all women in South African Society were, and still are, marginalized by the mere fact of their sex, both at home and in their careers. Although definite steps are in place to achieve not only racial equity, but also gender equity, there still exist a large degree of gender discrimination against females of all races. Women tend to find themselves clustered in junior, part-time and temporary positions, often without access to technological information and or time to educate themselves or to be trained in information technology.

3. Breaking Barriers: The Role of the Community Library and Information Service in South Africa

Community Library and Information Services in South Africa are playing a vital role in empowering especially women by ensuring that they are informed and able to take financial care of themselves. The ongoing circle of poverty, illiteracy and disease can be broken only by getting women to really and actively participate in the information society as the influence of the mother on a child is the only factor really impacting on transforming a society. Policies, legislation, programmes etc. can attempt to empower a society, but true participation and empowerment can only come from inside a society and an individual.

Community Libraries in South Africa are increasingly becoming the link between the "uneducated individual" and the information highway.

Community Libraries are fulfilling the vital role of addressing community needs on a very basic level, making it less fearful and daunting to access information than on a more formal level. It is firstly necessary to have a clear view of the barriers preventing easy access for women to information in general:

3.1 Barriers experienced in information delivery to women

Lack of time

Lack of financial resources

Lack of access to training

Illiteracy

Technological illiteracy

Fear of technology

Crime

Language barrier

Lack of telephone and information infrastructure

Lack of effective channels of communication

Public Libraries perceived to be a luxury and not a basic right

Views of women as being intellectually inferior

Women perceived as having a second-class status

Lack of self-worth and self trust

Lack of interest

Women are unaware of the value of information and knowledge

Lack of support from partners and families

Lack of a culture of reading and learning

These are but a few barriers that have to be broken. The situation is further complicated by the fact that the status of the Community Library and Information Service in South Africa is not perceived as to be of great importance. No legislation exists enforcing the rendering of Community Library and Information Services. Budget cuts firstly affects this specific service delivery while demands on the service from the community is ever increasing. Alternative and innovative ways have to be found to address the ever changing and increasing needs of the communities.

Service rendering has to change from being book focused to finding other ways of information dissemination as the South African currency is plunging drastically. Very limited resources are available to concentrate on empowering women in the information world, as there are always more visible priorities to attend to.

3.2. Finding ways to break barriers

The Tshwane Community Library and Information Services have come a long way towards breaking these barriers. The Library Service has moved, and is still moving rapidly away from the traditional western Library service delivery and is breaking ground in finding a true South African model of service delivery, concentrating on the diverse cultural needs of all citizens in order to satisfy all information needs.

3.2.1. Provision of information services

Special emphasis is given to information dissemination concentrating on women's needs. This information is available on a basic level and attempts to provide quick and effective answers and guidance with everyday real life problems:

Survival information

Business information (entrepreneurial information)

Legal information

Community information

Municipal services

Career information

Job opportunities

Housing opportunities

Heritage information

Health issues

General enquiries

Information packages

Research projects

In order to make information accessible to especially women, it is firstly essential to reach the women, to make them aware of the importance of information in their lives. It is not viable to wait that women approach the Community Library, as in most cases due to all the reasons listed above and more, they will simply not come. It is therefore very important to form and utilised network of stakeholders and to infiltrated the community on all levels:

Some examples of such stakeholders are:

Formal and informal educational institutions

Church groups

NGO's

Governmental bodies

Womans associations

Shebeens (Local pubs)

Places of work

3.2.2. Support to Education

Educational services enable people to educate themselves. Services are:

Educare

Support to formal education

Adult-Basic Education

Provision of study facilities

Informal education

Youth services

The Community Library is further putting emphasis on providing support to education. 40% of women in the Greater Tshwane area is illiterate or semi literate. All attempts are made to allow people to educate themselves. Literacy training, Life skills and Adult Basic Education programmes are offered in partnership with stakeholders, reaching over 2000 learners per month. 89% of these learners are women between 30 and 90. These programmes concentrate on entrepreneural empowerment in order to assist the learners to become economically self sustainable and independant from abusive home environments.

3.2.3. The establishment and maintenance of a reading and learning culture

One of the most important barriers is the lack of a culture of reading and learning. The verbal tradition in early African society has kept folklore and heritage alive. With Colonisation and the urbanilisation, this verbal transition from the elderly in the community is ending. With no access to books and other information material especially in rural areas, a very limited culture of reading exists. The access to television and computers in the urban areas further enhances this problem. The youth therefore has no sense of self-education and the value of information. Linked to the tendency that females are undereducated, this leads to a real problem as women are not able to install a culture of reading and learning in their children.

Regular awareness programmes like marches for literacy are initiated. During 2001 a total of more than 30 000 people were involved this way. Reading circles and programmes exists not only for children, but also for elderly and illiterate women. Books on tape are increasingly popular were a group of women get together to listen to these tapes while they are taught knitting or crocheting.

3.2.4. Outreach activities and programmes

The following key areas should be kept in mind when outreach activities are rendered and programmes are presented:

All activities and programmes should be presented as fun and non-threatening.

The Libraries itself should be as non-daunting as possible.

The status and dignity of the most uneducated and poor participant should maintained at all times.

Provision should always be made for childcare

Access to activities should be easy (financially and physically)

Time constraints should be taken into account

Level of entrance should be relevant to the average literacy rate and economic environment of the immediate community

The following very successful regular programmes are currently in place, reaching approximately 20 000 women on a monthly basis :

Born to Read programme

Basic and advanced literacy training

Entrepreneurial activities and training

Cultural development activities

Interest groups for teenage mothers and mothers to be

Extensive HIV/AIDS awareness campaigns

Reading circles for aged women

Feeding programmes

Counseling in women related matters with stakeholders

Practical instructions on various projects

Exhibitions on relevant topics

Skills workshops

In all cases the emphasis is on easy and relaxed way of self-education. Only when the women are comfortable with accessing basic information and attending regular sessions, attempts are made into progressing into a more advance stage of formal access to ICT. Computer classes, providing friendly access are offered by way of public private partnerships. Lack of funding for virtual villages are however extremely limited and this still poses as one of the major barriers into empowering women and the whole community in information technology.

4. Conclusion

South Africa has just celebrated eight years of democracy and freedom on 27 April 2002. The Country has come a long way, but women have still not found true democracy and independency. As long as every newspaper daily reports on rape of women and children, AIDS deaths etc., this country will not be truly democratic. As long as women are forbidden by their partners to use contraceptives, as long as women do not know where babies coming from because they are denied access to basic information, women will not be truly citizens of this country.

The women of South Africa are, however, strong. Women of all races are standing together, utilizing all the opportunities coming their way in order to ensure that their children have that have been denied to them for a very long time, that is the power of being informed. The Tshwane Community Library and Information Service is committed towards empowering women and the children of this Country by providing access to information and teaching women the power and joy of being informed.

V. WOMEN'S INFORMATION NEEDS: A SOCIETAL AND FEMINIST ISSUE

INFORMATION NEEDS OF WOMEN:
ADDRESSING DIVERSE FACTORS IN THE INDIAN CONTEXT

Kalpana Dasgupta

Director, Central Secretariat Library

Department of Culture, Government of India

and President, Indian Library Association

New Delhi, India (2001)

Abstract

The information needs of women and their views on available information have hardly been studied as a research topic or as a critical issue within the information system. It is surely a pity that the need for information and access to information have not been taken as a serious matter in the field of library and information services. In the Indian context it is even more so because, other than the academic and scientific sector where information is a scholarly commodity and the user is a serious information seeker whether a man or a women, the information need of an ordinary woman is seldom understood or appreciated. The status of women being a major subject of debate in India is dependent on several factors. However, in this paper I wish to address the diverse factors which will ultimately influence the information seeking behaviour of women.

1. Information needs of Women in the Society

(1) What information do women need? This concept of information need can be of different types. Need for traditional information and need for personal and other development oriented information. In the Indian context there are diverse factors which influence information need of women and their information seeking pattern. The social, economic and familial factors mostly influence women's behaviour in India.

(2) In the social sector the following factors are of prime importance:

(a) caste, (b) class, (c) urban, (d) rural, (e) literate/educated, (f) illiterate/uneducated

(3) The economic sector reveals another set of diversity:

(a) employed, (b) unemployed, (c) employed in organized sector, (d) employed in the unorganized sector, (e) self employed, and (f) house wife

(4) India being a family-oriented society, the women's lives are greatly influenced by the familial norms and hierarchy. This mainly accounts for women-oriented issues such as health, parenting and child care, domestic requirements and house keeping, family planning, legal security, crime and safety, migration and mobility.

2. Hierarchical Structure of the Indian Society

Indian society has had a hierarchical structure as a part of the Hindu religion. The caste hierarchies have been spelt out with religious approval. Therefore, in a society divided on the basis of caste hierarchy, women in each caste generally hold the lowest position. However, historically the status of women has depended over a period of time on factors such as regional development, matriarchy, British penetration, women's education, social reforms and economic independence. However, a dichotomy prevails in the field of economic independence. The lower caste women have historically been economically independent in the real sense of the term. The 20th century saw changes in the socio-economic condition of women within the caste and class structure. Therefore, the diversity can be narrowed down to basically five categories of women while discussing their information needs:

Urban elite

Educated urban middleclass

Educated rural elite

Educated rural/semi urban middleclass

Uneducated rural poor.

These categories of women have different types of information need and its use according to the social, economic and familial structure.

2.1 Urban Educated Elite

This group of women have specific information needs which encompass information regarding educational particulars, career and other counseling, legal rights and aid, self-awareness, high standards of consumerism, house keeping, recreation and culture, etc. These women are part of the higher rung of the socio-economic ladder and generally enjoy social and economic security.

2.2 Urban Educated Middleclass

The women of this class of Indian citizens are facing the maximum difficulties within the social system because they face the problems such as discrimination, sexism and violence. However, they strive within the traditional system to come up to a level which will help them to change their status. Though their main concern is the traditional womanly approaches to life, they have specific requirements for information on education and schooling, health, social security, discrimination and gender relations, childcare and family relationships, family planning and birth control, legal aid, house keeping and house hold maintenance and more. Women of this group often work in the organized sector at the middle level. The job opportunities availed of are mainly traditional in nature and usually those which are not likely to tilt the economic scenario of the familial hierarchical structure. In this group many women are home-based workers or house wives which makes them invisible and their information needs inconsequential to many academic research. These women unfortunately face maximum social pressures which are often insurmountable. They face discrimination since birth, are victims of dowry problems and are constantly facing discrimination at all levels. They need the broadest spectrum of information concerning gender sensitization, legal awareness/aid/facilities, economic/

employment opportunities, education and career orientations. These women need information support to break loose the gripping socio-economic and familial stereotypes.

2.3 Educated Semi-urban/Rural Middle Class

Socio economic development has influenced the lives of the women residing on the periphery of the urban society i.e. the suburban areas and in forward-looking rural society. The women here face similar problems and discriminations faced by their urban middleclass counterparts but the grip of the double standards of a traditional society is much more. The young women are exposed to formal education mainly because education upto a level has better marriage prospect. Majority of these women are expected to follow all traditional norms of behaviour without challenging any of it. To get them out of that stupor exposure to information about their innumerable rights and opportunities will have to be given.

2.4 Educated Rural Elite

A large majority of Indians are still within the feudal structure of the village society. The village of the yester years has seen a very systematic growth of feudal families which were the elites in villages in different parts of India. These families are very highly educated and cultured in their breeding and many well-known men and women of India have come from this background. During and after the social reform movements in the 19th century and the uprising for India's independence in the early 20th century women of these families were actively involved in these activities. The information needs of these women were surely at par with their men though the caste structure and family hierarchy remained very rigid in spite of the liberalization process.

The educated rural elite had a very different information requirement from the rest of the rural society. Their women were gradually educated and sent to cities for education. They were involved in reformatory activities in the women's movement and in the Independence movement of India. Historically also even before the British or the colonial days and spreading of western education among women, the women of the rural elite often used information in a very systematic manner because the rural women looked up to these wives, mothers and daughters of elitist families as teachers and instructors and benevolent persons within the social structure. Therefore, the information requirement of women in the village society were often channelized through these elitist women. Unfortunately this very effective class of women is fast receding from the rural scenario because the younger generation of these families have migrated to the urban sector and have become visitors to the rural society.

2.5 Uneducated Rural Poor

In this category the caste and class structure get totally merged. The poor women in a village society are economically independent but they have hardly any time or ability to seek information. Whatever they learn is through oral wisdom of the family hierarchy. The family hierarchical structure again gives a very diverse picture in the family relationship of women. The eldest woman or the matriarch is the epitome of wisdom and all information is sought from her. Her information is also gathered from the previous generation. Therefore, generation after generation it is the oral information which is sought and given. Inter personal communication is most important and that generally happens within the family or within a community. The women of the rural poor do not enjoy economic security because most of them work in the unorganized sector i.e., the lowest rung in the economic ladder. Many of them have skills in rural craft and are part of the family activity. The wages and other facilities in the agricultural, forestry and other sectors are discriminatory and there is no fixed relationship between the employer and the employee. It is unlikely that the women of this group will make efforts to seek information outside their restricted boundaries.

3. The Role of Librarian and Information Professional

With such a diverse spectrum of information seeking environment it is very difficult to pin down the exact type of library or exact type of librarian needed to cater to information for all women of such a diverse social structure. However, in the Indian situation we need the following:

(a) Well-developed modern library and information dissemination facilities

The role of librarian/information officer will call for a workable blend of a traditional librarian and electronic media savvy information generator and disseminator. Well-organized libraries are necessary in the academic sector, special libraries in scientific & research sector and government sector to cater to the needs of the scholarly, sophisticated and well-informed women. There is seldom any special requirement because the realm of multifarious activities undertaken by women of this group deal mainly with development and other spheres of national/regional goals.

(b) Public libraries in the new information seeking environment

Well-equipped public libraries and information centers are essential support systems in the information environment for all types of urban and semi urban women specially those who are out of the formal employment and academic circles. A public librarian must be able to empathise with the hesitant and often confused women information seekers. He/she should be personally gender sensitized to be able to handle a new type of clientele which has so far been mainly dependent on traditional and family oriented information.

In many areas, public libraries will have to set up a special area exclusively for women because women of traditional background are not allowed to utilize facilities common to men and women. The libraries have to keep a broad spectrum of information sources to cater to information requirement for traditional womanly pursuits as well as education and career orientation, legal rights and aid, job opportunities etc.

(c) Information/communication centre at the rural level

The most challenging role of the library professional will be in the rural sector. The literacy level among women is very low and in many parts of India it is abysmal. The librarian will have to be a communicator and not a librarian in the traditional sense. He/she has to climb down from the ivory tower where literacy and formal education can be taken for granted. The rural women have economic role as well as traditional familial roles. The library-cum information/communication centre must be equipped with necessary information in different media i.e., printed material for the neo literates, audio visual and electronic material for those who are not comfortable with the written word. The information professional must be aware of the local needs and furnish necessary information in comprehensible language and content. Oral and visual communication will be the most important mode of information transfer. Physically, the centre must be easily approachable to women who may have the chance to visit. To a large majority, the required information may have to reach the clientele in different innovative repackaged forum which is within the comprehension level of women.

4. Right to Information

Right to information is of great interest and debate in all of South Asia. A detailed legislation on this issue which spells out instruction for implementation is the need of the hour. There have been efforts in all these countries to funnel information through governmental and non-governmental channels. Even a relevant bill was drafted in India entitled 'Freedom of Information Bill, 1997' but it has not been enacted as yet. In this debate, the information need of women as a special group should be spelt out. In all the countries of South Asia other than the problem of illiteracy the complex barrier of multiple languages and religious diversity make information generation, information repackaging and dissemination even more challenging, specially among women. Therefore, if Right to Information has to be fructified, the automatic corollary will be Information Management in the right perspective and in the right manner. The role of librarians is crucial in this new environment.

5. Need for Research

The urgent need to study the information needs and the information seeking behaviour of women of diverse situations and backgrounds has to be understood by academicians, activists as well as governmental and non-governmental organizations. National and international efforts have to be channeled in that direction without any more delay.

WOMEN'S HEALTHCARE, CENSORSHIP, AND THE LIBRARY: PROBLEMS, ISSUES, QUESTIONS

Nancy Kuhl

Reference/Instruction Librarian

Robert Frost Library, Amherst College

Amherst, MA, USA

Abstract

Censorship of information dealing with women's reproductive health, birth control, abortion, and other family planning issues is widespread in the U.S. and abroad. Even in highly industrialized nations where women seemingly have access to a range of healthcare choices, subtle censorship of information regarding birth control, abortion, sexuality, and other issues prevent women from accessing thorough, current, accurate, and unbiased information about these subject areas. In many parts of the world, censorship is overt and woman and girls lack access to even basic information about their bodies, sexuality, and family planning.

This paper will explore various contemporary and historical examples of the censorship of information about reproductive heath and family planning. Such examples include, but are not limited to, the following: the censorship of Margaret Sanger and other pioneers of women's healthcare and birth control; the challenges faced by women attempting to produce culture- or nation-specific editions of books like Our Bodies, Ourselves (published in the U.S. by the Boston Women's Health Book Collective); the misinformation and propaganda surrounding the FDA approval of RU 486, the so-called "abortion pill"; and the "global gag rule" whereby U.S. family planning assistance is denied to international organizations that provide information about abortion services or perform abortions (even if they are funded by other, non-US sources). The role of libraries in providing access to information about family planning, women's health, and related issues is somewhat unclear at this time. Though libraries in the United States and abroad are often advocates for free access to information of all kinds, the political and social implications of women's reproductive health issues can make such advocacy difficult if not impossible.

Because family planning and reproductive health issues are influenced by social, cultural, political, and religious factors, libraries, which hope to provide access to information in these areas will face significant challenges and risks. This paper will consider the extent to which libraries are meeting women's information needs in these areas. The essay will examine possible roles libraries can and should play in the fight to provide healthcare information to women and girls all over the world. A commitment to providing access to controversial information is not without consequence (consider, in the U.S., the threat to cut federal funding to libraries that do not use Internet filters-most of which prevent access to information about birth control, abortion, and related topics). "Family Planning, Censorship, and the Library" will explore the risks libraries and librarians face in providing women with access to controversial information.

Finally, the paper will also discuss the part library associations, such as IFLA and ALA, might play in providing women world-wide with much-needed information and in combating all kinds of censorship in these subject areas.

Introduction

In a recent issue of *American Libraries*, Nancy Kranich, sitting president of the American Library Association, acknowledged the critical role that librarians play in preventing censorship and ensuring that individuals have unlimited access to all manner of information. "Librarians", Kranich wrote "must act as trailblazers in promoting access to information, and serve as watchdogs in protecting the public's information rights" (Kranich 7). Nowhere is the need for "trailblazers in promoting access to information" more apparent than in the area of women's healthcare information. In the U.S. and abroad, women's access to authoritative, clear, and thorough information about reproductive health and sexuality are increasingly under attack by religious organizations, political groups, and governmental agencies. In her essay, "Censorship and Manipulation of Reproductive Health Information: An Issue of Human Rights and Women's Health", Lynn P. Freedman tells us that "in the last century, contraception and abortion have been one key site of the struggle over reproductive sexuality ... one key to controlling access to contraception and abortion is to control information about them and their uses" (31). Though censorship of information about women's health is not a new phenomenon, it is increasingly aggressive and destructive to women and girls.

In 1914, Margaret Sanger, founder of Planned Parenthood, was arrested for publishing The Woman Rebel, a magazine addressing women's need for information about methods of preventing conception (Chesler 99). The Woman Rebel violated the aggressive anti-vice laws, known as the Comstock Laws, which preventing distribution of information about contraceptive methods. Articles which were said to violate the Comstock Laws had title such as: "The Prevention of Conception"; "Open Discussion"; "Abortion in the United States"; and "Can You Afford to Have a Large Family?" (Sanger 87). From our vantage, nearly one hundred years later – when more than sixty percent of women in the U.S. use some form of birth control (Life 84) – the censorship of such materials seems very old fashioned. And yet, even now, long after Sanger started her struggle to make birth control available, women are regularly denied information about family planning and other healthcare issues.

The censorship of information dealing with women's reproductive health is, in fact, widespread in the U.S. and abroad. Even in highly industrialized nations where women seemingly have access to a range of healthcare choices, subtle censorship of information regarding birth control, abortion, sexuality, and sexually transmitted diseases prevent women from accessing complete, current, and unbiased information about these subject areas. In many parts of the world, censorship is overt and woman and girls lack access to even basic information about their bodies, sexuality, and family planning.

Examples of the censorship of information about reproductive health and family planning are abundant. In many cases, such as the censorship of Margaret Sanger and other pioneers of women's healthcare, the suppression of information about family planning is quite overt. Yet, in other cases, the restriction of information is more inconspicuous and more complicated, as in the case of the misinformation and propaganda surrounding the FDA approval of RU 486, the so-called "abortion pill". Regardless of the form the limiting of information takes or the source controlling information about women's health issues, such censorship serves to limit women's ability to make informed choices about healthcare. In addition, restrictions on family planning information violate women's rights to control their bodies, their fertility, and their sexuality.

The goal of "Women's Healthcare, Censorship, and the Library" is to explore a number of examples of the censorship of women's healthcare issues, and to investigate issues and questions related to those examples. This paper will look primarily at censorship in the U.S., however the problems and issues discussed herein are international in scope, and some international examples will be examined. Though I will consider and examine the roles libraries have played and might yet play in preventing such censorship, my goal is to call attention to problems that exist more than it is to propose solutions to those problems. There is still much research that must be done in the areas discussed in this paper, and the appropriate courses of action available to libraries in preventing the censorship of women's health information will be clear only in the light of such research.

Concealed and Obscured: Clinical Healthcare Information

In the United States and abroad, information dealing with the complex and sensitive subjects of birth control methods and abortion is often compromised, limited, pulled from circulation, or prevented from reaching the women who need it. Perhaps the most famous example of the censoring of clinical information about women's healthcare is that of Margaret Sanger who was censored and silenced throughout her lifetime by both religious and governmental forces.

By making it nearly impossible to legally discuss the topic of birth control, the Comstock Laws insured that women would be unable to gain access to information about birth control and thus, would be unable to control unwanted pregnancies. Sanger continually challenged the Comstock Laws by publishing The Woman Rebel and pamphlets dealing with specific methods of birth control. In 1917, Sanger served 30 days in a workhouse for maintaining a clinic that distributed information about birth control. Sanger's various conflicts with the law indicate her determination to "put information and power into the hands of women", at any cost (Steinem 93).

The United States government wasn't Sanger's only adversary. Leaders of the Catholic Church, according to a recent issues of the Sanger Papers Project Newsletter, frequently challenged Sanger in various ways and arranged to have many of her speaking engagements cancelled (1). The Catholic Church's efforts to prevent discussion of birth control, and specifically their efforts to silence Sanger, led to her most memorable protest against censorship. At a lecture in Boston, Sanger appeared on stage with her mouth taped shut. In her comments, which were written out for the audience, Sanger stated that "to inflict silence upon a woman is indeed drastic punishment ... I have been gagged...yet every time, more people have listened to me ... more people have lifted up their own voices" (2).

As recently as 1994, members of the Catholic Church were still trying to censor Margaret Sanger. That year, Bishop Robert Carlson tried to have a poster of Sanger removed form the library at St. Thomas University in Minnesota. In spite of Bishop Carlson's objections in which he "likened the Sanger poster ... to honoring Adolph Hitler, " the poster was defended by the library's Director and was not removed (Gaughan 2). Many alumni of the University threatened to withdraw financial contributions to the University unless the library removed the poster (1). This contemporary attempt to censor Margaret Sanger is evidence of a climate hostile to free access to information about women's health issues. This climate, of course, is not limited to the Catholic community.

The problem of denying women access to information about reproductive heath is, in fact, international in scope. One terrifically important and far-reaching example of this is the so-called "Global Gag Rule", which serves to "deny U.S. family planning funds to foreign organizations if they use other, non-U.S. funds to provide legal abortion services or to participate in policy debates over abortion in their own countries" (Lasher 3). The significance of the global gag rule cannot be overstated; women worldwide will be denied access to information and healthcare services as a result of the enactment of this policy. The global gag rule demonstrates the alarming power that a minority of conservatives in the U.S. has to restrict women's access to critical information about family planning all over the world.

In addition to restrictions resulting from outside forces, individual countries often present barriers to women's access to health care information. Governmental agencies often impose laws or enact healthcare practices that prevent women from gaining access to information about reproductive heath. In Ireland, for example, "the government did not publish any informational materials on family planning until January 1994" (Coliver 164). Because of strict laws prohibiting pornographic publications, in Kenya "family planning materials may be censored if [they are] found to be obscene or contrary to public morality" (Kabeberi-Macharia 189). In Algeria, information about family planning "was provided in order to promote the government's interests", and thus little attention was paid to the information needs of individual women (Coliver 109).

In her study of reproductive heath information in Brazil, Rachael Reichmann notes that the lack of information about reproductive health issues in that country is "not so much a result of active government suppression of information as of government indifference or omission" (121). Though information is not actively censored, "the absence of adequate information about alternative methods of contraception ... has lead to high sterilization and abortion rates" (Reichmann 132). And while women in Brazil can easily gain access to birth control pills, information about proper use of the pill, side effects, and efficacy is often unavailable or inadequate. "The great majority of women Brazilian women have used the pill" Reichmann tells us, "but often incorrectly and rarely with medical supervision" (126).

In the U.S., as well as abroad, efforts have frequently been made to censor women's health information. Conservative politicians and "pro life" activists have worked to prevent free access to information about abortion and birth control methods. An increasingly conservative climate in U.S. politics acts, in many ways, as a threat to women's and girls' access to information about health issues. Planned Parenthood, for instance, is regularly challenged with regard to providing information about abortion and birth control to minors. There is much debate, too, about whether or not health workers in public schools should be able to provide information about birth control and sexually transmitted diseases. In addition, recently proposed adoption legislation would prevent family planning clinics from providing clients with information about abortion. According to The Guttmacher Report on Public Policy, this legislation, is "directly aimed at denying women facing crisis pregnancy full information about their options – apparently on the basis of the notion that the best way to promote adoption is to prevent family planning providers from discussing abortion" (1). Of course, preventing discussion about healthcare options only serves to promote ignorance and strip women of choices.

In many countries, including the United States, a lack of appropriate education exacerbates the already significant problem of inadequate information. In Poland, "education about reproductive matters, including contraceptive methods, has always been poor. Popular misunderstandings abound: many think that the pill poses a high risk of cancer; others think that it promotes the growth of facial hair" (Coliver and Nowicka 280). Studies in Chile have found that although "adolescents increasingly have had sexual relations at earlier ages, they have not had access to more information" and educational resources about birth control, STDs, and reproductive health (Iriate and Alexander 147).

Education about sexuality and health is lacking in the U.S. as well, where it is increasingly under attack by conservative groups. In fact, sex education "in all grades is much less likely to cover birth control, abortion, how to obtain contraceptive and STD services, and sexual orientation than it was in the late 1980s" (USA Today 1). Teenagers in the U.S. are so poorly informed about their reproductive choices that "in a 1990 study – conducted more than 15 years after abortion was legalized on a national basis – many teenagers thought abortion was illegal and none said abortion was legal in all 50 states" (Pine and Fischler 307).

Though these cases clearly reflect insufficient access to information, some examples of withheld information are less clearly defined. The misinformation associated with intrauterine devices (IUDs) as contraceptive methods in the U.S. is one such instance. Though IUDs are among the most effective birth control methods and are the "most popular form of reversible birth control in the world", they are not frequently used in the United States (Motamed 1). IUDs are, in fact, "used by 85 million to 100 million women" worldwide and "fewer than 1 million women" in the United States (Canavan 1).

Though at first glance it seems likely that the IUD is unpopular in the U.S. as a result of the frequent occurrence of pelvic inflammatory disease during the 1960s and 1970s which was associated with one "poorly researched IUD: the Dalkon Shield" (Motamed 1), further investigation, reveals another possible reason that the IUD has not been well promoted in the United States. Planned Parenthood publications assert that IUDs are useful as a method of emergency contraception, a method that can prevent pregnancy "up to five days after unprotected intercourse" (2). Considering the recent controversy surrounding such emergency contraceptive methods as the hormone pill RU486 (the so-called "abortion pill"), and the Preven emergency contraception kit (which caught the country's attention when Wal-Mart refused to stock it), it seems that political pressures may play a role in preventing large-scale marketing and distribution of information about the IUD as a contraceptive method and as an effective emergency contraceptive.

Contraception and abortion are only one area in which women are denied the information necessary to make informed choices about their health. Studies have shown that in the U.S., "22 percent of pregnancies end in a C[esarean]-section, when authorities, including the U.S. Department of Health and Human Services, have indicated that no more than 15 percent are medically necessary" (Brink 1). In parts of Great Britain, Cesarean section rates are as high as 20 percent (Lancet 1). In some regions in Latin America, Cesarean births account for up to 40 percent of the total births (Belizan et al 3).

Though there are complex social, cultural, and economic reasons for the worldwide increase in Cesarean section deliveries, the general lack of accurate and thorough information available to women is one component of the problem. In his response to a recent study of C-section births in Latin America, Arachu Castro states that "the increase in cesarean sections can … be regarded as a process in which women are finally given less information and less choice and in which obstetricians appropriate the central role of childbirth at the expense of the women" (11).

In addition to these areas, we must consider other women's health issues: the problems associated with silicon breast implants, the sometimes fatal side effects of the diet drug combination Fen-Phen which was marketed, in the U.S., primary to women, and the high rate of unnecessary hysterectomy (a recent study stated that hysterectomy recommendations were "inappropriate in 70% of the cases" studied [Contemporary OB/GYN 1]). We might also examine the treatment of Sexually Transmitted Diseases, especially AIDS, and the medical profession's sometimes-questionable handling of women's sexuality and lesbianism. Though these are complex healthcare issues, it seems clear that women are, in many cases, not well informed by their doctors or the medical industry at large. This is a subtle and destructive form of censorship, which prevents women from making informed decisions about healthcare.

Banned and Blocked: Censoring Popular and Informal Information Sources

The censorship of clinical and medical information by healthcare agencies and providers, religious groups, and government agencies is only part of the problem. The same, or like-minded, institutions often censor other informational outlets – popular materials, personal accounts, self-help resources, informal educational information. Preventing access to these materials and resources is as destructive as the censorship of more traditional sources of medical information.

The Boston Women's Health Book Collective recognized women's need for easily understood information about healthcare and sexuality and created Our Bodies, Ourselves in the early 1970s in an effort to meet that need. The book, the writers claimed, was a response to "doctors who were condescending, paternalistic, judgmental, and non-informative" (Diskin and Sanford 1). In their essay, "Women's Bodies and Feminist Subversions: The Influence of Our Bodies, Ourselves: A Book by and for Women", Linda Gordon and Barrie Thorne state that before Our Bodies, Ourselves, "there was virtually no open discussion of sex and reproduction in schools or the popular media, and physicians condescended to women and regularly withheld medical information from female patients" (323). Since the first edition was published, Our Bodies, Ourselves has become so important to women that some 15 versions of it currently exist – in various languages and addressing age- and culture-specific issues – and others are being written by women around the world. In spite of this number of editions and the demand for quality healthcare information from informal or non-traditional sources, Our Bodies, Ourselves has been frequently challenged and censored.

Internationally, the need for books like Our Bodies, Ourselves is great, and the women who write these books face many challenges to provide healthcare information to women in extremely hostile environments. In her essay, "Our Bodies, Ourselves in Beijing: Breaking the Silences", Jennifer J. Yanco tells us that "state censorship is a big issue in many countries…in many societies, the open treatment of women's sexuality … is grounds for censorship. For many groups, treatment of lesbianism guarantees that their book will not be published" (Yanco 5). As a result of such state censorship and deeply ingrained social taboos, women in many parts of the world have no forum in which to discuss issues of health and sexuality.

And social taboo is only part of the problem. In some parts of the world, women face the challenge of "creating an environment that is safe from outside dangers. There are cultural/political/social contexts where it's not simply uncomfortable to speak about sexuality; it is actually dangerous" (4). In such environments, the perceived need to prevent women from gaining access to information about their bodies and their health is deemed so important, it actually warrants violence against those who would provide such access.

In the United States, as well as in other countries, demand for useful reproductive heath information is great and yet women's access to informal information about healthcare is frequently challenged. Political and economic factors in the healthcare industry have increasingly "cut down [women's] access to health information" (OBOS '92 14). And access to non-traditional sources of information is often restricted. Our Bodies, Ourselves, for example, has faced censorship challenges many times as have books for young adults such as Deal with It! A Whole New Approach to Your Body, Brain, and Life as a Gurl by Esther Drill, Heather McDonald, and Rebecca Odes and It's Perfectly Normal: A Book About Changing Bodies, Growing Up, Sex, and Sexual Health by Robie H. Harris. In spite of being positive, extremely well reviewed sources of information for young adults – of Deal With It, one critic wrote: "the main message concerns accepting diversity in bodies and lifestyles, taking responsibility, and finding help when you need it" (Cornog 218); It's Perfectly Normal is described as "intelligent, amiable and carefully researched" (PW 248) – these books have been challenged in some public schools and libraries.

Censorship of popular materials is not limited to informational resources such as Our Bodies, Ourselves. In The Right to Know: Human Rights and Access to Reproductive Health Information, Sandra Coliver recounts an instance of censorship in Ireland:

In May 1992, Easons, the largest national distributor to retail news agents, hoarded and refused to offer for sale virtually all imported copies of an issues of the London *Guardian* newspaper when they arrived at the airport. The issue included a full-page advertisement with addresses and telephone numbers of Marie Stopes clinics, which provide abortion services in the UK. (171)

Popular women's magazines have been censored in Ireland as well. For instance, blank pages appear in Irish editions of Cosmopolitan in place of advertisements for abortion services and birth control (171).

In the United States, novels and autobiographical books that deal with female sexuality, reproductive health, and similar subject matter have been censored, challenged and banned. Books dealing with rape, incest, birth control, and masturbation have been "targeted for removal from school curricula or library shelves, condemned in churches and forbidden to the faithful, rejected or expurgated by publishers, [and] challenged in court" (Wachsberger ix). The Bluest Eye, by Noble Prizewinner Toni Morrison, has been banned in an Alaska high school because "parents complained that the language was 'obscene' and that it contained explicit sexual episodes" (Sova 12). Renowned young adult author Judy Blume's books have been challenged because of their frank discussion of female sexuality: Forever has been challenged because it "contained 'four-letter words and talked about masturbation [and] birth control'" (52). Blume's Blubber and Then Again, Maybe I Won't have also been frequently banned and challenged in public schools and libraries based on sexual content and language. Margaret Atwood's The Handmaid's Tale was challenged in one case because it was deemed to be "sexually explicit" and in another because "the main character of the novel was a woman and young men were unable to relate to her" (73).

The list of books banned and challenged because of controversial sexual content or because they deal candidly with sensitive issues that are of interest to girls and women is long and includes important works such as The Color Purple by Alice Walker, The Bell Jar by Sylvia Plath, Still I Rise and I Know Why the Caged Bird Sings by Maya Angelou and the anonymously written Go Ask Alice, to name only a few examples (Foerstel 179, 190, 218; Sova 264, 265, 266, 267). Preventing access to these informal sources of information about women's heath issues is as deeply problematic as preventing women and girls from accessing clinical information about healthcare.

The Internet filtering systems in use in some U.S. schools and libraries censor countless additional women's health resources, many of which are designed to make healthcare information clear and accessible to the general public. Filters, which claim to prevent users from accessing pornographic materials, often censor materials dealing with legitimate healthcare and sexuality issues such as abortion, AIDS and other sexually transmitted diseases, lesbianism, and safe sex. In his informal study of various Internet filters, Geoffrey Nunberg found that

SurfWatch has blocked safe-sex information pages at Washington University, the University of Illinois Health Center, and the Allegheny University Hospitals, and Cyber Patrol has blocked the HIV/AIDS information page of the Journal of American Medical association and the site of Planned Parenthood. Smartfilter blocks the safe-sex page of the Johns Hopkins Medical School research group on sexually transmitted diseases. The filters have also blocked numerous sites associated with feminism or gay and lesbian rights. Both I-Gear and CYBERsitter have blocked the site of the National Organization for Women (CYBERsitter cites the "lesbian bias" of the group). I-Gear has blocked the Harvard Gay and Lesbian Caucus, BESS has blocked the Gay and Lesbian Prisoner Project, and NetNanny has blocked Internet discussion groups on AIDS and feminism. (7)

As Internet filters become more widely used, more and more women and girls (especially those who rely on public school and libraries for Internet service) will only have access to the information that can slip through Internet filtering systems. Because Internet filters censor information about breast cancer, abortion, STDs, and nearly all topics having anything to do with women's bodies, their use in public libraries has a significant impact on women's ability to locate Internet resources dealing with health issues.

Women's Healthcare, Censorship, and the Library

Libraries, librarians, and professional library associations are famous for fighting censorship and for being advocates for free and equal access to information. Nevertheless, libraries have, perhaps unwittingly, played a role in preventing women from accessing healthcare information. Unclear subject headings, librarian discomfort with sensitive subject matter, and failure to develop and maintain collections of current materials all contribute to create a library environment where women may not have access to the healthcare information they need.

In the areas of women's health and sexuality, Library of Congress Subject Headings (LCSH) are seriously flawed. The headings are, in many cases, unclear, clinical, or too broad to be useful. In some cases, the headings reveal subtle biases that serve to obscure important issues; when one searches for books with the heading "Women – Health and Hygiene", for example, the LCSHs direct her to see also "Beauty, Personal". Conceptual pairings such as this undermine the importance of women's healthcare issues and may even keep women from finding necessary healthcare information resources.

In some cases, LCSHs dealing with women's healthcare and sexuality are simply unclear. A heading like "Sex Instruction" for example, sounds like it would be used to describe guides to having good sex rather than information resources about reproductive health. Actually, the heading is used to describe both kinds of books: titles like Dr. Ruth's Guide to Good Sex and Facts of Life for Children share this heading. In another example, the heading "Sex Customs – United States", is used to describe such diverse titles as High Risk: An Anthology Of Forbidden Writings, The Hite Report: A Nationwide Study Of Female Sexuality, and Sex and the College Girl. Still other headings, like "Women – Sexual Behavior", "Hygiene, Sexual", and "Women – Diseases" are very clinical and, finally, not apt to be very useful in many cases. While reference librarians could surely help a patron decipher subject headings, women may be reluctant to ask for assistance with matters of personal healthcare and sexuality.

Yet, some librarians may, for a variety of reasons, prefer not to answer questions about abortion, birth control, lesbianism, or other sensitive issues. In her essay "The Invisibles: Lesbian Women as Library Users", Heike Seidel states that "many lesbians fear subliminal or openly discriminatory behavior ... by library staff [and] lesbians feel discriminated against when made invisible in library collections" (3-4). In this way, instead of helping women find information, librarians may actually help to prevent women from accessing information.

In spite of these issues, there can be little doubt that libraries, librarians, and professional library associations are among the most active individuals and institutions fighting censorship today. By adopting the Library Bill of Right, which states, "Libraries should challenge censorship in the fulfillment of their responsibility to provide information and enlightenment" (ALA), many libraries in the U.S. indicate their commitment to providing free and unfettered access to information of all kinds. In the current debate over Internet filters, perhaps the most contentious and far-reaching censorship battle in recent history, the American Library Association and many individual libraries and librarians have been at the forefront, risking library funding and political support to provide free access to electronic information and to prevent censorship of Internet resources.

With regard to preventing and fighting censorship, libraries in the U.S. are at their best when dealing with the overt censorship of books and other library materials (through public challenges and attempts to remove particular books from libraries) and with the censorship and restriction of Internet resources through the use of Internet filtering software. The American Library Association has official positions and policies for addressing these two forms of censorship and is well equipped to support individual libraries and librarians in various ways when they come under fire for resisting internet filtering or censorship of controversial titles.

Libraries and librarians have been less active in addressing other, more subtle kinds of censorship, like the examples discussed in this paper. It is, in fact, quite unclear at this time what role libraries can and should play in providing access to information about family planning, women's health, and related issues. Though libraries in the United States and abroad are often advocates for free access to information of all kinds, the political and social implications of women's reproductive health issues can make such advocacy difficult if not impossible. Because family planning and reproductive health issues are influenced by social, cultural, political, and religious factors, libraries that hope to provide access to information in these areas will face significant challenges and risks.

Nevertheless, there are possible avenues of activism against censorship of women's health resources that libraries, librarians, and especially library associations might explore. Librarians and library associations might work to find new ways to act as information advocates for women, including joining women's rights coalitions and organizations, lobbying politicians, and supporting anti-censorship and pro-women's rights groups. In addition, libraries and library associations might work, locally, nationally, and internationally to form partnerships with healthcare providers, human rights workers, and women's organizations. Such partnerships might enable libraries to take more active roles in advocating for reproductive health information, relevant education in public schools, and community education programs.

In addition to working outside the library with community organizations, much can be done within the library community to prevent censorship of women's healthcare resources. A comparative study of LC subject headings and Sears Subject headings should be conducted to give library professionals a greater sense of the ways current headings might obscure information rather than create access to it. Such a study might lead to positive changes in subject headings and heading assignments. Libraries and librarians can combat censorship by collecting current materials in sensitive subject areas and displaying those materials periodically. And, of course, librarians can, and should, speak out against bias and discrimination in library policies and among library staff.

Conclusions

In 1990, *Life* Magazine included Sanger on its list of "The 100 Most Important Americans of the Twentieth Century". In a recent special edition titled "Time 100: Leaders and Revolutionaries of the 20th Century", *Time* Magazine named Margaret Sanger as one the most influential people of the twentieth century. In spite of the fact that our culture currently views Margaret Sanger as a hero, women's access to information about birth control specifically and healthcare in general is often in jeopardy. In her discussion of Sanger for the Time Magazine tribute, Gloria Steinem writes

One can imagine Sanger's response to the anti-choice lobby and congressional leadership that opposes abortion, sex education in schools, and federally funded contraceptive programs that would make abortion less necessary ... and that holds hostage the entire U.S. billion-dollar debt to the United Nations in the hope of attaching an antiabortion rider. As in her day, the question seems to be less about what gets decided than who has the power to make the decision. (84)

Steinem's statement reminds us, also, of the many healthcare workers who have been victims of assault and attempted murder and those who have been murdered as a result of their efforts to provide women free access to healthcare. It is impossible to ignore the consistent problems associated with women's access to healthcare and information in light of this violence.

Though censorship in all its forms is dangerous, the censorship of information about women's health issues is an actual threat to the health and well being of the women who are denied access to information. Margaret Sanger's struggle to make information about contraception available to all women was a fight for control and power as much as it was for information. That struggle continues, as girls' and women's access to information is challenged and restricted.

"Access to information is a right only in the abstract", Nancy Kranich tells us. "It is up to librarians to ensure that this abstract concept becomes concrete, and to continuously communicate the importance of access to information" (Kranich 7). Whether librarians will strive to make concrete women's rights to healthcare information – and thus greater control over their bodies, health, and well being – remains to be seen. At a time when conservative politicians and right-wing groups threaten women's rights, libraries and librarians can be powerful allies to women all over the world. The risks to libraries, however, may prove to be too great.

References

Works Cited/Consulted

"Abstinence-Only Sex Education is Not Enough". USA Today Magazine Jan. 2001: 2 pp. Online. Gale Group. Expanded Academic ASAP. A69698387. 19 April 01.

American Library Association Council. "Library Bill of Rights". 1996. http://www.ala.org/work/freedom/lbr.html. 25 March 01.

Belizan, Jose M., Fernando Althabe, Fernando C. Barros, and Sophie Alexander. "Rates and Implications of Caesarean Sections in Latin America". British Medical Journal 27 November 1999: 13 pp. Online. Gale Group. Health Reference Center. A58358818.

Boston Women's Health Book Collective. The New Our Bodies, Ourselves: Updated and Expanded for the '90's. NY: Simon and Schuster, 1992.

Brink, Susan. "C-Sections Rise but May Not be the Kindest Cut". U.S. News & World Report 4 September 2000: 2 pp. Online. Gale Group. Health Reference Center. A64788049.

"Caesarean Section on the Rise". Editorial. The Lancet 18 November 2000: 2 pp. Online. Gale Group. Health Reference Center. A67161697. 10 April 2001.

Cammack, Diana R. "The Right to Know: Malawi". Coliver 207-230.

Castro, Arachu. "Commentary: Increase in Caesarean Sections May Reflect Medical Control Not Woman's Choice". (Response to "Rates and Implications of Caesarean Sections in Latin America"). British Medical Journal 27 November 1999: 13 pp. Online. Gale Group. Health Reference Center. A58358818.

Chesler, Ellen. Woman of Valor: Margaret Sanger and the Birth Control Movement in America. NY: Anchor Double Day, 1992.

Coliver, Sandra, Ed. The Right to Know: Human Rights and Access to Reproductive Health Information. London: Univ. of Pennsylvania Press, 1995.

— and Wanda Nowicka. "The Right to Know: Poland". Coliver 268-288.

Cornog, Martha. Rev. of Deal With It! A Whole New Approach to Your Body, Brain, and Life as a Gurl. By Esther Drill et al. Library Journal 1 September 1999: 218.

Diskin, Wilma and Wendy Coppedge Sanford. Preface. Our Bodies, Ourselves by The Boston Women's Health Collective. NY: Simon and Schuster, 1973. 1-4.

"The Demonization of Margaret Sanger". Margaret Sanger Papers Project Newsletter 16 (1997): 2 pp. http://www.nyu.edu/projects/sanger/demon.htm 27 April 2001.

Foerstel, Herbert N. Banned in the U.S.A.: A Reference Guide to Book Censorship in Schools and Public Libraries. Westport: Greenwood Press, 1994.

Freedman, Lynn P. "Censorship and Manipulation of Reproductive Health Information: An Issue of Human Rights and Women's Health". In Coliver, pp. 1-31.

Gaughan, Thomas M. "ALA's Sanger Poster Sparks Value Clash In Catholic Library". American Libraries 24.11 (1993): 1 pp. Online. Gale Group. Expanded Academic ASAP. A14708691. 9 January 01.

Gordon, Linda and Barrie Thorne. "Women's Bodies and Feminist Subversions: The Influence of Our Bodies, Ourselves: A Book by and for Women". Contemporary Sociology 25.3 (1996): 322.

"Hysterectomy is Often Wrongly Recommended". Contemporary OB/GYN 45.6 (2000): 1 pp. Online. Gale Group. Health Reference Center. A63772156. 10 April 2001.

Iriate, Claudia and Lucy Alexander. "The Right to Know: Chile". In Coliver, pp. 142-158.

Kabeberi-Macharia, Janet W. "The Right to Know: Kenya". In Coliver, pp. 181-206.

Kennedy, David M. Birth Control in America: The Career of Margaret Sanger. New Haven: Yale Univ. Press, 1970.

Kranich, Nancy. "ALA President's Message: Celebrate Freedom of Information Day, March 16". American Libraries 32.3 (2001): 7.

Lasher, Craig. "Playing with People's Lives: How Politics have Shaped the U.S. Response". Free Inquiry 19.2 (1999): 5 pp. Online. Gale Group. Expanded Academic ASAP. A54421577. 9 January 2001.

"Margaret Sanger: The Fighter who Helped Women and Men Plan their Families". Life 13:12 (1990): 84.

Melody, M.E. and Linda M. Peterson. Teaching America About Sex: Marriage Guides and Sex Manuals from the Late Victorians to Dr. Ruth. New York: New York Univ. Press, 1999.

Motamed, Susan. "100 Million Women Can't Be Wrong: What Most American Women Don't Know About the IUD". Planned Parenthood Dot Org Website 1999. http://www.plannedparenthood.org/articles/IUD.html. 27 April 01.

Nunberg, Geoffrey. "The Internet Filter Farce". The American Prospect 12:1 (2001): 7 pp. Online. Gale Group. Expanded Academic ASAP. A69652750. 29 April 01.

Pine, Rachael N. and Lori F. Fischler. "The Right to Know: the United States of America". In Coliver, pp. 289-326.

Powderly, Kathleen E. "Contraceptive Policy and Ethics: Illustrations from American History". The Hastings Center Report 25:1 (1995): 4pp. Online. Gale Group. A16650815. 19 April 01.

Reichmann, Rebecca. "The Right to Know: Brazil". In Coliver, pp. 121-141.

Review of It's Perfectly Normal: A Book about Changing Bodies, Growing Up, Sex, and Sexual Health. By Robie H. Harris. Publisher's Weekly. 18 July 1994: 248.

Sanger, Margaret. My Fight for Birth Control. NY: Farrar and Rinehart, 1931.

"Sanger, Censorship, and the Catholic Church: The Latest Battle in a Long War". Margaret Sanger Papers Project Newsletter 6 (1993/4). 2pp. http://www.nyu.edu/projects/sanger/censor.htm. 27 April 01.

Seidel, Heike. "The Invisibles: Lesbian Women as Library Users". The Progressive Librarian 14 (1998): 5pp. http:www.libr.org/PL/14_Seidel.html. 27 April 01.

"Spate of Proposed Adoption Legislation Would Gag Family Planning Clinics and Divert Necessary Resources". The Guttmacher Report on Public Policy 29 Oct. 1999: 2 pp. http://www.agi-usa.org/pubs/archives/newsreleasetgr0205.html. 19 April 01.

Sova, Dawn B. Banned Books: Literature Suppressed on Sexual Grounds. Ed. Ken Wachsberger. New York: Facts on File, 1998.

Steinem, Gloria. "Margaret Sanger: Her Crusade to Legalize Birth Control Spurred the Movement for Women's Liberation". Time. April 13 1998: 93-4.

Wachsberger, Ken, Ed. Introduction. Banned Books: Literature Suppressed on Sexual Grounds. By Dawn B. Sova. New York: Facts on File, 1998. ix-x.

Yanco, Jennifer J. "Our Bodies, Ourselves in Beijing: Breaking the Silences". Feminist Studies. 22:3 (1996): 511-18.

VI. KEY TO THE FUTURE: EDUCATION

GENDER AND EQUITY IN THE LIBRARY AND INFORMATION STUDIES CURRICULUM: BUILDING CONFIDENCE FOR THE FUTURE

Anne Goulding *and* **Marigold Cleeve**

Department of Information and Library Studies,

Loughborough University

Loughborough, U.K. (1997)

Abstract

Women may numerically dominate the information professional, but powerful positions in administration and management are dominated by men. Various explanations and solutions have been proffered for this state of affairs but the issue of how the information and library studies (ILS) curriculum contributes to, or could help remedy matters, has not been investigated.

Drawing on a national survey of lecturers and students in UK departments of ILS, this paper explores the extent to which ILS curricula include consideration of gender issues and equity. Starting from the premise that lecturers in higher education have a vital role to play in transforming the beliefs and values of those they teach, this paper examines how the curriculum can be developed to raise students' awareness of equity issues. It is argued that women's attitudes towards their careers can be positively influenced by their formative experiences at departments of ILS, which have a responsibility to encourage students to critically analyze their personal and especially their professional experiences.

1. Introduction

The position of women in the library profession has long been a "sex oddity" (Ritchie, 1979). Despite the numerical domination of the library and information workforce by women, their advancement into positions of senior management has been notoriously slow. According to the British Library Association (LA), in 1991 75 per cent of its members were women and yet only 4.5 per cent earned over £20,000, compared with 19 per cent of male LA members (Library Association, 1991). Explanations offered for the lack of female senior managers in libraries, and in the wider workforce, are many. They include:

career interruptions

family commitments

lack of networking

inflexible working arrangements

recruitment practices

lack of role models

male work cultures

lack of networks

prejudice

outdated attitudes

perception of women's management styles

women's own lack of commitment

women's lack of determination to succeed

women's lack of confidence. (MSC, 1981; Poland, 1996; McDermott, 1994).

Strategies aimed at overcoming barriers to women's advancement have also been various. Part-time working and job sharing, for example, have been advocated as the means of tackling the problems of inflexible working arrangements. Better childcare support from either the Government or employers would, it is argued, help those trying to balance work and family roles. The increasing number of organisational equal opportunities policies have, hopefully, addressed inequities in recruitment policies and raised awareness amongst male managers of the barriers women face and the benefits of a more equitable workforce. Mentoring programmes and networking can promote female role models and, together with female-only training and better career counseling, address the issues of women's own aspirations and confidence in their ability.

Many of the solutions advocated to combat inequality in the workforce focus on organisational barriers (structures and practices), and/or barriers deriving from women's 'traditional' familial roles. Although overcoming these is essential to ensure the higher reaches of work are accessible for women, as Sarah Pritchard (1989) comments, true transformation of the workplace will not come from merely adding more women, the underlying nature of that workplace also needs to be transformed. Women cannot challenge the status quo, however, unless they know what they are confronting and are given the intellectual means to do so. This entails empowering women by helping them towards a critical understanding of the structures of domination affecting their lives in order that they might be challenged (Taylor, 1989). The empowerment of women thus depends on information and education.

This paper will argue that the education system has the opportunity and the responsibility to promote change and that departments of information and library studies (ILS) can, and should, play a major role in equipping their female students with the necessary awareness and skills to analyse and challenge their own experiences at home, in society, in education and, critically, in the library and information workplace. The paper will discuss the potential of this approach, and will assess how viable it is in the UK by drawing on the results of a national survey of ILS lecturers and students.

2. Challenging Gender Inequality

Gender equity is concerned with the promotion of personal, social, cultural, political and economic equality for all, regardless of sex. The term 'gender equity' emerged from a growing recognition of pervasive gender inequities in society that have resulted in the systematic devaluation of attitudes, activities, and abilities associated with women (Gender Equity, 1997). Achieving gender equity requires challenging the underlying assumptions about gender within society, and one focus for change has been the traditional school and university curriculum which, it is argued, "fails to reflect the experiences and contribution of women in history and in contemporary society" (Taylor, 1989). It has been suggested that there is a relationship between the social construction of knowledge in the curriculum, and the social reproduction of gender relations in society (Dewar, 1987). Within the ILS sector, Hannigan (1994, p. 297) asserts: "The basic premises upon which librarianship and information science have been built are structured on white, middle-class, male paradigms that have systematically, if unconsciously, silenced and excluded women."

A gender inclusive curriculum, therefore, would not only promote an awareness of the position of women in libraries but should also "…empower them to challenge systematic biases and to question their own socialisation concerning the value of women. " (Canadian Journal of Information Science, 1992, p. 30)

The content of the curriculum is not the only concern when attempting to promote gender equity, the learning environment is also important. Poole and Isaacs (1993) suggest that class-room dynamics can reinforce stereotypical roles and attitudes, as can out-of-class communications and relations. Individual teacher's own attitudes and beliefs can also have a considerable impact on how, or if, gender issues are presented. Lecturers in higher education thus have a vital role to play in transforming the beliefs and values of those they teach. The remainder of this paper will investigate these issues in relation to the ILS curriculum and how it is taught in the UK based on data gathered in a national survey of lecturers and students in departments of information and library studies.

3. Gender Equity in Departments of Information and Library Studies in the United Kingdom

In 1996-1997 a study based at Loughborough University investigated the extent to which ILS curricula in UK departments of Information and Library Studies include consideration of gender issues and equity. There were three main foci to the study:

The overt curriculum: to what extent issues of gender and equity are included in the ILS teaching agenda.

The hidden curriculum: how lecturers view the inclusion of issues of gender and equity into their curriculum; to what extent gender is a consideration in lecturers' formal and informal relationships with students.

Student attitudes: how interested ILS students are in gender issues; how relevant they consider these issues; if interest varies according to age, sex, programme of study.

3.1 Methodology

3.1.1 Literature search

Literature from the fields of library and information science, the sociology of education, women's studies, psychology and management was reviewed to identify the main issues surrounding the incorporation of gender issues in the higher education curriculum and its effect on students' awareness of how gender impacts on their personal and professional lives.

3.1.2 Mail questionnaire

A mail questionnaire (appendix A) was sent to academic staff at 18 UK library schools. The sampling frame used was the BAILER directory. Questionnaires were sent to all staff on the BAILER lists unless it was known that they were no longer actively teaching. 252 questionnaires were distributed. There was a 42 per cent response rate (49 per cent female, 46 per cent male, 5 per cent did not declare their sex). Although this appears low, questionnaires were erroneously sent to staff who had either retired or left after compilation of the BAILER directory, or who had no teaching responsibilities but were included in the list of academic staff.

The questionnaire was designed to investigate how lecturers regarded gender issues, their importance to them personally, and how they dealt with them in their teaching. Specifically, the questionnaire covered the following:

if gender and equity featured in respondents' teaching

if respondents were happy with the amount of time devoted to gender issues

how gender issues were presented in their department's curriculum

the use of gender-neutral language

their perceptions of students' views of gender issues

classroom dynamics.

3.1.3 Case studies

Case studies were carried out in two departments from which the questionnaire return rate had been high. At both departments, six academic staff were interviewed on a one-to-one basis. At department A a focus group was held with seven postgraduate students (all female), at department B a focus group was held with seven undergraduates (six female, one male). The interviews and focus groups pursued topics of interest that had arisen from the questionnaire and from the literature review.

3.2 Results

3.2.1 The overt and hidden curriculum

3.2.1.1 Coverage of gender and equity in the ILS curriculum

The issues of gender and gender equity featured in many different areas of the ILS curriculum including:

the information society

the information industries

library management

marketing and business planning

public libraries

international information studies

arts management.

Human resource management was the area most likely to incorporate awareness of gender issues with an emphasis on employment law, but also included in consideration of topics such as training and development, communications and people skills. The comments of one of the student focus groups, however, raises a question about how effective some of the teaching is:

We've touched on [equal opportunities] in one lecture on human resource management, about people. It was an absolute joke, it really was. We got nothing. 'Well, there's the Race Relations Act' and so and so, and so and so, only just, 'and that makes sure nobody discriminates against people because of their ethnic background'. But, I thought, I knew that before, and then it's exactly the same about, 'then there's the Sex Discrimination Act and that stops discrimination by sex'. It was like that, it was, and I found it absolutely humiliating.

If coverage of gender issues is felt to be tokenistic or simplistic it is unlikely that it will have the desired effect of raising questions in students' minds about gender relations in society and at work, and their attitudes towards them. In some departments, issues of gender and equity did not feature in some areas of the curriculum where it might be expected, including:

information technology

electronic publishing

human-computer interaction

public relations and corporate communication

health information management.

All of these could incorporate gender issues as a relevant and interesting aspect of the module. Fifty-four (54) per cent of respondents reported that they did consider aspects of gender and equity in their teaching, although the amount of time devoted to gender issues varied (Table 1).

Table 1: Time devoted to gender issues per academic year by respondents who included consideration of gender issues in their teaching (%).

More than 2 hours	33
1–2 hours	21
Less than 1 hour	46

Respondents were asked if they were satisfied with this amount of time and if they intended to increase coverage. In response, the time-pressured nature of the curriculum was often commented upon, e.g.:

I am not satisfied about the amount of time I devote to most of what I teach at postgraduate level because of the compressed nature of the programme. (Male)

Others were dissatisfied for other reasons:

I have a double module on gender and communication validated but I'm not allowed to run it. (Female)

Extended coverage was being considered in a number of areas, including: research methodology; job design; attitudes to technology; communications; library history; consumer health information; women and information in the Third World.

There does appear to be, therefore, scope for increasing the gender-related content in many modules taught in ILS departments. More interesting, perhaps, are the comments of those who either did not plan to extend coverage of gender issues, spent less than one hour per academic year teaching them, or who did not feature gender and equity at all:

Does not justify more time in the context of the class. (Male, specialising in IT and society)

No extension of coverage as it [i.e. readership studies, library history] is retrospective in context, not current. (Male)

Although there are gender implications in management I don't find it necessary to address although I use a couple of videos which include gender assumptions which I highlight as weaknesses. (Male)

These comments speak for themselves, but the notion that gender has no relevance to a module examining the development of library and information work is quite astonishing. More worrying is the idea that a lecturer can choose to ignore the gender implications of management issues and that "a couple of videos" are enough to sensitise students to gender relations in the workplace.

The individual topics taught within modules that did include consideration of gender issues varied enormously. The questionnaire listed topics that might be considered gender related, and also asked respondents to note any other relevant topics that they taught (Table 2).

Table 2: Number of respondents teaching specified gender-related topics

Presentation skills	41
Equal opportunities and employment law	20
Assertiveness/confidence building	19
Women and IT	17
Stereotyping in literature	16
Contribution of women librarians	12
Women's publishing houses	11
Women writers	10
Sexual harassment	10

21 respondents noted that they taught other topics which they regarded as being gender related, including:

images of women in the media

women's contribution to the Internet

gender in children's literature

community information

women as users of information/libraries

women in the information society.

Those academics who think gender issues are irrelevant to their subject area may learn from the efforts of others who manage to address gender in a wide range of modules.

One student focus group felt that gender issues were often introduced with little thought given to how they related to the rest of the module:

S5 It's like this, um, 'Let's throw something in. Let's add in some human resource management, and we'll throw that in'.

This comment reinforces the point that the introduction of gender issues needs to be planned so that they are properly integrated rather than being merely 'bolted on'.

3.2.1.2 Support for, and awareness of, coverage of gender and equity in the ILS curriculum

Lecturers' own attitudes may well have an effect on how, or if, gender issues are considered in the curriculum. Generally, respondents were supportive of the inclusion of gender issues in the ILS curriculum (Table 3).

Table 3: Support for inclusion of gender issues in the ILS curriculum (% of respondents).

Very supportive	30
Generally supportive	63
Not supportive	7

Female academics tended to be very supportive while male academics tended to be supportive in general. These figures would appear to be in conflict with those above. Although an overwhelming 93 per cent of respondents declared themselves supportive of gender issues in the curriculum, only 54 per cent reported including consideration of the issues in their teaching. It would appear that staff often supported the inclusion of gender and equity in the curriculum as long as they did not have to teach it. It is also possible that staff believed these issues are being covered when in fact they were not.

This assertion is supported by the fact that 54 per cent of respondents were not aware whether gender and equity issues were presented in the curriculum of their department. One respondent noted that she was "weakly aware of others outside my own orbit". This sentiment was echoed by lecturers interviewed as part of the case studies. Although programme co-ordinators were generally aware of what their colleagues taught, individual academics without programme-wide responsibilities often had little idea of the content of their colleagues' lecture courses.

3.2.1.3 Presentation of gender and equity issues in the ILS curriculum

Respondents who were aware of the inclusion of gender and equity issues were asked how these topics were presented in the curriculum. The majority said that discussion of these issues were included throughout the programme where appropriate (table 4). 18 per cent noted that their department invited a special guest lecturer, while 22 per cent said that a one-off lecture (on, for example, equal opportunities in the library profession) was given.

Table 4: Presentation of gender and equity issues in the ILS curriculum (% of respondents)

Special (guest) lecturer	18
One-off gender/equity lecture	22
Discussion of facets of gender issues throughout course	60

How accurate these figures are is open to question. Once again, awareness of the content of colleagues' modules appears to be quite low, one respondent noting, for example:

[I am] not conversant with lecture schedules of colleagues who are likely to teach this.

It is also possible that guest lecturers talk to specific groups only and their lectures are not advertised or open to all. This was commented upon by one of the student focus groups:

S4 Well, we've just had a lecture on women and information in Europe. [Laughter]

MC That's pure coincidence. [Laughter]

S3 But that's only available to 4 out of 28, so the others haven't even had it.

When guest lecturers are likely to be speaking of issues of relevance to the wider student population, staff should consider advertising the talk more widely.

Staff who included consideration of gender in their teaching used a mixture of methods to present these issues (Table 5).

Table 5: Methods used to teach gender and equity (% of respondents)

Theoretical approach	40
Anecdotal/experiential approach	34
Other	26

Academics often used more than one method. The use of role models was a significant feature of the study. Acting as a role model was considered particularly important amongst the female lecturers. One noted on her questionnaire, for example:

I think being a strong, powerful and authoritative figure, i.e. woman in the workplace, I am giving off the necessary vibes.

The use of role models is problematic, however, as Poole and Isaacs (1993) note, because it cannot be assumed that role models will be accepted. Students will not necessarily view the role models provided as particularly desirable or relevant to their own situation. The problems associated with role modelling were expressed well by one female lecturer in interview:

I think that's another important thing, if you have a lot of women students, female students, that they do have good role models. Because I think they can see that they can do it, they can get on and they have got a role to play.

In a previous exchange, however, this lecturer had commented:

I always remember somebody saying to me in the library where I worked at the time how pleased women must be about Margaret Thatcher [Laughter]. I was absolutely flabbergasted. Because, I mean, anybody less like a role model for any young women I just wouldn't want to find, I have to say that. I mean her whole way of dealing with her colleagues and dealing with things, it's almost put the women's movement back years, because it was actually the worst of everything.

As this lecturer obviously resented Baroness Thatcher being held up as a role model for her, there is no reason to suppose that female students will or should accept the role models being presented to them in the form of female academics.

The importance of mentoring was also discussed in interviews with staff. Female staff often mentioned the issue of 'clubability' and the old boy network, making the point that for women networking was often more difficult:

...[women are] not clubbable in the way that men are so, you know, they miss out on all the gossip in the gent's toilets … when I was on the Library Association Council I used to go to the meetings and I always used to have to rush off before the end so I could catch my train home again so that I could pick my son up from the child-minder...

In these circumstances, the argument for the establishment for a female network of support and mentors is persuasive.

Staff in the case study interviews also talked of how important the issue of gender equity was in their personal lives and how this extended to their formal and informal relations at work:

I have to admit that my wife has been very influential on me on this because as far as I'm concerned I need to get the relationships right at work with friends and at home, and for me it's a whole. And I hate to be liberal in one domain and bigoted in another. (Male)

Here, the lecturer is displaying aspects of the feminist view that 'the personal is political' and it is to be hoped that lecturers adhering to this viewpoint will encourage formal and/or informal discussion with students on changes in gender roles at home and at work over the last few decades.

3.2.1.4 Language

The questionnaire asked staff their views of the importance of gender-neutral language. As Dale Spender (1980, p. 162) argues, "For women to become visible, it is necessary that they become linguistically visible".

Women can feel alienated and excluded when male-oriented terminology is used as it supports the visibility and primacy of males. The importance of using as inclusive terms as possible is, therefore, clear.

The majority of staff felt the use of gender-neutral language to be important although there were differences of opinion about its relative importance with regard to lectures, students' work, and course materials (see Table 6).

Table 6: Importance of use of gender-neutral language (% of respondents)

	Very important	Average importance	Of no importance
In lectures	70	25	5
In students' work	51	41	8
In course materials	70	24	6

Worrying, however, is the (admittedly small) proportion of staff in these female dominated departments who felt this issue to be of no importance, especially with regard to students' work. Both student focus groups said that they had not been told specifically about the importance of gender neutral language, and the students had mixed views about its importance:

MC Have you ever had mentioned to you about, in the workplace, keeping to gender-neutral languages, that sort of thing?

S6 No.

S7 No.

MC Right. Do you think that sort of thing's important? Supposing I sat here and started talking about, well, manpower, for example?

S3 Well it doesn't worry me.

S4 It doesn't, no.

S3 It's actually stupid to say something like Chairperson. I'm quite happy with Chairman.

S5 I disagree. I think it's quite important to start using certain words, but every word, it's just too awkward.... When I did my first degree a lecturer stood up and he said 'he' every single example,'he this, he that'. After 6 weeks of that it starts really annoying you. If you're seeing him twice a week for six weeks, and it's 'he, he, he' and then this, he says 'man' and he actually means 'human', and it really gets up your nose.

As the same student later commented, by using these terms the lecturer is excluding half of society.

As long as individuals speak the language of the dominant order, society will reproduce itself in fairly constant form. Using 'he' and 'man' renders women linguistically invisible and promotes male imagery at the expense of female imagery so that the world is assumed male unless proven otherwise. It also makes women outsiders (Spender, 1980). Lecturers have a responsibility to ensure that their own language is an inclusive as possible. They also need to be sure that students are aware of the importance of using gender-neutral language and, perhaps most importantly, they realise why it is important.

3.2.1.5 Classroom dynamics

Staff were asked about classroom dynamics between male and female students. The results of numerous studies have found that men talk more than women in classroom situations (James and Drakich, 1993). Whether this is because this is a way of exercising dominance over women, or because women feel they will be judged negatively as too assertive is a matter of debate. Lecturers should, however, be aware of the possibility of domination of classroom interactions by males and the detrimental effect this can have on women. There was a fairly even split between those who had encountered problems with male/female classroom interactions (including students/student and lecturer/student interaction), and those who had not (see Table 7).

Table 7. The frequency of problems encountered with classroom interaction
(% of respondents)

Frequently	3
Occasionally	48
Never	49

Those respondents who commented on difficulties with student/student interactions sometimes mentioned problems with males' reactions in teaching situations, e.g.:

From inappropriate courtship behaviour to out and out harassment. Male domination of seminars and discussions. (Female)

Some male students can become insecure and aggressive if their attitudes are challenged. (Female)

More often, however, it was felt that in a female-dominated subject, the men in the class may feel excluded:

Males in a mainly female cohort occasionally feel threatened. (Female)

Lecturers also commented that mature and overseas students may be the cause of difficulties:

Male students on PG courses sometimes appear to doubt the ability of female staff. Overseas male undergraduates tend to patronise female lecturers. (Female)

The staff interviewed for the case studies often commented that their teaching style and the dynamics of the class did sometimes change according to the gender of the group:

I find it quite – when it's a mixed group, I think the boys – I don't know if they cramp the girls' style or what. Certainly with male groups I find them to be more formal or the only sort of relaxation that come in is through the guys trying to make witty comments or be smart and impress each other. Whereas, with the girls, I find when there's no men around there's more honesty. (Female)

Although none of the staff interviewed would favour single-sex teaching, the nature of class dynamics between the sexes and the effect that this can have on the women's participation does need to be taken into account.

3.2.2 Student Attitudes

3.2.2.1 Student viewpoint of gender issues

Respondents to the questionnaire believed that students were interested in gender issues to a degree (Table 8) and that students perceived gender issues as relevant (Table 9).

Table 8: Lecturers' opinion of student interest in gender issues
(% of respondents)

Very interested	9
Fairly interested	58
Not at all interested	7
Don't know	26

Table 9: Lecturers' opinion of relevance of gender issues to students
(% of respondents)

Very relevant	8
Fairly relevant	61
Of no relevance	5
Don't know	26

The number of staff who had little idea of their students' attitudes towards these issues is interesting suggesting that questions around gender and equity are not a matter for discussion for some staff.

Respondents often felt that attitudes towards gender issues varied according to sex, age and year of study and explained their answers in various ways:

> Some women are very touchy about it, mostly in mid-20s or older (40+) returnees. (Anon)

> Female students and black students are clearly more aware, interested than white male students. (Female)

It is interesting that in the first quote the female students' attitude is termed 'touchy' while in the second it is 'aware' and 'interested'. This perhaps says more about the respondents' own attitudes to gender issues than those of their students. Other comments included:

> Age – the older they are (men) the more sexist they are. 18 year-old men are a bit more laid back (90s man?) (Male)

> Mature women have opinions, young men do not, or worse. (Male)

The sentiment in the second quote, i.e. that gender issues are not a matter of debate these days, was echoed by other respondents, e.g.:

> Summed up by one student's remark: It's uncool to be feminist these days. (Female)
> I've been lecturing for six years and gender/glass ceiling seems to be far less of an issue than it used to be. (Female)

Library Association figures and those of Poland (1996) would dispute the view that the battle for equality has been won, and staff interviewed generally agreed that there was still a need for consciousness raising although how receptive students were was another question, as pointed out by an interviewee:

> It's just awful. It just goes over [students'] heads, they haven't got a clue about it. And they think you're getting on your soap box if you sort of introduce this at all… So in a sense, where they are is where we were with regard to the Second World War or something, so it's that sort of generation gap maybe. (Female)

Although staff thinks that students generally do perceive gender issues to be of relevance and interest, anecdotal evidence suggests that 'post-feminist' attitudes are common within the student body. This reinforces the need for an exploration of perceptions of gender and equal opportunities within the curriculum so that students are encouraged to develop understanding and insight into the relevance of gender for the personal and professional lives.

3.2.2.2 Student performance

Staff was asked about perceived differences between male and female performance with the aim of ascertaining if there was any stereotypical attitudes or assumptions with regard to the relative ability of the sexes. The power of the education process to reinforce gender stereotypes was noted by one interviewee when asked about the interests of the different genders:

> I think that an expectation on their part, and on staff part, and academic staff part, and I think that together we all combine to, this is my very personal view, that together we all combine to kind of reinforce some of these gender biases. (Male)

The majority of respondents (60%) believed that male and female students performed equally well in all subjects of the curriculum. Of those who believed there was a difference in performance, female students were often considered to perform better in all areas of the curriculum, e.g.:

> Females do better in all subjects. Better quality female than male students in all respects: motivation, literacy, application and general intelligence. (Male)

Male students were often considered better at IT related subjects and, by one respondent, at presentation work:

> [Male students do better in] oral presentations etc. Males are more confident and articulate even when they have prepared very little. [Female students do better in] tasks involving research, study etc. The females in general are harder working and more organised... Girls are encouraged to be demure; not loud, to carry out tasks etc.; males are allowed to be loud; outgoing, take the lead etc. (Female)

Here, the lecturer is acknowledging that stereotypes, and expectations of those stereotypes, can play a significant role in performance. The lack of confidence among female students was picked up in an interview:

> In a sense, I think women tend to be terribly hung up on everything. They want to be really good at things and if they're unsure then they're scared about it and they're unsure and they're unconfident whereas if men are unsure about things they just go, 'Ah well, I'll get by and it will be okay, I can reason my way out of a situation.' (Female)

The reasons why the female students are underconfident need to be addressed and remedial action taken to redress them. By including gender as an aspect of the curriculum, it is to be hoped that the female students will recognise how the views and roles of women have been socially constructed, and thus give them the wherewithal to take issue with continuing discrimination and stereotypical attitudes in their work and personal relationships.

4 Conclusions

The results of this study suggest that although gender is included in the teaching curriculum of departments of information and library studies, there is no co-ordinated effort to ensure that issues of equity are systematically raised and addressed. There is little doubt that teaching staff (particularly the female staff) are concerned about the position of women in the information professions and committed to change. Whether the teaching curriculum is the most appropriate vehicle for promoting issues of gender and equity is a matter of debate, however.

With appropriate planning, the curriculum can create an opportunity for students to consider their own and other people's sex and gender related experiences and assumptions. The curriculum can assist the professional and personal development of students by a process of exploration and exchange of experiences and analysis, encouraging each student to identify the influence of gender role socialisation in their own development and behaviour in a variety of professional and social contexts. The ILS lecturer can help in this process by providing students with a knowledge of:

gender inequality from a historical perspective

gender and equity in the workplace and particularly with reference to information work

policies and action which promote equal opportunities in professional contexts.

Apart from those subjects with a specifically equal opportunities content (e.g. human resource management), gender and equity issues can also be integrated into courses dealing with special subjects, e.g. library history, acquisitions and stock management, information technology, the internet. Departments should also consider drawing up guidelines for the use of gender-neutral language and ensure that all students are aware of the importance of inclusive terminology. In addition, there should be encouragement for female students to participate fully in professional events and networking including standing for office on committees.

Thought does need to be given as to how to include gender issues in the curriculum, whether to deal with them in a separate module or integrate them into all courses. Separate courses may appeal to those with a particular interest in the area but the integrated approach would ensure that all student (and staff) were exposed to gender issues which, judging by the complacency that some staff and apparently students display about the position of women in the profession, may well be necessary.

By including issues of gender and equity in the ILS curriculum, lecturers will be giving female students the intellectual means to challenge the status quo and question the inequalities that still exist in the information professions. Armed with knowledge of why things are the way they are, females entering the profession in the future should be confident about their ability and equipped to challenge the barriers to advancement that still exist.

References

Canadian Journal of Information Science, 1992. Librarianship as a woman's profession: strategies of empowerment, Canadian Journal of Information Science, 17(930), pp. 1-41.

Dewar, A. , 1987. The social construction of gender in physical education. Women's Studies International Forum, 10(4), pp. 453-465.

Gender Equity, 1997. URL: http://www.est.giv.bc.ca/equity/intro.html

Hannigan, J. A. , 1994. A feminist standpoint for library and information science. Wilson Library Bulletin. Journal of Education for Library and Information Science, 35(4), pp. 297-319.

James, D. and Drakich, J. , 1993, Understanding gender differences in amount of talk: a critical review of research. In: Tannen, D., ed. Gender and Conversational Interaction. Oxford: OUP, 1993, pp. 281-312

Library Association, 1991. Equal Opportunities in the Library Profession, London: Library Association.

Manpower Services Commission, 1981. No Barriers Here? London: MSC.

McDermott, E, 1994. Who needs equal opportunities? Libraries do. New Library World, 94(1112), pp. 9-14.

Poland, F. et al, 1996. Women and Senior Management. London: Library Association.

Poole, M., and Isaacs, D. , 1993. The gender agenda in teacher education. British Journal of Sociology of Education, 14(3), pp. 275-284.

Pritchard, S. , 1989. The impact of feminism on women in the profession. Library Journal, 114(13), pp. 76-77.

Ritchie, S. , 1979. 2,000:1, a sex oddity, Assistant Librarian, 71(3), pp. 38-41.

Spender, D. , 1980. Man Made Language. London: Routledge & Kegan Paul.

Taylor, S. , 1989. Empowering girls and young women: the challenge of the gender-inclusive curriculum. Journal of Curriculum Studies, 21(5), pp. 441-456.

NATIONAL VOCATIONAL QUALIFICATIONS (NVQs): ONE ROUTE TO IMPROVE THE STATUS OF WOMEN IN LIBRARIES?

Sandra Parker and *Catherine Hare*, Project Directors

Pat Gannon-Leary, Senior Research Assistant

School of Information Studies, University of Northumbria at Newcastle,

Newcastle, U.K. (2000)

Abstract

While Information and Library Services are female-dominated, the roles occupied by women employed in the sector are frequently those of library assistants rather than those at a higher level. Reasons for this are many including: career breaks, family commitments and reduced working hours. However, skills and qualifications remain an important element and any further education embarked upon by women needs to be flexible to fit in with both their public and private lives.

National Vocational Qualifications (NVQs) were introduced in Great Britain in the 1980s as a means of increasing the skills of the workforce. They are based on occupational competence and are assessed in the workplace, which is an ideal pattern for many women.

Might NVQs in Library and Information Services not only redress the U.K. skills imbalance as compared to other developed countries (another aim of their introduction) but also redress the balance of males : females in the higher echelons of the profession? This paper considers this question in the light of findings of the INSIST project, a one-year Government funded project conducted at the University of Northumbria, which investigated the benefits of the qualifications.

1. Introduction

National Vocational Qualifications (NVQS) and Scottish Vocational Qualifications (SVQS) were introduced in Great Britain in the 1980s because it was thought that increasing the skills of the workforce was the way to improve the economic health of the country; to redress the imbalance as compared to other developed countries; and to co-ordinate a growing number of "confusing" qualifications. The Department of Education and Science in the UK set up some 160 organisations called Lead Bodies to represent occupational sectors and to lead the way in developing S/NVQs with particular responsibility for developing the standards of work-based practice for the sector. The one for the information occupational sector was the Information and Library Services Lead Body. The information sector is wide ranging and this was reflected within the Lead Body which was subdivided into the specialist areas of Information and Library Services (ILS), Archives, Records and Tourist Information. Each specialist area was represented by nominated professionals and practitioners in the field.

The ILS Lead Body started work in April 1991, but it was not until the summer of 1995, after development, discussion and testing, that the first S/NVQS from the standards were approved. The extent and diversity of the ILS sector is reflected in the suite of 11 awards ranging from Levels 2 to 4 and covering information and library services (IILS)(1995), records services and records management (1997), and archives (1997). Despite their relatively recent development, the occupational standards and awards have been adopted across the sector with the establishment of assessment centres and registration of candidates at all levels. The Information and Library Service S/NVQs were developed first and, to date, they have had the greatest uptake. By December 1998 ILS S/NVQs had evolved to the extent that there were 165 assessment centres with the numbers of candidates at each site ranging from a minimum of one to a maximum of 26 (level 2), 29 (level 3) and 8 (level 4).

These NVQ's have been particularly helpful to paraprofessional or Library technician staff to achieve recognition. They often have long periods of service with key skills, but have no formal qualifications. Currently the registration for these awards is at least 90% women.

2. What Is an SVQ or NVQ and What Is Involved in Getting One?

NVQs measure skills that are directly relevant to the everyday world of work (Arundale 1995). They are competence based (Dakers 1994b and 1994c) and measure whether a person can carry out his or her work to the defined national standards of current best practice (Dakers 1997b). They emphasize achievement rather than theory (Trevett 1996b) but candidates have to show both that they have the skills to do the job and that they have the necessary knowledge to do it well and in a range of circumstances. (Scarsbrook in Trevett 1996b).

The NVQ standards are broken down into five levels which range from the application of basic skills (at levels 1 and 2); level 3 for more senior staff with greater responsibility including the control and guidance of others (Herzog 1996); to a high degree of professional understanding comparable to full academic degrees at level 4 (Arundale 1995a and 1995b). Further details of each level are given in a number of articles including Dakers & Hare (1996), Fries (1995), Harrison (1994), Herzog (1995). Level 2 is currently the first Information and Library level used and is intended for library assistants. It is particularly helpful as induction training. It covers processing materials, identifying and providing information and working with users. Level 3 is intended for senior library assistants or information officers/executives and covers providing and organising information, solving problems for users and maintaining quality standards together with five optional units. Level 4 is intended for library, customer services or information managers. (Lobban 1997) A level 5 qualification for senior managers was under discussion but appears to have been shelved.

At each level, NVQs are broken down into a series of units, which describe separate functions within an individual's job role (Stott 1996). These are grouped into Core and Mandatory Units, where work is considered as essential regardless of the kind of service being provided, and Optional Units which allow for specialist activities, such as the IT units for someone working in a hi-tech Business Information Unit (Trevett 1997d). For example at level 2 for information and library staff the Mandatory Units are:

Process material for use.

Identify and provide information/material required by user.

Develop positive working relationships with customers.

Optional Units are:

Maintain arrangement of information/material.

Secure information/material.

Contribute to the maintenance of a supportive environment for users.

Direct users.

Issue and recover loan material.

Maintain data in a computer system.

(Information and Library Services Lead Body. Information Organisations and Libraries: Scottish and National Vocational Qualifications levels 2-4. NB: These awards are due to be revised in January 2001).

Units are further broken down into a number of elements, usually from two to five elements. The element is the smallest assessable component of an NVQ, although it cannot gain independent certification or be transferable: the unit is the smallest component which can be transferred (Herzog 1996).

Each element contains statements about performance criteria, range and underpinning knowledge and understanding, and assessment guidance. [To gain an ILS S/NVQ at level 2, for example, the candidate must provide evidence for each element of the six units, which meets the requirements of those elements (Stott 1996)].

Each unit is a 'mini qualification' and an individual can take just one or two units from an NVQ if this suits their purpose. They could combine units from different NVQs if this was valuable for them. They will be awarded the full NVQ only if they complete all the core and mandatory units designated for that level NVQ but, where they prefer to 'pick and mix' their own units, they get a certificate for each unit they have successfully completed (Herzog 1996)

3. The Benefits to Women

On the job

A benefit frequently referred to is not having to take extended time off the job (Harrison 1994). Coker (1997) found enthusiasm for a flexible and accessible qualification equivalent to a professional one that can be acquired on the job. Goulding & Kerslake (1996) feel NVQs may give flexible workers a chance to gain qualifications. This is particularly suitable for part-time workers and volunteers many of whom are women (Fries 1995). A manager quoted in Coker (1997) from a survey by Drury suggests NVQs will give recognition to people not able to study for other qualifications e.g. City & Guilds or Library and Information Assistants' Certificate (LIAC), which requires time-off, travel and study time.

Dakers (1995b), while promoting the value of NVQs for those working in United Kingdom school libraries, stresses the opportunity they offer for people to obtain qualifications in recognition for skills acquired while doing a particular job. "NVQs are tailor-made for those who cannot get away to do some formal training course because they have to mind the library. They are ideal for the part-time employee".

Flexible

Another benefit of S/NVQs for the individual is that they are flexible and can be achieved at a pace to suit the trainee (Harrison 1994) Anyone can take an NVQ regardless of age, sex, language or ability. Units can be gained gradually as there are no set timescales (Jones

1994) (although in practice certain deadlines may be useful). Fries (1995) believes that S/NVQS are useful for the voluntary sector where limited resources, part-time workers and volunteers are the norm and she also suggests it would be possible for individuals to undertake an S/NVQ even if it were not offered by their employer if they were prepared to pay for it themselves. However in Goulding & Kerslake's survey (1996) a school library manager believed that the work the qualifications involves for part-time workers who already gave a lot to their jobs, and have families would be just too much.

Existing Skills May Gain Exemption

Existing skills or qualifications may gain exemption from some parts of NVQs by means Accreditation of Prior Learning (APL) (Information and Library Services Lead Body 1996h). There is however some debate as to how far APL is possible (Totterdell 1997 and Scarsbrook 1997).

Costs

Because NVQ's are most often assessed in the workplace and are relevant to employers needs, the employer will often meet costs. Also they do not entail leaving employment and undertaking a expensive College education.

Career Progression and Development

Dakers (1993) and Trevett (1997) suggest that NVQ's offer, for the first time career development for the paraprofessional. Dakers also claims that those staff who can see internal means of career progression are more likely to stay in post and be absent less often. The Assessment Centre at the University of Northumbria, School of Information Studies offers a linked qualification. Candidates completing NVQ level 4 are then qualified to enter the B.Sc. Information and Communication degree in the third (final) year, their NVQ being accredited as equivalent to the first two years of the degree syllabus. The only candidate to have progressed so far and about to obtain a degree by this route is a mature woman working in an academic library.

4. Some Disadvantages

Jargon and Language

This is an oft-repeated criticism, as the standards are national and sometimes function across many occupations sectors e.g. Customer care, the language is sometimes complex and jargon based. This has improved with new editions.

Time Consuming

Because they are intended to being pursued while doing a job, some employers and candidates under estimate the amount of time that is needed. 'I've just started doing the NVQ but I am finding it difficult to find the time' On average the research found that Level 2 took 6 month to complete, Level 3 two years and level 4 four years. Candidates found that they needed 4-5 hours a week to complete the work. Some employers gave half a day as study leave and this was found to be very successful.

Practical Versus Underlying Theory

It is the emphasis on practical competence that has led to criticism from those who are worried about lack of theoretical underpinning. Elkin (1994) dislikes the mechanistic approach "and lack of encouragement of any vision or broadening of horizons". Wilson (1995) worries that there is no mention of the need for imagination, creativity, innovation or analytical thought, especially for managers at levels 4 and 5. Muddiman (1995) thinks that "...2001 may well see in libraries the emergence of the jobber, who knows how but not why".

However, the performance evidence refers to the desirability of portfolios showing underpinning knowledge and understanding: to carry out a task well, people need to know why they are doing it and what to do when things go wrong. Totterdell (1997) writes about using City and Guilds to provide theoretical underpinning for level 2 and, to a lesser extent, level 3. She says that Sandra Parker (LA president in 1996) "was right when she described ILS-NVQs as being as well as rather than instead of existing qualifications". Trevett (1996b) suggests that underpinning knowledge and skills gaps are best delivered in the workplace via training methods such as induction periods, working alongside more experienced staff, coaching, organised job swaps, staff meetings, study sessions and open learning.

5. Conclusions

Women have long formed the majority of the workforce in this sector. They have largely been undervalued, underpaid, under-educated and under-trained. This competence-based form of on the job training undoubtedly offers a way forward that has not been possible before. It is hoped that employers will welcome these developments and support women appropriately with fees and the necessary time to achieve recognition of their skills.

References

Arundale, J. (1995a) National Vocational Qualifications: What's it all about? Assignation, 13 (1), p. 34-6. refs.

Arundale, J. (1995b) Getting your S/NVO: a guide for candidates in the information and library sector. Library Association Publishing.

Dakers, H. (1997b) The library as a key to exploiting economic resources: global competence in the library oils the lock. EFLA Journal, 23 (1), p. 30-5. il.refs.

Dakers, H. (I 996c) NVOs and how to get them. Kogan Page.

Dakers, H. (1995b) National Vocational Qualifications. What is in them for school libraries? School Librarian, 43 (2), p. 45.

Dakers, H. (1994b) A matter of competence. Library Association Record, 98(6), p. 446-7.

Dakers, H. and Hare, C.E. (1996) NVQs for records management revealed. Records Management Journal, 6 (2), p. I 1 1-29. refs.

Elkin, J. (1994) Higher-level NVQS: cause for concern? Librarian Career Development, 2 (4), p. 32-3.

Fries, C. (1995) National Vocational Qualifications (NVQS) for information and library services. Assignation, 12 (3), p. 5-7.

Goulding, A. and Kerslake, E. (1996) Flexible information workers: training and equal opportunities. Librarian Career Development, 4 (2), p. 5-12. refs.

Hare, C. and Rhodes, G. (1996) Forging a partnership with HE. Library Association Record, (9), p. 466-8. il.refs.

Harrison, C.T. (1994) S/NVQs and professional qualifications in library and information Services. Librarian Career Development, 2 (4), p. 24-8. refs.

Herzog, J. (1 996) Implementing S/NVQs in the information and library sector: a guide for employers. Library Association Publishing.

Herzog, J. (I 995) The development of NVQs/SVQs. School Librarian, 43 (2), p. 46-8.

Information and Library services Lead Body (1997) Time to review the ILS S/NVQs. Newsletter, Winter

Jones, B. (1994) National Vocational Qualifications (NVQs): an introduction for library and information workers. Bulletin of the Association of British Theological and Philosophical Libraries, 3 (3), p. 3-8. refs.

Lobban, M. (1997) Scottish and National Vocational Qualifications (S/NVQs). In: Training Library Assistants. Library Association Publishing. Chapter 5. p. 25-30.

McKeever, L.(1997) Customer care training at the new Bibliotheque Nationale de France. Personnel Training and Education, 14(2), p. 10-12.

Muddiman, D. (1995) Information and library education: a manifesto for the Millennium. New Library World, 96 (1119), p. 26-31. refs.

Scarsbrook, P. (1997) NVQ Comments and update. Personnel Training and Education, 14(3), p. 15.

Stott, H. (1996b) Review of Getting Your S/NVO: a guide for candidates in the information and library sector by J. Arundale. Managing Information, 3 (5), p. 50.

Totterdell, A. (1997) NVQ'S: A response to Steve Lee. Personnel Training and Education 14 (3) 1997, p. 14-15.

Trevett, A. (1997a) Offering the ILS S/NVQs; some do's and don'ts for college library services. COFHE Bulletin, 81 (Summer), p. 2-3.

Trevett, A. (1997b) Using the ELS S/NVQs. School Librarian, 45 (2), p. 69-70. refs.

Trevett, A. (1997d). Taking stock: Using the information and library services S/NVQs for acquisitions staff. Libraries and the Book Trade. 6 (1). p. 33-5.

Trevett, A. (1996b) Where are we up to with S/NVQs in libraries? Personnel Training and Education, 13(2), p. 9-10.

Wilson, T.D. (I 995) Are NVQs for robots? Library Association Record, 97 (7) July, p. 38-41.

WOMEN'S ISSUES IN CONTEMPORARY CHINA:
THE CASE OF FEMALE UNIVERSITY LIBRARIANS IN BEIJING

Zhang Li Xin

Librarian, Foreign Languages Department,

Beijing Normal University,

Beijing, P.R. China (1997)

Introduction

I am a librarian and have been working in a library for twenty years. I therefore want to present in this paper the situation of female librarians in China like myself. It was the Beijing IFLA Conference that opened my eyes, made me understand the situation of librarians in different places all over the world, and stimulated me into write about Chinese librarians, especially female librarians, their work and their life. Because this is the first time I am writing a paper like this and also because it is generally difficult to obtain materials containing gender statistics in China, it has been a challenge for me to provide a clear picture of the situation of women librarians in China. I do hope, however, to tell you as much as I can and to get your advice for improving this work. In addition, please let me know of any questions that you may have, and maybe next time, with your input, my paper will improve greatly.

I would first like to introduce myself, my work, and life experience, because just as I was growing up my country, the People's Republic of China, was changing dramatically. I think my personal background can help you gain insight into Chinese history and reality.

I was born in 1956. My own road to women's studies has been tumultuous but never boring. Because schools were closed down during the Cultural Revolution (1966-1977), I lost, at age of 10, the chance to continue my schooling. So at age 14 I took the next best option – I became a female soldier in the Chinese Army. The schools opened up again, and, when I was 20, I returned to Beijing from Sichuan Province, worked at Beijing Normal University as a librarian and began my middle and high school studies. At 26 years, I passed the college entrance exam, became a university student(studying in my free time, as I was working full time), and began studying English . It was only in 1993 that I discovered the world feminist movement through translating articles on it.

Learning about women's studies and the feminist movement was, and continues to be, a source of inspiration and knowledge for me. It seems to me that I was searching for this for so long, but didn't know what I was looking for until I found it. I think that women's studies in China is to be looked at differently than women's studies in other countries. It is, in some ways, much more difficult to do research and obtain data. Because women's studies in mainland China is always subject to the national policy, it sometimes looks as if there existed no problems and little research has been carried out to show the real life of women.

Market Economy Changes Women's Situation

In 1978, China initiated a set of economic reforms that led to the opening up of China and the development of a market economy. Unfortunately many new social problems began to emerge at the same time. For instance, reforms led to the emergence of a large number of migrant workers from rural areas and a wide range of concomitant problems. These migrant workers, many of whom are women, come to the cities in large numbers, hoping to improve their economic situation.

Another women's issue emerging from the economic reforms is the impact local industry has had on women, particularly the current situation of women workers in state enterprises. In recent years, a large number of women have lost their jobs due to the poor economic performance of these enterprises. Economic reforms have also led to the discrimination against women in the work environment.

Alongside these new issues emerging from economic changes, the previously existing problems which Chinese women face in marriage and sexual relationships remain significant areas deserving attention.

Women's Studies in China

Liu Bohong, a researcher at the All-China Women's Federation, has noted that the development of women's studies in China has occurred in two stages: the initial stage covering the early 1980s to 1990 and the second stage thereafter making a phase of strengthening and consolidation. Since the 1970s, when China first opened its doors to the outside world, western ideas have circulated in China. In this atmosphere, and as the free market has become more powerful, the scope of the government's control has lessened, women's studies and other individual, activities, not originating in government circles have emerged.

Sexual Discrimination and Employment

In 1993, Wenhuibao (a newspaper) began a discussion of the problems of sexual discrimination and unemployment among women. Professor Tao Jie, of Peking University, noted at a workshop that, in the factories, women are the first to be laid off when staff is being reduced, because employing female workers is more expensive than employing male workers. For instance, if a female worker goes on maternity leave, the factory has to pay 1500 Yuan in wages and additional benefits.

Recently, it has been found that even female university students are facing discrimination. Because of the limited quota for employment of new staff in each research department or work unit, priority is usually given to male students, when graduates are being recruited. Many reasons are given by the work-units for giving priority to male graduates over female graduates. It is said that it is not convenient for women to go into business, that female students can not do physical work, and that female students are likely to get married and have children in the immediate future.

Education of Girls – and Mothers

Another area where discrimination is obvious is the education of girls. Why is it that fewer girls than boys attend school? The problem here is poverty. However, there also some families, even though they are not very poor, that still resist sending female children to school.

This is a result of the traditional thinking that boys and men are more important than girls and women, and that even women with no education can still perform the traditional function of giving birth to children.

As a result, mothers (most of the women living in rural area) often have little education, and it will often not occur to them to send their daughters to school. At the same time, these relatively uneducated women normally get married early, have many children and need their daughters to help them with the housework, thus creating what has become a vicious cycle in some areas of China.

Owing to constraints in social development and the influence of traditional believes, the conditions for Chinese women in present day Chinese society are still not wholly satisfactory. There still remains a long way to go before Chinese women can become fully emancipated. Female self-improvement is a strategic task fundamental to the protection of women's rights and interests.

Women Librarians

On the whole, the Chinese revolution and socialism have made the experiences of Chinese women unique. Even within China, women in different realms of society have different experiences. This paper is looking at the experience of women working in libraries. Below I describe the situation of librarians at Beijing Normal University and give a picture of their work and life.

Most female librarians in China are found in cities and, in Beijing, most of them work in colleges, universities and institutions. Libraries in China can be separated into three categories: public libraries, school libraries and company

libraries. Most of the libraries belong to the state, though a few are in private hands. The problems discussed above are not as prominent for women working in libraries as they are for women in other workplaces. Libraries are supported by the state; and thus, the change to a market economy has had less impact in this area. For example, female librarians are less affected by unemployment than women in other sectors. Although the quota for employment of librarians has been lowered in recent years, the number of librarians has also been decreasing for other reasons. Many have retired and often almost no new staff has been employed to replace them.

When I interviewed the president of BNU library and asked him if the library hires new staff on equal basis, regardless of gender, he said that he prefers male staff. Hardly any men, however, want to work in the library, so that, in the end, men and women are essentially equal in the librarians' employment process. Many people believe that being a librarian is a women's position and that women are well suited working in this area. China still is a developing country, however, and librarians must do much physical labor. Thus, women's work in the library is very hard.

The Beijing Normal University Library

There are 130 librarians in BNU's library, 30 of whom are male. Even though they are in the minority it is the men who are usually the first ones to be considered for promotion. When I interviewed the female librarians however, they all said that there was no discrimination in the work place and also no sexual harassment. Why is it then that women are considered best suited to perform library work by our society? I believe this is because work conditions for librarians in China are not adequate. The salary is low, heavy work is involved, and there is hardly any chance of promotion. In a sense, it is a form of discrimination against women, but even though many people have been living in this situation for a long time they do not see it as a problem.

In the wake of economic reforms, librarians' salaries have been increased. The lowest salary for a librarian at BNU rose from 80 Yuan in 1979 to 800 Yuan (about US$100) in 1997. A research librarian's salary rose from 100 Yuan in 1979 to 1000 Yuan in 1997. Compared with staff working in companies these salaries are extremely low, but compared with factory workers or the jobless workers from failing state enterprises, these salaries are significantly higher.

The president of BNU said that the library is facing a number of difficulties and may not continue to exist. The library is short of funds and the low salary is a significant obstruct to maintaining quality employees. The library sponsored 1tenof its staff for M.A degree programs, however none of them returned to work in the library at the end of their studies. Thus continuing education has become also a major problem. If the library does not send people to training course to obtain new skills, it cannot improve the quality of its work. If people are sent for further training, however, they usually do not come back. A table below is showing the educational background and position of BNU library staff.

Table 1. BNU Library – Librarians' Educational Situation

	Age 20–29		Age 30–39		Age 40–49		Age 50–59	
Total	18		39		35		18	
	M*	F*	M	F	M	F	M	F
	7	11	6	33	8	27	9	9
Educ. degree								
M.A.	1				1			
B.A.	3	5	1	17	3	10	1	
C*	3	5	3	10	1	9	6	6
HS*			2	6	1	5	1	2
MS*		1			2	3	1	1

From Table 1. we can detract that out of the 130 librarians in the BNU library, the only three people who hold an MA degree are male; 28 females and 13 males have a B.A.

degree; 26 females and 8 males have 2 years of higher education; 12 females and 4 males have graduated from high school, and 4 females and 2 males have graduated from middle school.

Table 2. Beijing Normal University – Librarians' Positions

	Age 20–29		Age 30–39		Age 40–49		Age 50–59	
Total	18		39		35		18	
	M*	**F***	**M**	**F**	**M**	**F**	**M**	**F**
	7	11	6	33	8	27	9	9
RL*					1	1	5	4
L*	2	5	1	18	4	15	4	4
SL*	2	8	2	11	2	8		
Other	1		2	5	1	3		1

Key: *M = Male, F = Female, RL* = Research Librarian, at the level of professor, L* = Librarian, SL = Assistant Librarian*

Table 2 shows that 5 females and 6 males are research librarians (same level as professor); 42 females and 6 males are librarians; 27 females and 6 males are assistant librarians; another 9 females and 4 males have no official title. Twenty female librarians returned my questionnaire. They come from three different age groups; 11 women were between 30 and 40 years old; 6 were between 40 and 50 years old; and 3 were between 50 and 60 years old. There were no respondents among the 20 and 30 years old.

Questionnaire. Questions and Answers

A. Work Situation

Why are you working in the library?

Among the 20 persons, 2 answered that they have to work, because they graduated in library science, and 7 answered, that they were placed here. In China, most students will be placed by the government upon graduation. Normally, once a worker is assigned to a department, this is a position for lifetime. This situation was more prevailing before the 1980s, but now students have more choices; but they have also more difficulty in finding good jobs. Normally, every big department has its own support system, for example, each department is in charge of housing, children's education, shopping center, canteen, etc. Institutions such as BNU also have a department that manages the staff housing, the nursery school, the primary school, and the three middle schools. Sometimes a university appears to be like a closed society. You don't have to leave the campus – everything can be done there. The retired university staff receives a pension. Those who started working before 1949 receive 100% of their previous salary and those who started after 1949 receive 80%. Five persons said that they were working in the library, because they like to red books. One librarian said that she had been crazy to join the staff and that she regretted working as librarian. Two persons said that they loved their work and the work environment was good.

Are you satisfied with working in the library?

Twelve respondents said they were satisfied, 5 were dissatisfied, and 3 said they didn't know.

What kind of job would you choose if you were given the opportunity to choose again?

Six persons said they would still choose to work in library; 5 said they would like to teach; 2 said they would like to go into business; 3 would like to work with children and music; 4 said they didn't know.

What do you think about your work environment (including library building equipment and staff and staff relations)?

Thirteen said they were satisfied; 4 were dissatisfied; 3 answered they didn't know.

Is your salary satisfactory?

This is a most interesting question for female librarians , and this is also were the biggest problem for them arises. There was only one woman, above 50 years old, who was satisfied with her salary, 18 women were dissatisfied, 1 said she didn't know.

When did you start working in the library? How long did you work in the library?

The women with the longest work experience could look back on 32 years work, the one with the shortest on 6 years. Compared with women in other countries, Chinese women's work experience tends to be longer. Except for six-months maternity leave, Chinese women work their whole lives, from the day they graduate until the day they retire. Female librarians retire at the age of 55, research librarians at the age of 60.

Do you feel there is sex discrimination in your work place?

Except for one woman who said "yes", other women all said "no". Although almost all women said there was no discrimination in their work place, I think this is not quite realistic. In my opinion they are merely not aware of the discrimination. There are 130 staff in BNU library, only 30 of them are male. However among those 30 male librarians, one is the library's president, two are vice-president, and other two section heads. Only four women are section heads. The most important positions of the library are occupied by men. This library still is a man's environment.

What annoys you most in your work?

Intensity of the work, I was named 7 times, long working hours 9 times, a low salary 19 times, no prospect of promotion, assigned housing too far away from work 2 times.

B. Marriage Situation

Among the 20 female librarians who answered, 19 are married, one is single. Two of the married women have 2 children, all others have one child. When asked how many children they would like to have, 9 women said one, 4 women said 2, 2 women said 2-3. The above tell us a little about the family life of female librarians. I believe that one child policy is beneficial to most women. It has liberated women from duties and allowed many women in the cities to work. However, the problem is that after they finish work women still need to go shopping and cook (in China dinner still requires two hours to cook). The library closes at 5 PM, most families have dinner at 20:30) and take care of their children. This double burden women for the most part have to carry by themselves. Some women hope that some day when they go home to cook and take care of their child, they will be happy because they will not need to do double work.

How long was your maternity leave?

Seven women had a 6-month maternity leave, 5 women had a three-month, and 7 women had a 56 days maternity leave (during the maternity leave women receive their full salary except bonuses. Women will decide how long they want to be on maternity leave)

Who in the family makes the decision on how the money is spent?

Seven decide for themselves, 13 decide jointly with their husbands.

Who cares for your child/children?

Seventeen women said they do it themselves, 1 said her mother-in-low was helping, 1 said her maid was helping.

Who does the cooking?

Twelve said they did cooking themselves, 4 said their husband cooks, 3 said both they and their husband cook.

Who does the washing?

Fourteen said they themselves wash, 2 said their husband, 3 said both they and their husbands do washing.

What do you like to do in your free time?

Eleven women like to watch TV, take care child/children and knit sweaters; 1 likes to read books and play with her child; 3 read books and watch TV; 1 likes to write and go shopping; 3 like to listen to music and go out; 1 likes to read books, watch TV, and clean house.

Conclusion

Although the figures and the survey presented above are very limited, they give a glimpse into female librarian's working situation. I have a particular interest in the human rights of Chinese rural women. During my field research in Haogeng Village (Anhui Province), I found that there was an extremely large gap between the educational levels of men and women, and that situation was accepted as normal by both men and women. I believe that the most important thing is to make women aware of the injustice of this situation and to become able to better their own situation.

I have attended the Intercultural Course on Women and Society in Manila, Philippines in 1995. I was also among the participants of the IFLA Conference 1996 in Beijing. Before that conference, I was not sure that it is important to be a librarian. At this conference everyone was very friendly, helpful and kind, really exellent people. I'm thrilled that I'm entering the library world. Altogether, the library field seems a logical extension to me.

LIBRARIES FOR LIFE IN THE PAPUA NEW GUINEA INFORMATION SOCIETY?

Margaret Obi

Strand Leader/Senior Lecturer

Information and Communication Science Strand

University of Papua New Guinea

Papua New Guinea (2002)

Introduction

"Libraries for life" in today's Papua New Guinea information society is not an impossible goal to strive for to achieve with today's new and old information and communication technologies. However, in order for this to happen, a number of issues and concepts will need to be asked in an ettempt to find some answers.

There are three issues that need immediate attention. They are:

1. What is "an information society" and what is its significance for Papua New Guinea?

2. What is information literacy and its relevance for Papua New Guinea's information society?

3. What is the role of women as information professionals participating in a democratic Papua New Guinea society?

These three questions need to be answered to provide some understanding of whether or not libraries are used as a way of life in the Papua New Guinea society.

Student assignments from two of the courses, which I have developed and taught since 2000, will be used as the main data for this paper. These courses are Information Society and Information Literacy. Both these courses were originally developed as librarianship courses. Due to the rationalisation programme at the University of Papua New Guinea and the need by the Information and Communication Sciences Strand to attract student members, the content of both courses now cater for students in all disciplines within the main campus at Waigani.

Table 1. Students in Information Society and Information Literacy from 2000–2002

Course	Year 2000	Year 2001	Year 2002	Total
*37.1000/39.2254 Information Literacy	16/40	3/23	3/81	22/144
*37.2000/39.2251 Information Society	5/85	1/45	5/40	11/170
	21/125	4/68	8/121	33/314

NB. The number of students majoring in librarianship is in **bold**.

Papua New Guinea as an "Information Society"?

In the absence of a Papua New Guinea authorship in/on "information society", the views of students taking the second year course 37.000/39.2251 Information Society at the University of Papua New Guinea were sought through the use of course assignments over a period of three years from 2000-2002. The purpose of these assignments was to encourage students to evaluate concepts and/or definitions used by non Papua New Guinean authors and to identify the relevancy of these concepts to the Papua New Guinea situation, in particular, as an information society.

To assist students' understanding of the concept of "information society", the writings of four authors – Cronin (1985), Martin (1985 & 1995), Feather (1994) and Webster (1994) – were presented through lectures, readings and class discussion. Whilst the materila may be outdated, the concepts used by the above authors were adequate for our purposes. Materials accessed through the Internet facility and conference papers collected from my attendance were used to update the discussion on "information society".

A matrix was drawn up depicting the various criteria for an information society used by these authors. Students were then asked to use these criteria to test whether or not the criteria used to identify a society as an "information society" in the "western" world could be the same criteria to determine Papua New Guinea as an information society. The Solomon Island students were asked to do the same for their country.

Table 2. Criteria for an Information Society

Cronin (1985)	Martin (1985)	Feather (1994)	Webster (1994)	Martin (1995)
Technology	Technology		Technology	Technology
Socio-economic	Social			Social
	Economic	Economic	Economic	Economic
	Political	Political		Political
	Cultural		Cultural	Cultural
Information workforce		Information professional	Occupational	
			Spatial	
		History		

Assignments similar to the ones for this year were given to the students in the previous years for this purpose. The first assignment asked, "Using the criteria of western auhorship, discuss whether or not your village community is an information society". The results from the assignments suggested the following.

Technology

Each student identified their village community as either their mother's or their father's village. The technologies used within this community varied depending on the geo-political location of each one. For example, the Manus Island villages use the garamut to notify people of messages – public information they wanted communicated. They also used the canoe to travel from island to island. In the Highlands of Papua New Guinea, shouting from one hilltop to another was the mode for public information. On the coastal regions of the country, the conch shell was used for public information. For private and personal information, the human being was the best message carrier to ensure the confidentiality and privacy of the message. The types of technology found in these village communities were adequate to sustain a local way of life.

Most students acknowledged that accepting and adapting to change in whatever form was necessary to sustain their village communities.

Social, Cultural and Political

Students identified the social and political networks, that each of their families created and maintained, were to ensure that an amicable and harmonious relationship was enjoyed by all. For example, the maintenance of peace between warring clans in most cases would result in the marriage of children of the chiefs. This union strengthened social, political and cultural linkages. Indirectly, it created another linkage as trading partners. This is evidenced in the "hiri" between the Gulf and Central provinces, the "moka" in the Highlands regions and the "kula" in the Trobriand Islands of Papua New Guinea.

Regarding the economics of information, it was agreed by all students, that the barter and exchange system ensured a continuous flow of "value of each item exchanged" information. These exchanges were not only tangible goods such as a "bunch of banana" for a "basket of seashells", but in non-tangible items such "chants for chants" or a "song and dance" for a "song and dance", a "method of fishing" that was not practiced in a certain area for a "gardening method".

Feather's history dimension posed a challenge for the students. Without a written language, their oral histories were used for this assignment. Carvings of totem poles, masks, canoes, etc., knots in ropes to keep count of days; using sun to tell the time, weather patterns, seasonal growth of vegetation, the physical changes to the male and female body, etc., all communicated information that was interpreted and put into rituals, ceremonies for everyday living in the community.

The findings of this first assignment strongly indicate that the criteria used by Cronin, Feather, Martin and Webster can be used to identify a village community on Papua New Guinea as an information society. These criteria are integral components in defining an "information society".

Students concluded that though their folk technologies may have a low level of impact and the information flow may be fit for the village pace of life, it was adequate and relevant to ensuring a village community's way of life.

Two other criteria – language and change – were also deemed necessary criteria to determine whether a society was an information society or not. The reasons given by students were that language was and must be a pre-requisite for communicating information and that village communities must accept change to sustain itself. Change can be in the form of, e.g. for fishing villages, a different angle in the throwing of a spear, or making a smaller eyelet when making a net to catch shrimp, or a different irrigation method in order to get a better harvest and a better life.

Another interesting outcome of this assignment relates to Webster's spatial criteria. Whilst Webster's (1994, p. 12) "major emphasis is on the information networks that connect locations and, as consequence, have dramatic effects on the organisation of time and space", students translated spatial as social, cultural and political positions to determine who the opinion leaders were and their hierarchical relationships in their village communities. These spatial relationships formalised information and communication linkages within families, clans and the village community. Students used only their oral information and communication resources and networks to answer this question. Formalised sources of information such as the library school or health centre were not considered and thus were not significant to answering this assignment.

The second assignment asked this year's students to "Determine the type of non-cultural information (i.e., any information that is not from Papua New Guinea or the Solomn Islands) that was being used by these two countries". The same eight criteria, i.e. technology, social, economic, political, cultural, occupational, history and spatial, were used to identify information related to them that were being used in both countries. For each criterion, students were able to identify information, not originally from within Papua New Guinea or the Solomon Islands that was being used in and by both countries. For technology, students identified the computer, online for Internet and e-mail access, and off-line for CD-ROM and word processing use; satellite and cable communications, telephones, mobile phones; radio and television, as being non-indigenous in both Papua New Guinea and the Solomon Islands. Radio and television could not be used to communicate private, i.e. confidential information unless it was in a coded format. A minority of students, which includes librarianship students in the three years of the course being taught, identified libraries as repositories; books, journals etc. in libraries and newspapers as sources of information. These information and communication technologies helped in communicating outside technological, social, economic, political, historical and cultural information in the two countries. This information helped to create new jobs such as social workers, economists, politicians in a non-traditional parliamentary system, computer workers, teachers, and librarians, doctors and lawyers.

The computer networks, television and newspapers particularly narrowed the spatial divide in Papua New Guinea and the Solomon Islands. However, it widened the digital divide between those who had access to computer, telephone and television facilities and those who did not.

Students agreed that despite the geographical/spatial locations of both the Solomon Islands and Papua New Guinea, both countries were recipients of all types of information that was not originally from within the countries. The evidence from the two assignments using eight criteria suggested very strongly that both Papua New Guinea and the Solomon Islands are information societies, whether it is within a community dealing with village issues or a nation dealing with national and international issues.

Relevance of Information Literacy for the PNG Information Society

The significance of Papua New Guinea as an information society paves the way for the question two: "What is Information Literacy and its relevance for Papua New Guinea as a society?" My grassroots definition of "information literacy" can be written as "when you hear, see, feel, touch and taste something and you react either negatively or positively to these sensations to meet a particular need". In an orally oriented society such as Papua New Guinea, this grassroots definition is adequate although it must be complemented with the most common definition found in the literature, namely "the ability to locate, process and use information effectively and purposefully". (Doyle, 1994; Browne, 1986; Kirk, Poston-Anderson and Yerbury, 1990; Brevik, 1992 and Todd, 1995)

The significance of Papua New Guinea being an information society is dependent on it also being an information literate society. This means that Papua New Guinea must be literate in all forms of literacy whether it is oral, visual, computer, technological, or functional. It also means that a person must have the skills to read and write and understand that particular language used for communication purposes.

Various models and standards for information literacy have been developed. For our purposes, in the Information Literacy classes, the Big6Model by Eisenberg and Berkowitz and the January 18, 2000 ACRL Information Literacy Competency Standards for Higher Education were used. Three ACRL standards were stressed: information literacy, independent learning and being socially responsible with information. The Big6Model, including task definition, identification, location, use, synthesis and evaluation, was used for its simplicity to help achieve the three standards.

As a pre-test to idenntify their information literacy skills, students in the first year course on Information Literacy were asked to locate "A code for etics" for the profession they hoped to enter after graduating. Of the forty students in the class this year, at least five students used the library as their first port of call. The rest asked freinds, lecturers, searched their rooms, and senior students in the same disciplines to assist them. The library search skills of this year's students do not differ from the 200 and 2001 students.

Students this year were given two assignments based on research using oral sources of information and on library-based research using the Big6Model. The aim of these assignments was to see whether or not the Mig6Model could be used for oral based research as well as library-based research. In the oral based research students were able to identify and locate information, how to use, synthesise and evaluate information that posed problems. The question asked, "Using oral based research, identify an area of cultural interest that you would like to know more about", e.g., on brideprice, land entitlement, fishing techniques, grass-skirt making, etc.

The library based research posed a few problems, although students were able to identify and define their task. They were not able to locate, use, synthesise and evaluate information that created problems. Perhaps, this was due to the fact that students did not have adequate library use knowledge and skills that included computer use, identifying bibliographical details of a book and using them correctly, and use of reference sources.

I had assumed in my first year of teaching information literacy that students would have this knowledge and skills before coming to the university but was proved wrong. As a remedy, major types and sources of information were included in the course outline for years 2001 and 2002 for Information Literacy. Other problems emerged: their English language reading and writing skills to enhance the standards of information literacy and independent learning skills, acknowledgement of intellectual property of others and plagiarism for the standard of social responsibility. As a linear model, following the Big6Model was not a problem. The problem, however, lay in transferring this research model to other courses. This became evident when these same students taking the Information Society course in year two were not following any research method, let alone the Big6Model! Readings placed on Library reserve as background information were not often referred to unless students were informed they would be used in the examination. Perhaps, a retrospective look at the background of information use and information literacy in Papua New Guinea is necessary to understand the situation at the University.

In a 1998 article, I argued that for Papua New Guinea to become an information literate society at least six factors "seem to influence the role of libraries and librarians as agents for information literacy in the country":

1. The information knowledge base of the LIS professionals

2. The library systems and services

3. Government and non-government support

4. Communication and information infrastructure

5. The library and information professionals

6. The social, cultural and economic environment.

Three of these: library systems and services and communication, information infrastructure, and government and non-government support, need some explanation to undertsnad the inadequate information literacy skills at the University of Papua New Guinea. Firstly, even after almost twenty-seven years of national independence, library systems and services still cannot adequately meet the information needs, even though we have found that there is an abundant supply of information in the country. The problem is perhaps in the inadequate funding, logistical and sustainable support, moral and attitudinal support for library systems and services by all concerned, i.e., library and information workers and government and non-government decision-makers in library services.

Schools at all levels, with the exception of private schools, do not have adequate library and information resources. In most cases, schools are without librarians and library resources. The worst is the situation in elementary and community/ primary schools where independent literacy should be established.

Lack of good, systematic library and information services is a challenge to all students, who go through the educational system, entering the university education with insufficient library and research skills – not any fault of theirs. The current government has not provided for an adequate library and information services infrastructure for them to utilise. Most of these students have depended on class texts and lectures and notes to see them through to the university level.

Students in both the Information Society and Information Literacy classes have information literacy skills with oral based research skills using the first two and, perhaps to some extent, the third step, locating of sources, using the Big6Model. Even then, using, synthesizing, evaluating and writing information correctly is still a challenge. Students have tried to sustain these new knowledges through difficult circumstances, which also place a strain on them when they graduate from the university, because they will still be exposed to inadequate public library services. However, they have used a good library service at the university level and would have been exposed to a wider knowledge base of information sources and how to access these sources both nationally and internationally.

Women Information Professionals. Being information literate is relevant and necessary to perpetuate an information society. These new graduate are the information professionals who will perpetuate the new society.. Among them are women information professionals. What is the role of women as information professionals participating in a democratic Papua New Guinea Society? Though female student numbers (see Table 3) are low, they are significant in that they reveal that women are exposed to how to identify and use information and to their role as information professionals. In my classes, I didn't differentiate between male and females roles as I saw them all as potential information professionals. As part of their final assessment in exams students were asked, "What do you see your role as an information professional in the information society" in the Information Society class and "What do you see your role as an information professional in enhancing information literacy" in the Information Literacy class. The purpose of these questions was to assess for knowledge acquired in these classes about the role of information professional and whether or not each student saw himself or herself as a potential information professional.

Most students wrote that they did not know that they would become information professional. They identified librarians and journalists as information professionals but not social workers, geologists, microbiologists and chemists. For each course two principles of the Constitution of Papua New Guinea were emphasised: integral human development and equal participation. Issues relating to women as information professionals were presented and discussed in class. For example, there were mothers and married women in both courses for three years. Mothers had babysitting and spouse problems but these didn't hinder studies. Student fathers almost never were faced with "housekeeping" duties compared to student mothers. Of 110 female students, the husbands of 2 women would constantly phone or write to say that his wife could not attend classes. One female student frequently reported that her husband had to do babysitting instead of going to work so that she could attend classes. Because their role was addressed in the constitutional context of the integral human development and equal participation, the issue of gender was given cursory attention.

Table 3.. UNPG Students in Information Literacy and Information Society from 2000–2002

Course	Year 2000	Year 2001	Year 2002	Total
*37.1000/39.2254 Information Literacy	16/40	4/ 23	33/81	63/144
*37.2000/39.2251 Information Society	21/85	21/45	15/ 40	57 /170
	37/ 125	25/68	48/ 121	110/314

NB. The number of female students is in **bold.**

Most women did see their role as faciliatory, mediatory and as en educator. Women students stressed the educator role especially for the subject areas they were going into. The biochemistry, microbiology and environment studies female students felt that because they were venturing into male dominated areas, they felt very strongly that awareness was a priority area for their work. Whatever role women play in the profession they take up, women are all information professionals as mothers, microbiologists, librarians, journalists, geologists, etc. Each and every role that they play is vital to enhancing either Papua New Guinea or the Solomon Islands as an information society. Integral to this is the maintenance of an information literacy environment.

Conclusion

Whilst libraries have not played an important role in the education and social life of the students in courses on Information Society and Information Literacy, these students now have been exposed to both these courses. As information professionals, men and women, they now have the knowledge, skills and attitudes to be responsible citizens in using information effectively and purposefully in Papua New Guinea and the Solomon Island societies.

References

Association of College and Research Libraries (ACRL) Board, January 18, 2000. Approved the Information Literacy Competency Standards for Higher Education Standards, Performance Indicators, and Outcomes.

Brevik, P.S. Information Literacy: what's it all about. In The Information Literacy: the Australian Agenda. Proceedings of conference conducted by the University of South Australia Library held at Adelaide College of TAFE 2-4 December, 1992, pp. 6-8.

Browne, M. Disciplinary Study in Information Science: a foundation for the education of information professionals. Education for Information, 4, 1986, pp. 305-318.

Cronin, Blaise. The information society. Aslib Proceedings, 38(4), 1986, pp. 121-129.

Doyle, C.S. Information literacy in an information society: a concept for an information age. Syracuse University, 1994, pp. 53-78.

Eisenberg, Michael B. and Berkowitz, Robert E. Curriculum initiative: an agenda and strategy for library media programs. Ablex, 1988.

Feather, John. The Information Society – a study of continuity and change. London: Library Association Publishing, 1994.

Kirk, J., Poston-Anderson, B. and Yerbury, H. Into the 21st century library and information services in schools. Australian Library and Information Association, 1990.

Martin, William J. The global information society. AslibGower, 1995.

Martin, Willaim J. The information society. Aslib, 1988.

Obi, Margaret J.P. LIS Professionals as agents for information literacy: a new perspective for Papua New Guinea? Libri 48(3), 1998, pp. 131-139.

Todd, R.J. Information literacy: philosophy, principles, and practice. School Libraries Worldwide 1, 1995, pp. 54-68.

Webster, Frank. What information society? The Information Society 10, 1994, pp. 1-23.

(Editor's note: *Course descriptions available on IFLANET and from the Author.*)

INFORMATION USE IN GENDER AND DEVELOPMENT:
A STUDY OF BEHAVIORAL PATTERN

Rochna Srivastava

Head, Department of Library and Information Science

Isabella Thoburn College

Lucknow, India (2002)

Abstract

Need of assesing reading habits in the field of Women's Studies was felt due to tremendous expansion in research and action, its wide scope and multidisciplinary nature resulting into information explosion. Moreover, in the field of Women's Studies, categories of usersand their needs are different at different levels. Information needs of researchers on women's issues are different from that of women workers working at grass root level in remote areas. This study aims at investigating personal reading habits of those working in the field of Women's Studies and at determining the use pattern of documentary sources of information. It also aims at finding behavioral pattern of those engaged in research work, teaching or social action work in this field. Structured interview method is used for collecting data. The respondents selected for this study are faculty members, post-graduate students as well as those working in non-governmental organizations.

Introduction

The progress of any subject is impeded unless new knowledge generated by research flows freely, quickly and timely among the user community. An information system, therefore, must bring into attention the newly generated information to the users as soon as it is generated because nascent information by its very nature is perishable. Assessment of reading habits of its users is an important task of any efficient information retrieval system so that information needs of its users may be identified and the information available in different types of formats and through a variety of channels may be provided to the users.

Reading habits of scholars in any field depend both on their personal characteristics as well as characteristics of specialty in which they work. Though personal characteristics of scholars is one of the important factors which contributes towards reading habits, but subject characteristics also have definite impact on reading habits of scholars in any field. It has been noticed that the more interdisciplinary the subject studied, the more scattered is its literature and therefore, the larger is the amount of material to be examined in order to keep abreast of recent developments. It is because of this reason, any person working in any interdisciplinary field has to read more.

The amount of reading done by scholars have wide variations. While some of them may be highly literature oriented others may not. The amount of reading varies substantially not only among the persons working in different disciplines but also among those working in the same discipline. The factors responsible for such variations have been identified as education, research experience, age, motivation, intelligence and persistence. But age and seniority have more influence on the reading habits than other characteristics. Many surveys have revealed the fact that the older scientists make less use of literature than the younger ones.

Need of Assessing Reading Habits and Information Use in the Field of Women's Studies (WS)

In a field like Women's Studies (WS), where tremendous expansion in research and action is taking place for women's development resulting into information explosion, it becomes more important to improve dissemination of information and to design an effective system to control and organize the information. A substantial quality of information, generated in this field as the subject, has very wide scope because of its multidisciplinary, interdisciplinary, cross-cultural and inter-regional nature. Moreover, information requirements are voluminous and of a very diverse nature. Users, their categories and information needs are different at different levels. Information needs of researchers on women's issues are different from that of women workers working at the grass root level in remote areas. Not only this but information comes in a wide range of physical forms.

A majority of information in this field is available in the form of "grey literature" or "fugitive literature" which are not available through the traditional book trade channels. One important difference, between resources used in WS and many other subjects, is that WS has its roots both in scholarship and activism or the efforts of individuals and organizations to expand opportunities to women and bring about equity between genders. We, therefore, need to have a more complete understanding of the weaknesses and the strengths of the information channels used by scholars / activists in the field of WS so that unfulfilled or inadequate needs of users of information may be identified and most preferred channels of information in the field of WS may be noticed.

Objectives

The present study was undertaken to fulfill the following objectives:

- To investigate the personal reading habits of scholars / activists in the field of WS.

- To determine the use pattern of documentary sources of information in WS.

- To identify various sources of information used by those engaged in research work, teaching or social action work in the field of WS in India.

Scope

1. This study will help NGOs / Institutions in the field of WS in better "Collection Development" of their libraries on the basis of information use pattern.

2. The present study will make librarians / information scientists aware of the reading habits of those working in the field of WS. This will help them in catering to their information needs in a better way.

3. This study may also help in proportional allocation of funds in the libraries on the basis of use pattern of documentary sources.

4. With the help of this study:

   a) Journals may be subscribed in terms of their relative use.

   b) Acquisition policy of the centre may be formulated on the basis of their preferences of documentary sources of information.

   c) Services of the libraries / information centre may be improved and can be managed in a better way.

d) A large-scale national study in India can be suggested on the basis of the findings of this study.

e) Local networks on the focused subject may be established for the proper dissemination of information.

Methodology

For conducting survey the investigator used "Questionnaire Method". It was also thought proper to interview a few respondents so as to cross check the responses received through questionnaire. In order to ensure consistency in the organization of data and comparability in the findings, structured interview was preferred. The respondents selected for this study were Post-Graduate students of WS/ Teachers as well as those working in various Non Government Organizations of the country. Thus, information use pattern of both scholars and of field workers has been taken care of in the present study.

Break-up of Respondents

Out of total respondents (280), Social Action Group (SAG) constituted the majority (42.86%), followed by Faculty Members (FM) (31.43%) and post-graduate students of WS (25.71%). As is evident from Table 1 all FM and students belonged to five prestigious institutions of India in the field of WS, whereas, respondents of SAG group were taken from 24 NGOs of the country. (Appendix 1)

Table 1 Institution and Category-wise break-up of respondents

CATEGORIES OF USERS
INSTITUTIONS

	FM		STUDENTS		SAG		TOTAL	
	No.	%	No.	%	No.	%	No.	%
ITC, Lucknow	44	50	27	37.5	–	–	71	25.36
Depts. Of WS, Lucknow University	26	29.55	26	36.11	–	–	52	18.57
SNDT Univ., Mumbai	5	5.68	12	16.67	–	–	17	6.07
Jadavpur Univ., Kolkata	5	5.68	7	9.72	–	–	12	4.29
CWDS, New Delhi	8	9.09	–	–	4	3.33	12	4.29
NGOs (List of 24 NGOs attached)	–	–	–	–	166	96.67	116	41.42
TOTAL	88	100	72	100	120	100	280	100
	88	31.43	72	25.71	120	42.86	280	100

AGE OF RESPONDENTS

Age-wise breakup of respondents shows that FM were older than students and SAG.

SEX OF RESPONDENTS

Appreciable number of males was found to be present when they were analyzed according to their sex. This shows that not only females but also males are becoming sensitive towards women related issues.

MEMBERSHIPS OF PROFESSIONAL BODIES / SOCIETIES

Table 2 shows that more seniors were members of professional bodies than the junior ones. This indicates that professionalism increases with age and experience. A healthy trend was noticed in this study that appreciably higher numbers of FM were found to be the members of international professional bodies.

(Editor's note: *Tables 2 to 20 are available on IFLANET Conference proceedings 2002 and from the Author.*)

CONFERENCES / SEMINARS ATTENDED

It is clear from Table 3 that appreciably higher number of respondents (94.29%) attended conferences or workshops. Further, more number of FM attended international and national conferences than students and SAG, attending more regional or local conferences.

TYPE OF PUBLICATIONS

Table 4 shows that majority of respondents (51.43%) published articles in the journals as compared to research works published by 42.86% respondents. As was expected, more SAG published reports because the kind of work they do was project oriented for which they were required to submit a report.

PERSONAL SUBSCRIPTION OF PERIODICALS

It was pleasing to note that a good number of respondents 54.29% were found to be subscribing to periodicals on WS. As is evident from Table 5, more number of FM subscribed periodicals than other categories of respondents. This again confirms the findings of other surveys that type of work and seniority has impact on personal subscription habits of scientists.

Out of 54.29% respondents subscribing to periodicals, all of them were found to be subscribing to Indian journals.

WAYS FOR KEEPING ABREAST OF LATEST DEVELOPMENTS

The present study reflects that scanning of current issues of periodicals and participation in seminars / workshops are the most dominating ways for keeping abreast of latest developments in the field of WS (Table 6).

PREFERRED CHANNELS OF INFORMATION

The present study reveals that libraries are the most preferred channel of information amongst scholars in WS as they are mostly dependent on libraries of either their institution or any other library for getting desired information (Table 7). It is also interesting to note that use of informal channel of information such as taking help of teacher/friend/colleague is also one of the frequently used and popular methods for getting desired information in the field of WS.

FREQUENCY OF VISITS TO INSTITUTION'S LIBRARY

This study confirms the findings of many reading habits' surveys that older scientists make less use of literature and are less frequent visitor of the library than the younger ones. While majority of students and SAG visit their institution's library daily, most of the FM use library only twice a week. (Table 8)

AVERAGE TIME SPENT ON EACH LIBRARY VISIT

It is also found in this study that approximately 50% scholars in the field of WS spent between 1 to 5 hours in the library during each visit (Table 9). It is interesting to note that though the FM were less frequent visitors of the library but, they were found to be spending more time during each visit.

PURPOSE OF VISITING THE LIBRARY

While inquiring about the purpose of visiting the library, it was found that most of the students visit the library for obtaining information for writing a paper, whereas, maximum number of SAG visit library for background material needed for preparing a proposal for a new project (Table 10). FM visit the library for varying purposes.

RELEVANCE OF INFORMATION OBTAINED FROM LIBRARIES

It was also noticed in this study that substantially higher number of scholars in WS get desired information from their own library (Table 11). While most of the FM and SAG are capable of locating desired information from their respective libraries, maximum number of students is seldom successful and hence they take the help of other libraries also. FM and SAG also used libraries of other than their own institute at the time of need. (Table 12) The reason for the students not getting the desired information from only one library may be the lack of syllabus oriented reading material in this newly emerged field.

LIBRARIES USEFUL IN THE FIELD OF WOMEN'S STUDIES (WS)

One of the most important findings of this study is that it identifies most preferred libraries being frequently used by the scholars of WS in the country. Appendix 2 shows list of such libraries in India in order of preference.

SOURCES OF INFORMATION USED

This study reflects that journals/newsletter/bulletins, dictionaries/thesaurus, directories, handbooks, statistical sources, theses/dissertations, books/monographs and government publications are the most preferred sources of information in WS. (Table 13) While all the FM make use of all these sources of information, students and SAG prefer journals/ newsletter/ bulletins, dictionaries/thesaurus, directories and statistical sources only. This may reflect that seniors and more experienced persons in the field of WS make use of variety of sources than the younger ones.

USE OF GOVERNMENT PUBLICATIONS

Government publications are substantially used documents in the field of WS. More number of FM use these publication than other categories of respondents. It is also noticed that committees and commissions reports and policy documents are the most preferred type of Government publications in WS (table 14). It may be because of the fact that committees /commission reports and policy documents on women issues contain firsthand information on that particular issue for which they are constituted and hence are most sought.

Majority of the respondents (71.43%) indicated that they come to know about the existence of Government Publications through Reviews given in journals/ newspapers (Table 15). It is happy to note that the scholars of WS also use personal contacts for getting information about the existence of government publications, which is a very healthy pattern. A list of most used government publications in the field of WS in the country was also prepared on the basis of respondents' preferences for the same. (Appendix 3)

Table 16 indicates that all categories of respondents come to know about the forthcoming conferences through personal means, bulletin / newsletters etc. FM and SAG were found to be more professional as they make more use of newsletters.

Legal rights of and the offences relating to women and their legal remedies is one of the thrust areas in the filed of WS. It was therefore, necessary to determine the pattern and use of legal sources by the scholars/activists in the field of WS. It was noticed that FM and SAG make use of legal sources of information substantially (Table 17). While FM and SAG use all type of legal sources – bare acts and statutes, commentaries an acts and statutes and law reports containing case laws equally, students use only bare acts and law reports (Table 18) for locating a particular legal provision or case law on any point. Secondary publications such as digests of case laws were found to be popular among most of the respondents. Besides, commentaries on specific laws or help of lawyers were also found to be the main sources of locating a particular legal provision or case law (Table 19). Newspapers were found to be the chief source of information regarding new legislation/amendments (Table 20).

MOST PREFERRED PERIODICALS IN THE FIELD OF WS

A list of frequently used periodicals in order of preference has also been derived (Appendix 4) in this study on the basis of preferences of periodical given by the respondents. It was happy to note that periodicals published by NGOs occupied very high ranks in this list. "Manushi", "Chetna News", "Mahila Samakhya Newsletter", "Sahbhagi

Ki Chitthi", "Roshni", "Nari Samvad", "Kurushetra" and "Saheli" published by NGOs find place in the list of frequently used periodicals derived in this study.

All this reflects that NGOs are doing very good work in the field of WS and are brining out useful publications in the form of periodicals or otherwise. A glance through Appendix 4 also reflects the multidisciplinary nature of WS as the periodicals pertaining to the field of sociology, law, health, economics, social sciences, political science etc. do appear in this list.

INDEXING / ABSTRACTING SOURCES AND SERVICES

In WS, with a few exceptions, comprehensive secondary services are almost non-existent. Two indexing sources, namely, 'Guide to Women's Studies' and 'Women Studies Index' brought out by SNDT Women's University, Mumbai were found to be heavily used by the users. Besides, two in-house current awareness bulletins of Jadavpur University, Kolkata and Center for Women's Development Studies, New Delhi, were also found to be used on topics such as rape, dowry, violence against women etc. Appendix 5 reflects some indexing and abstracting sources and services used in WS.

BIBLIOGRAPHICAL SOURCES AND SERVICES

The present study indicates a shift from general to thematic and subject bibliographies. It was found that with the development and expansion of WS, the need for focused and thematic bibliographies increased. Most of the bibliographies found to be used were in English language. However, few bibliographies in other regional languages were also found to be used. Bibliographic services as mentioned by the respondents were those brought out by documentation centers/libraries. Some of them are of: SNDT Women's University Library, Mumbai, National Social Science Documentation Center (NASSDOC), New Delhi, and National Library, Calcutta. "Bibliographic Reprints: Women" in two parts brought out by NASSDOC was also found useful as was indicated by few respondents.

DICTIONARIES / THESAURI

The present study establishes dictionaries/thesauri as an important source of information in the field of WS as all the respondents use them. Unfortunately, none of the dictionaries/thesauri used was of Indian origin. This is due to the fact that no comprehensive dictionary / thesauri on WS is published from India. (Appendix 6)

DIRECTORIES

It is noticed that all the respondents use directories in order to know who is doing what and where in the field of WS. Most of the directories used by them were found to be of Indian origin. The reason being that quite a few directories indicating training institutes in WS, Women's originations and institutions for women in India have been brought out in recent years.

Moreover, scholars/activists working in this field find Indian information more relevant than global information. A list of frequently used directories in order of preference is given in Appendix 7.

HAND BOOKS AND RESOURCE GUIDES

Handbooks and resource guides were used only by 92.14% of respondents. It is interesting to note that not only Indian but International handbook and resource guides published from other countries were also found to be used. Appendix 8 reveals the most used handbook/ resource guides in the field of WS.

BIOGRAPHICAL SOURCES

Most of the respondents indicated that they use biographical sources to find out the contributions made and positions held of the biographed person. It was also revealed that international sources were found inadequate for not covering the biographies of Indians adequately, whereas, Indian sources were found to be inadequate for less prominent Indian personalities. A list of frequently used biographical sources in the field of WS is given in order of preference. (Appendix 9)

STATISTICAL RESOURCES

The present study reveals that statistical resources are frequently used sources in the field of WS. Nature of job is seen to be influencing the use of these sources. While FM use these resources to support their teaching and learning, activist group use them for their research activities and to expand opportunities to women and to bring about equity between genders. It was happy to note that the respondents use both national as well as international statistical resources as is evident from Appendix 10.

THESES AND DISSERTATION

Table 21 Use of Theses / Dissertations

Categories	Yes		No		Total	
	No.	%	No.	%	No.	%
FM (88)	88	100	–	–	88	100
Students (72)	70	97.22	2	2.78	72	100
SAG (120)	93	77.5	27	22.5	20	100
Total (280)	251	89.64	29	10.36	280	100

Table 21 shows that appreciably higher number of respondents in the field of WS makes use of theses/dissertations as sources of information. More use of these sources by FM and students may be because of the reason that their work is more academic and theses/dissertations are more suitable for their information needs. When asked about sources of getting information about theses and dissertations, majority of respondents quoted two important publications brought out by the Association of Indian Universities, whereas, quite a few responded that they get information about theses/ dissertations from teachers/friends/colleagues. (Appendix 11)

RESOURCES ON THE NET

The present study also indicates the substantial use of Internet resources in the field of WS. These women's studies resources included databases, e-journals, reports, discussions, curricula, reading lists, information "brochures" etc. available on the Net. Information centers, bookshops, publishers, universities, directories were also found to be used by the respondents.

Most of the e-journals used by the respondents were free or partially free journals. While "Aviva" (http://www.aviva.org/); "Advancing women in Leadership" (http://www.advancingwomen.com/awl.html) were the journals freely available, "Feminist Studies" etc. are partially free journals used by the respondents. Another important site, which was mentioned, by most of the respondents was (http://www.sosig.ac.uk/subjects/feminism.html). This freely available Internet service aiming at selecting high quality Internet information for students, academics, researchers and practitioners in the social sciences, business and law is a part of the UK Resource Discovery Network SAWNET (South Asian Women's Network) (http://www.umiacs.umd.edu/users/sawweb/sawnet/) was found to be used by majority of the respondents as it covers India also. This site was useful for reviews, news about south Asian women, legal issues, bookshelf, domestic violence, south Asian women's organization, home page of SAWNET members, divorce, health, career, grants and funding.

FeMiNa (http://www.femina.com) providing respondents with a comprehensive searchable directory of links to female friendly sites and information on the web is also worth mentioning.

National Organization for Women (NOW) (http://now.org/now/home.html) the largest organization of feminist activities in the U. S. having 500,000 contributing members and 550 chapters in all 50 states was found useful for new releases, legislative updates and NOW Times action alerts. Another site mentioned was The UN Internet Gateway on the Advancement and Empowerment of women (http://www.un.org/womenwatch). Few sites of international organizations, national bodies and of women's organizations proved to be rich sources for the users working on women related issues. For example reports of International Labor Organization, UNICEF, Govt. of India's ninth plan, University Grants Commission, India etc. On line databases like Gender (http://www.uni-koeln.de) and library data bases of women's studies' centers providing information about their catalogues, conferences, courses, topical bibliographies were also mentioned by the users. For example SNDT Women's University Library, Mumbai, Center for Women's Development Studies, New Delhi, Madras

Institute of Development Studies, Chennai, International Center for Research on Women, New Delhi etc. Besides these, some sites of Indian NGOs were also used by majority of respondents. They are: Single Women's Organization, Ahmedabad; Joint Women's Programme, Bangalore; Streelekha, Mumbai; Maitree, Kolkata; The Center for Feminist Legal Research, New Delhi; IFSHA, Kali and WISCOMP (Women in Security Conflict Management and Peace), New Delhi; Research Institute for Women, Goa.

FINDINGS

1. The present study reveals that factors like age, seniority and nature of job influence the reading habits of those working in the field of WS. Further, not only females but also males are becoming sensitive towards women related issues.

2. It is noticed that more seniors are members of professional bodies than the junior ones indicating that professionalism increases with age and experience. Appreciably higher number of FM is found to be the members of international professional bodies.

3. Majority of respondents attended conferences / workshops but it is interesting to note that seniority and designation have impact on the type of conferences attended.

4. Another important finding is that Activist group publish more reports than students and FM because of their project oriented work where they are required to submit a report at the end of the project, whereas, FM publish more number of articles in the journals of WS.

5. More than half of the respondents are found to be subscribing to only Indian journals. Factors like seniority and age influence their journal subscription habits also.

6. The present study reveals that scholars in the field of WS are mostly dependent on libraries of either their institution or any other library for getting desired information.

7. This study confirms the findings of many reading habits' surveys that older scientist make less use of literature and are less frequent visitors of their libraries. It is interesting to note that though the FM were less visitors of the library, they are found to be spending more time during each visit than others. Purpose of visiting the library differs according to categories of respondents.

8. One of the most important findings of this study is that it identifies a number of libraries, which are being frequently used by the scholars of WS in the country and hence it may be presumed that these libraries contain useful collection on women related issues.. The 5 important libraries identified by respondents are:

> National Library, Kolkata
>
> Asiatic Library, Mumbai
>
> SNDT Women's University Library, Mumbai
>
> Center for Women's Development Studies, New Delhi (CWDS)
>
> National Social Science Documentation Center, New Delhi (NASSDOC)

9. This study reflects that periodicals/newsletters/bulletins; directories; dictionaries/ thesaurus; statistical resources; handbooks/resource guides and books/monographs are most preferred sources of information in WS.

10. Though Internet resources are used by only 48.57% of respondents, they are found to be very useful for getting latest information on women related issues. Comparatively lesser use of Internet resources shows that the intrinsic value of information channels depends mainly on its accessibility.

11. Nature of job is seen to be influencing the usage of documentary sources of information.

12. Use of indexing/ abstracting services in the field of WS is found to be very low (40%). This is due to non-availability of any comprehensive abstracting service on WS published

from India. Various multidisciplinary and interdisciplinary indexing services available in the country were also used for the topics like rape, dowry, violence against women etc.

13. Journals published from NGOs occupied higher ranks in the list of most preferred journals of WS. Not only this but periodicals pertaining to the fields of sociology, law, health, economics, political science etc. did appear in the list of frequently used periodicals reflecting multidisciplinary nature of WS.

14. Another important finding of the present study is that primary periodicals published from India are more preferred by the scholars as compared to other international journals. Heavy reliance on Indian journals shows that scholars of WS find Indian information and coverage more relevant for their work rather than global information.

15. Appreciably higher percentage of users (98.57%) use statistical sources, which shows that statistical data plays a very important role in effective measurement and monitoring of the status of women but at the same time majority of respondents complained of nonavailability of up-to-date and meaningful Indian data due to various limitations of data collecting agencies. It is happy to note that those working in the field of WS in India are using both national and international statistical resources. FM where use these resources to support their teaching and learning, activist group use them for their research activities and to expand opportunities to women and to bring about equity between genders.

16. This study also indicates a shift from general to thematic and subject bibliographies. It is found that with the development and expansion of WS, the need for focused and thematic bibliographies increased. Most of the bibliographies found to be used are in English language, however, few bibliographies in other regional languages are also found to be used.

17. It is surprising to note that though all the respondents use dictionaries/thesauri, none of them is of Indian origin. It is due to the fact that no comprehensive dictionary/thesauri in WS is published from India.

18. On the contrary, respondents preferred Indian directories indicating Indian training institutions in WS, women's organizations and institutions for women in India as they find Indian information more relevant.

19. Biographical sources used are those of India, Asia and the Pacific. They use biographical sources to find out the contributions made and positions held of the biographee. Indian biographical sources, as mentioned by the respondents are found to be inadequate as they do not cover less prominent personalities, whereas, international biographical sources are found to be inadequate for not covering Indian personalities adequately.

20. Books/ monographs are found to be used by majority of respondents as they are published commercially. As the book trade channels in India are well developed and the infrastructure for bibliographical control exists, information published in the form of books presents the least difficulty and are easily available.

21. It is interesting to note that Indian scholars also use not only Indian but International handbooks and resource guides published from other countries.

22. Association of Indian University (AIU) plays a vital role in disseminating information about Indian theses/dissertations submitted to universities of India.

AGENDA FOR THE FUTURE DIRECTION

1. In order to satisfy the information requirements of those working in the field of WS, there is an urgent need for a constant dialogue between the users and the information professionals. This could be done by conducting regular surveys at various levels to assess the information requirements of users.

2. Directories covering human resources and organizations at national/regional and local level should be developed with comprehensive coverage and good mechanism for their updation. Regional centers of WS situated in various parts of the country may take up this task of compiling directories.

3. There is no abstracting service on WS coming out from India so far. Though a few women's studies' centers have started indexing services e.g. CWDS, New Delhi; Jadavpur University, Kolkata and All India Association of Christian Higher Education, New Delhi but it is necessary to initiate such abstracting services covering Indian literature on women related issues.

4. There has been a remarkable increase during the last few decades in the number of institutional and individual efforts made in publishing bibliographies on Indian women but the number of such bibliographies is still limited. Moreover, there is no proper bibliographical control. They are in mimeo form or are usually available directly from the 20 institutions. It is therefore suggested that more systematic efforts should be made in this area and certain standards should be maintained.

5. There is an urgent need to develop comprehensive computerized bibliographic databases covering Indian women literature so as to facilitate easy updating and exchange. Moreover, this database should be made available to concerned institutions.

6. Not only new data bases should be created but also existing sources of information on WS should be analyzed, evaluated and assessed and should be updated keeping in mind researchers' requirements in the field of WS.

7. Due to tremendous increase in the cost of publications and growing demands of users, it has become impossible for a single library to meet the demands and there is a wide gap between their needs and resources. It is therefore, suggested that libraries having resources on WS must resort to more cooperative measures for sharing their resources.

We must transform various loose and scattered library collections into an integrated structure with the help of technology available in the country, which will ensure greater accessibility to resources as well as maximum utilization of available funds.

FURTHER RESEARCH

1. It is suggested that systematic studies of the reading habits and use of literature by those working in the field of WS should be carried out in different geographical areas with different populations to get an overall and complete picture of their reading habits and information and literature use.

2. It is further suggested that separate studies using different variables may be carried out to determine the influence of each variable on the reading habits and use of literature in the field of WS.

APPENDIXES

Appendix – 1

LIST OF RESPONDED NGOs
1. Aastha Sansthan (Rajasthan)
2. All India Women's Conference, Lucknow (UP)
3. Centre for Communication Resource Development, Patna (Bihar)
4. DIOCESAN Social Work Centre, Lucknow (UP)
5. Energy Environment Technology International, Lucknow (UP)
6. Gandhian Institute of Studies, Varanasi (UP)
7. Giri Institute of Development Studies, Lucknow (UP)
8. Gobind Ballabh Pant University of Agriculture (Uttranchal)
9. ICCMRT
10. Institute of Social Studies Trust, New Delhi
11. Madhya Pradesh Institute of Social Science Research, Ujjain (MP)
12. Mahila Samakhya, Lucknow (UP)
13. National Council of Women in India, (UP)
14. NIPCCD, Reginal Centre, Lucknow (UP)
15. NIPCCD, New Delhi
16. Oxfam (India) Trust, Lucknow (UP)
17. Rajasthan Mahila Kalyan Mandal, Ajmer (Rajasthan)
18. Sahbhagi Shikshan Kendra, Lucknow (UP)
19. SSLNT Mahila Mahavidyalaya, Dhanbad (Bihar)
20. SURAKSHA, Lucknow (UP)
21. UNICEF, Lucknow (UP)
22. UNIFEM, New Delhi
23. UP Council for Child welfare, Lucknow (UP)
24. Uttar Pradesh Voluntary Action Network (UPVAN), Lucknow (UP)

Appendix – 2

LIBRARIES USEFUL IN THE FIELD OF WS IN ORDER OF PREFERENCE
1. National Library, Kolkata
2. Asiatic Library, Mumbai
3. SNDT Women's University Library, Mumbai
4. Center for Women's Development Studies, New Delhi
5. National Social Science Documentation Center, New Delhi
6. Institute of Social Studies Trust Library, New Delhi
7. Women's Library, Kolkata
8. Center for Rural Development Library, New Delhi
9. National Council for Educational Research and Training, New Delhi`
10. Indian Institute of Public Administration Library, New Delhi
11. Teen Murti Memorial Library, New Delhi
12. Jawaharlal Nehru University Library, New Delhi
13 Giri Institute of Development Studies, Lucknow

Appendix – 3

LIST OF FREQUENTLY USED GOVERNMENT PUBLICATIONS IN ORDER OF PREFERENCE

1. Policies, Programmes, Schemes, Legislation and Statistics on women. New Delhi. Documentation and Information Center, National Institute of Public Cooperation and Child Development, 1987

2. Committee on Status of women in India. Towards equality. Report of the Committee on Status of women in India. New Delhi. Ministry of Education and Social Welfare, Department of Welfare, 1975

3. Country Paper India: a Draft. Prepared for the 4th World Conference on Women, Beijing, 1995. Government of India, Department of Women and Child Development

4. National Policy on Education, 1986. Chapter 12, Education for women's equality. New Delhi. Ministry of Human Resource Development, Department of Education 1986.

5. Working Group of Social Welfare. New Delhi. Ministry of Social Welfare. 1980

6. National Advisory Committee on study of educational backwardness of girls in selected states. New Delhi. National Council for Educational Research and Training. 1981.

7. National Perspective Plan for Women 1988-2000 A.D. Report of the Core Group set up by the Department of Women and Child Development, Ministry of Human and Resource Development, Govt. of India. New Delhi. 1988

8. National Plan of Action for the SAARC decade of the girl child. 1991-2000 AD. New Delhi. Govt. of India, Ministry of Human Resource Development, Department of Women and Child Development. 1992

9. Working Group set up by the Planning Commission on employment of women. New Delhi. Women's Welfare and Development Bureau, Department of Social Welfare. 1978.

10. Committee on Adult Education Programmes for women. Report. New Delhi. Ministry of Education and Social Welfare.

Appendix – 4

LIST OF FREQUENTLY USED PERIODICALS IN ORDER OF PREFERENCE

Sr. no./ Name of Periodicals/ Rank

1. Manushi, English, New Delhi 1

2. Indian Journal of Gender Studies, English, New Delhi 2

3. Women's Link, English, New Delhi 2

4. RCWS Newsletter, English, Mumbai 3

5. Bulletin of the CWDS, English, New Delhi 3

6. Chetna News, English, Ahmedabad 4

7. Mahila Samakhya Newsletter, English, Lucknow 5

8. Women's Link Newsletter, English, New Delhi 5

9. School of Women's Studies Newsletter, English, Kolkata 6

10. Sahbhagi Ki Chitthi, Hindi, Lucknow 6

11. Indian Association for WS Newsletter, English, New Delhi 6

12. Asian Journal of Women's Studies, English, Seoul, Korea 6

13. Sakhi Varta, Hindi, Lucknow 7

14. Samajik, English, Pune 7

15. Roshni, Hindi and English, New Delhi 7

16. Women's Era, English, New Delhi 7

17. National Advocacy Study Centre Bulletin, English 8

18. Femina, English, Mumbai 8

19. Society, English, Mumbai 8

20. New Women, English 8

21. Legal News and Views, English, New Delhi 8

22. Nari Samvad, Hindi 8

23. Indian Journal of Sociology, English 8

24. Women's voice, English 8

25. Social Scientists, English 8

26. Kurushetra, English, New Delhi 8

27. Saheli, Hindi, 8

28. Journal of Gender Studies, English, New Delhi 8

29. Frontline, English, Chennai 8

30. Yojna, Hindi, English, New Delhi 8

31. E P W (Economic and Political Weekly), English, Mumbai 8

Appendix – 5

LIST OF FREQUENTLY USED INDEXING / ABSTRACTING SOURCES AND SERVICES IN ORDER OF PREFERENCE

1. Guide to Women's Studies, 1986: an index to select international journal, SNDT Women's University, Mumbai, 1988

2. Women's Studies Index, 1986: a guide to Indian periodical literature, SNDT Women's University Library, 1987

3. Women's Studies: a current awareness bulletin, Jadavpur University Library, Kolkata

4. CWDS Library Documentation Bulletin, Center for Women's Development, New Delhi

5. Guide to Indian Periodical Literature, Indian Documentation Services, Gurgaon, 1964

6. Sociological Literature South Asia 1992 / edited by T K Oommen & P K Jaiswal, New Delhi: SLSA Publication, 1993

7. Critical Review of Researches in Women's Studies 1975-1988, SNDT Women's University, Mumbai, 1989

8. Review of Researches in Women's Studies, Faculty of Home Science, Department of Child Development, M S University of Baroda, Gujrat, 1987

Appendix – 6

LIST OF FREQUENTLY USED DICTIONARIES / THESAURI IN ORDER OF PREFERENCE

1. Harlow: Longman, 1989

2. Women's Thesaurus: an index of language used to describe and locate information by and about women / edited by Mary Ellen, New York: Harper & Row, 1987

3. Women World: A dictionary of world about women / by Jane Mills, Women in Development Thesaurus / edited by Zurniaty Nasrul… [et. al.] Djakarta: Indonesian Institute of Science Center for Scientific Documentation and Information, 1991

4. A Feminist Dictionary / edited by Cheris Kramarae and Paula Treichler, London: Pandora, 1985

Appendix – 7

LIST OF FREQUENTLY USED DIRECTORIES IN ORDER OF PREFERENCE

1. Women's Studies in Indian Universities, 1984-89: A directory of UGC supported centers / cells, Mumbai: SNDT Women's University, 1990

2. Directory of Women's Organizations, Mumbai, SNDT Women's University, 1990

3. Directory of Women's Studies in India, Delhi: Association of Indian University, 1991

4. Directory of Training Institutions dealing with Women's Training, New Delhi: National Institute of Public Cooperation and Child Development, 1990

5. Women's Studies In India: a directory of Research Institutions/ compiled by Gulnaz A Khan and edited by S V Ramani Rao, New Delhi: Ashish, 1993

6. Women's Studies in India: A directory/ compiled by Suchitra Anant, S V Ramani Rao and Shikha Goel, New Delhi: Institute of Social Studies Trust, 1986

7. List of Voluntary Organizations working for the development / welfare of women/ prepared by National Commission for Women, New Delhi

8. Directories of training Institutions dealing with women's training, New Delhi: Jawaharlal Nehru University, Adult Continuing Education and Extension Unit, 1990

Appendix – 8

LIST OF FREQUENTLY USED HANDBOOKS AND RESOURCE GUIDES

IN ORDER OF PREFERENCE

1. Schemes for rural development scope for women: A handbook, New Delhi: UNICEF, 1982

2. Training schemes for women in the Government of India, New Delhi, National Institute of Public Cooperation and Child Development, Women's Development Division, 1989

3. Women's Studies In India: Information Sources, Services and programmes/ compiled by Anju Vyas and Sunita Singh, New Delhi: Sage, 1993

4. International Handbook of Women's Studies/ edited by Lou Lou Brown…[et.al.], New York: Harvester Wheatsheaf, 1993

5. Women in Third World: A directory of resources/ compiled and edited by Thomas P. Fenton and Marry J. Herfronn, Maryknoll: Orbis, 1987

6. Women's Studies: A guide to information sources/ Sarch Carter and Maureen Ritchie, London: Manshell, 1990

7. Assistance for women's development from national agencies: development programme, 3 Vol., Mumbai: Popular, 1992

Appendix – 9

LIST OF FREQUENTLY USED BIOGRAPHICAL SOURCES

IN ORDER OF PREFERENCE

1. Who's Who in Women's Studies in India, Mumbai: SNDT Women's University, 1984

2. Who's Who of Indian Women, Chennai: National Biographical Center, 1977

3. Women Social Scientists: Asia Pacific, Bangkok: UNESCO, 1987

4. Directory of Women Experts in Asia and the Pacific, Bangkok: United Nations Economic and Social Commission for Asia and the Pacific, 1987

5. Directory of Indian Women Today, New Delhi: India International, 1997

Appendix –10

LIST OF FREQUENTLY USED STATISTICAL RESOURCES IN ORDER OF PREFERENCE

1. Women in India: A statistical panorama, Prabash P Singh, New Delhi: Inter India, 1990

2. Women in India: A statistical profile, New Delhi: Ministry of Human resource Development, Department of Women and Child Development, 1988

3. Women and Development/ Sheel C Nuna, New Delhi: National Institute of Educational Planning and Administration, 1990

4. The World's Women 1970-1990: Trends and Statistics, New York: United Nations Publications, 1991

5. Handbook of International Data on Women/ Elise Boulding...[et.al.], New York: Wiley, 1976

6. Women in the World: An International Atlas/ Jani Seager and Ann Olson, London: Pluto, 1986

7. Statistics relating to employment and unemployment of women, New Delhi: Planning Commission, 1985

8. The Status of Women: Literacy and Employment/ Ashok Mitra, Mumbai: Allied, 1979

Appendix – 11

LIST OF FREQUENTLY USED DISSERTATION SOURCES IN ORDER OF PREFERENCE

1. Bibliography of Doctoral Dissertations, New Delhi: Association of Indian Universities (AIU)

2. University News, a weekly journal, New Delhi: Association of Indian Universities (AIU)

3. Women's Studies: A bibliography of dissertations 1870-1982, New York: Blackwell, 1985

4. Indian Dissertation Abstracts, New Delhi: Indian Council of Social Science Research, Quarterly

VII. INFORMATION SOCIETY, CULTURE AND ECONOMY: GLOBAL CHALLENGES

INFORMATION AND DOCUMENTATION ON WOMEN: A EUROPEAN NETWORK

Marieke Kramer

Director of Consultancy and Research

International Information Centre and Archives for the Women's Movement (IIAV)

Amsterdam, The Netherlands (1993)

Introduction

This paper is based on a study I carried out, in co-operation with my Danish colleague Jytte Larsen, for the Commission of the European Communities in 1991. The study was a joint venture of the Danish Women's Library (KVINFO), the Interdisciplinary Centre for Women's Studies, and the Dutch International Information Centre and Archives for the Women's Movement (IIAV).

One of the main goals of the IIAV, an information service with an international collection, is to enhance international co-operation and international exchange of information in the field of the position of women. To this purpose – and to the international audience I have today – I would like to take the opportunity to give you some facts about my own centre.

1. International Information Centre and Archives for the Women's Movement (IIAV)

IIAV is the central information service in the Netherlands on the position of women and women's studies. It is also the Dutch focal point for international exchange of information in several European networks.

The history of IIAV goes back to 1935, when the International Archives for the Women's Movement (IAV), emanating from the first women's liberation movement, was founded by three feminist women, who under the slogan "No documents, no history" wanted to establish an international documentation centre and library on all aspects of women's lives. They succeeded in amassing a considerable collection of books, periodicals and archives. However, during the World War II it was moved to Germany where it disappeared. (Part of our archives have been rediscovered, recently, in Moscow.) Only very little had been preserved, but with what was left a new start was made in 1945.

During the second feminist wave, in the 1970s, the need for first-hand, up-to-date information was recognized, which led to the founding of the Information and Docuemntation Centre for the Women's Movement (IDC) and of the journal LOVER which published, and still publishes, in each issue an extensive bibliography. These three organizations formed, in 1988, the basis for the central information service in the Netherlands, the IIAV. Since this merger, the IIAV with its academic library, documentation service and archives functions as the national resource centre on the position of women and women's studies. The IIAV is not only an important source for historical research but functions also as an intermediary latest, most current information and documentation on women's issues. This means that with the help of its catalogues, data bases and reference department the IIAV canprovide answers to queries such as

– the name of a feminist lawyer

– the latest information on women's health care in the Netherlands

– the situation of women's studies in Italy

– statistical data on abortion

– an overview of historical women's journals

– information on women's lives in the 1930s as written by women themselves, etc.

Services for Research and Consultancy. The IIAV provides two services around which its main activities are organized: Information Services, and Consultancy and Research. To give you an idea about the scope of these services, I will give you some statistics:

Collections and data bases include:

– Books and grey literature, 55.000 volumes. IIAV collects both fiction and non-fiction, Dutch and foreign books, covering all aspects of the position of women in the past and at present. The oldest publication has date 1578.

– Periodicals: 575 subscriptions. The current periodicals collection consists of 300 Dutch and 275 foreign titles; 200 of the current titles are being indexed and provided with an abstract.

– Thematic dossiers and newspaper clippings: 70 metres. The dossiers contain, among other things, pamphlets, press releases, clippings from five Dutch daily newspapers, and biographical information on 4000 women.

– Archives of women's organizations and individual women: 400 metres. This collection contains 200 archives from 1870 to the present and reflects the character of the women's movement by form as well as by contents. In addition, it contains a collection of unpublished documents written by 130 women about themselves: diaries, letters and autobiographies.

– Posters, photographs (13.500), slides, postcards. Part of this material is historical. IIAV has also well documented visual materials from the beginning of the second feminist movement to date. This collection is much in demand by the media.

Sources for Information

The records of the above mentioned publications and materials can be found in the IIAV online catalogues. In addition, the following sources of information are accessible:

– A bibliographic data base that contains titles of publications not represented in the collection.

– Ian inventory of current research: a data base of over 2000 project descriptions on Dutch research-in-progress.

– A data base of addresses that provides a "social map" of the women's movement in the Netherlands.

- A diary of events: a current survey of events, conferences, meetings, etc.
- A catalogue of periodical articles from Dutch historical journals.
- An international inventory of women's information and resource centres.

Usage of the IIAV

The centre has more than 7000 users, both Dutch and foreign, every year. Queries are dealt with by mail, telephone and fax, as well as in person at the information desk. There exist another way of keeping up-to-date with information processed by the IIAV: publications. The IIAV publishes several bibliographical journals, a.o. LOVER, a literary review journal with articles on current themes and an extensive bibliography. Other publications are topical lists of literature, guides, and a Dutch newsletter on women's information service.

Structure and Organization

The IIAV is subsidized by the Department of Emancipation Policy of the Ministry of Social Affairs and Employment. Also, it receives grants from the University of Amsterdam and the Ministry of Science. The staff of approximately 30 women working part-time is equivalent of 16 full-time posts.

2. Consultancy and Research

The second goal of the IIAV is to stimulate expertise and professionalim in the fiel od documentation and information on women, to stimulate exhange of knowledge and experience, and to enhance national and international co-operation. The IIAV also adbises on the development and management of women's collections and organizes courses and workshops.

On the national scale, there are projects together with other Dutch women's libraies, both regional and specialized, and with Dutch public libraries. Also, as a joint project with the Women's Studies department of the University of Utrecht, a Dutch Women's Thesaurus was developed. It's presently being used by ca. 12 Dutch and Belgian centres. At the international level, the IIAV co-operates in initiatives for the improvement of exchange of information by participating in advisory committees as a Documentation Working Party of the European Community and in international projects such as GRACE, a European women's studies data base.

As a consequence of its national and international functions, the IIAV participates in several official and unofficial networks and functions as a member of several advisory committees. As a consequence the IIAV is involved in one of the European initiatives for the improvement of exchange of which I was asked to tell you at this meeting.

3. European Co-operation

The importance of access to relevant information for the feminist movement, for women's studies and for equal opportunities policies has been recognize for a long time. The difficulties involved in obtaining relevant books, articles, reports, etc., on women in mainstream documentation are also well known. This has led women to establish their own libraries, archives and documentation centres.

The need to disseminate and exchange existing information on women and gender on an international basis has also become a major topic of interest, especially during last five years. In Europe there can be found many resource centres on women's information and several networks. Lately we have seen many initiatives to improve the existing situation. European co-operation in this area has become a topic on many agendas.

One of the initiatives taken was the Equal Opportunities Unit of the Commission of the European Communities (the administrative board of the European Community), a political and economic structure for co-operation of member states in the western Europe that has at the moment twelve member states(though the number of member states will probably increase in the near future): Belgium, Denmark, France, Germany, Greece, Italy, Luxemburg, The Netherlands, Portugal, Republic of Ireland, Spain, and the United Kingdom.

The Commission set up a Documentation Working Party with representatives from all member states. The goal was to devise ways to imrpove international exchange of information. In order to provide a solid base for future arrangements, it was decided, from the starting point onwards, that an inventory study should be carried out. This study, "Resources for providing information and documentation in the field of equal treatment for men and women in the European Community", was conducted by Jytte Larsen and myself from January to October 1991.

The aim of the study included the following:

- An analysis of the situation in the member states

- An analysis of the initiatives on the Community level and of some international institutions, and

- Recommendations for improving international exchange.

The main part of the study consisted of visits to libraries and resource centres in the Member States (of which 55 were visited) and consultations with experts at national level. Our goals were 1. to collect information on the situation, and 2. to identify national centres or focal points. We believed that co-ordination on national level were a precondition for exchange and co-operation at international level, and that it was necessary to have a national centre or a network structure within which exchange could be accomplished.

Some results are presented here from the following:

1. A survey of the situation in the Member States: different types of centres, their financial situation, the level of professionalism and computerization, bibliographic control of national publications, and existing forms of national and international co-operation

2. A survey of the situation at the European Community level: information services, plans and projects

3. A survey of the major national and international women's information services in the European Community, including financing, staff, size of collection, computerization, bibliographic control, and number of users.

Our findings indicated many similarities yet, at the same time, many differences in the history, organization, and so on, as follows:

In Europe, there exist three generations of women's information services. Each generation has its own characteristics:

- those that developed directly from the first wave of feminism (in the 1930s), including IIAV (Amsterdam), Fawcett Library (London), Bibliothéque Marguerite Durand (Paris), and are professional, publicly financed centres with large general collections,

- those that came in the wake of the second feminist movement (in the 1970s), are centres often short of funding and can work only with volunteers; subject specialization and a strong suitability for networking are their other characteristics,

- those set up by public bodies and organi zations, e.g., national organizations for equality policy (in the 1980s), are planned from the beginning on a professional basis with paid staff, are computerized, include information and documentation services, and function as national centres.

There exist some exceptions to the rule that include: centres that have their origin in national libraries (e.g., KVINFO), centres connected to women's studies departments of universities, and so on. The next generation will undoubtedly be international. This phenomenon has already begun with some international, factual data bases such as GRACE, for women's studies researchers and teachers, and IRIS, for vocational training programs for women.

4. Conclusions

There certainly exists a basis for co-operation and exchange:

- women's information centres have been established in all Member States, with an exception of Ireland

- in some Member States, national centres can be identified while in others the centres are organzied in national networks

- paid staff and professionally trained librarians were found in all major centres

- the international standards of cataloguing are being followed

- bibliographic control of relevant literature at a national level is the goal of the major centres, and

- co-operation at a national level has become common.

Among major obstacles are the following:

- the lack of national centres or national focal points, in some Member States

- the lack of sufficient financing

- the lack of standardized indexing and classification systems

- the lack of computerization, in some Member States, and

- the language barriers.

Based on the findings shown above, a phased approach to the improvement of information exchange has been recommended. The most important steps required, very briefly summarized, are the following:

5. Recommendations

1. Establishment of a European network of national centres

   Requests would be handled and information disseminated by these national centres.

   Exchanges would be facilitated by an electronic mailbox system.

   Interlibrary loan and co-operative national networks are a prerequisite.

2. Establishment of a European data base

   Must start with computerized centres and handle 20.000 records per year.

   The collections should include: recent non-fiction material: books, grey literature, periodical articles, audiovisual material, etc.

   The database should be made accessible in English and French.

3. On a national level it were necessary to develop national centres or focal points. At the European Community level, there is need for a group of subject specialists as a steering committee, and an expert group that will draft a multilingual list of keywords and to consider the extent to which data should be translated.

Future Considerations

After the presentation of the survey results, in October 1991, and the publication of the report [*] by the Commission, in March 1992, the Documentation Working Party, then composed exclusively of representatives of (potential) national centres or focal, points, met again in April 1992 to discuss the recommendations. In the second half of 1993 a follow-up meeting is planned to take place. We do not know what prospects there are of practical measures to be taken, but one of the positive results of the study is a greater awareness of collections and services in Europe. The report and the discussions of the results at several European meetings of representatives of women's libraries and documentation centres have also been an incentive for further ectivities by colleagues in the Member States.

This survey and initiative concerned the twelve Member States of the European Communities. Other European countries, e.g., Austria, Turkey) have interestinf women's libraries or flourishing networks. The Nordic countries: Denmark, Norway, Sweden and Finland, have started their own transnational co-operation project. There is also a growing group of recentrly founded centres in the Eastern European countries that are very keen on collaboration and exchange. Much has still to be done, and financial means for it still need to be found, but I hope that we ca inform about some progress at the next conference.

(*) The report can be ordered from: Equal Opportunities Unit (DG V. B. 4) Commission of the European Communities, 200 Rue de la Loi, 1049 Brussels, Belgium.

WOMEN IN DEVELOPMENT PROGRAMS AND PUBLICATIONS OF THE WORLD BANK AND THE IDB

Donald Ross

Chief, Reference and Information Services
Joint Library of the World Bank and the I.M.F.
Washington, D.C., USA (1994)

(Paper presented at the IFLA Government Information and Official Publications Section meeting on "Government Programmes and Publications on Women", organized jointly by the Round Table on Women's Issues)

Abstract

Since the United Nations Decade for Women, 1975-1985, the World Bank and the IDB have addressed the topic of women in development (WID) seriously. Each organisation commenced with the appointment of a specialist adviser on women in development, which led in turn to the drafting and adoption of plans of action on WID. These Advisers also undertook reviews of the reports written by their respective banks. The reviews indicated the rapid progress both organisations made in introducing WID concepts and concerns once they had turned their special attention to the issues involved. Plans of action, written guidelines and further reviews of project reports have been a major contribution to the better understanding by bank staff of these issues. Much of the written reporting on the subject from each organisation has influenced strongly the design and implementation strategies of projects, redirecting the focus of attention of the projects onto women. The development of a widespread application of WID concepts across their operational and research departments has established WID as a basic component of any loan project,so much so in the case of the World Bank that WID has been replaced with Gender Analysis and Policy Formulation (GAP). The valuable reports generated by the two organisations on WID, for the most part, are not available outside of the organisations.

Introduction

I have to commence with a confession. In the early 1980s, whilst I was learning my trade as the Intergovernmental Documents Librarian at the London School of Economics Library, I opened an unusual, tube-shaped package from the United Nations as part of the deposit of U.N. documents. From the tube I withdrew one of those many colourful posters, which like its postage stamps, the U.N. is so good at producing. This poster announced the United Nations Decade for Women, 1975–1985.

I hung the poster up on the wall of the Government Documents work space, but what I must confess is that I hung it up up-side-down and attached a note of unforgivable cynicism beside it, which read: "in the hope that a small amount of good may drop from this".

My presence here today attst to the fact that that small drop did indeed from the U.N. Decade for Women and in return fo my cynicism I have had the task of identifying what that good was and is. I feel suitably chastised and take great pleasure in having to pay for my cynicism in so appropriate a fashion as addressing this audience on the topic of "women in development: programmes and publications".

I am going to try to present an overview of the work of the World Bank and the Inter-American Development Bank in the field of women in development, or WID, as the phrase is so often reduced to in English. Let me very briefly describe these two organisations.

World Bank: Background for WID

The World Bank is, I am sure, well known to you all as the largest development agency in the world. It began life just over 50 years ago in July 1944 at a hotel in the United States' New England village of Bretton Woods, an event the consequences of which have been the subject of considerable comment and discussion recently. The name World Bank covers two organisations, namely the International Bank for Reconstruction and Development (IBRD) and the International Development Agency (IDA). The Multilateral Investment Guarantee Agency (MIGA), the International Centre for the Settlement of Investment Disputes (ICSID) and the International Finance Corporation (IFC) are associated organisations, which with the World Bank for the Worl Bank Group. From the original IBRD the others have grown as the World Bank has expanded its role as the largest single source of lending for development.

The Inter-American Development Bank (IDB) is a more recent arrival, established in 1959 as the world's first regional multilateral lending institution, designed to promote economic and social development in Latin America and the Caribbean under the banner of the Alliance for Progress.

Both organisations are active in Latin America and the Caribbean and both have women in development firmly upon their agendas. It was not always so however. Prior to 1975 women were not regarded as a subject of special relevance to development. But in 1975, with the commencement of the United Nations Decade for Women, the World Bankd adopted women in development" as an area of special emphasis. (1) In 1977 the post of Adviser on Women in Development was established. The purpose of this position was to review the Bank projects at an early stage to ensure that those relevant to women took account of important factors, so that the project

- responded to women's needs
- provided women with the opportunity to participate and share in the benefits
- overcame limitations on women's access to funds and services
- took account of women's role in a project and designed the project accordingly, and
- avoided any detrimental affects a project might otherwise have on the women involved.

The aim was to emphasise the need to make women an integral part of project design and implementation. The Adviser tried to review all education projects and more selectively those in agriculture, rural development, urban development, industry and population, health and nutrition. The work facing the Adviser and the attempts made by that office were described in a report by the Adviser entitled "Recognising the 'invisible' woman in development: the World Bank's experience" published in 1979. (2) The report identified 27 projects carried out in 23 countries between 1968 and 1978, identifying the importance of women in the development process

Between 1979 and 1988 a series of sectoral overviews, case studies and country profiles were conducted by the Adviser, brought together under the series titled "Notes on Women in Development" (3) which provided suggestions and guidelines for integrating women's issues into the Bank's projects. These were never made public and remain as internal documents today. One of the principal roles of the

Adciser was to sentise Bank staff to the role and needs of women in development. To this end a number of workshops were held such as those in 1981 and 1983. (4) These early steps were intended to promote the active attention of Bank staff to the role of women in Bank economic and sector work, which in turn provides the basis for formulating Bank policies, country assistance strategies and project design.

Women in Development Division Established

In 1987 a large scale re-organisation of the World Bank took place and in the course of it a more ambitious approach to women in development was adopted. A new Women in Development Division was established within the Population and Human Resources Department under a newly created vice-presidency for Policy, Planning and Research, thus identifying women in development as one of the Bank's "special operational emphases". The new Division undertook a number of tasks to establish a rationale and a conceptual framework for addressing women's issues. The purpose was to show that WID efforts by the Bank were practical, affordable and economically advantageous. Among other tasks, the Division reviewed the literature on women's issues, launched a research programme on women's agricultural productivity in Africa, and on women's education, employment and access to public services.

Four WID Areas Were Identified for Special Attention:

– Country action plans were to be undertaken to examine the situation of women in particular countries, to see how this related to the country's development strategy, how to assist women to increase their productivity and to offer recommendations to governments for action in key areas. The first country action plan was undertaken in Kenya, followed by Pakistan, which were to serve as models. The plans were to concentrate on the efficacy of the involvement of women in agriculture, education, family planning and health care and nutrition. Action plans for Banglades Women in Development and the h, Ethipia, Bolivia and the Gambia were to follow.

– The Bank also helped prepare the second phase of a national agricultural extension project in Kenya to bring the training and visit extension system more effectively to women smallholders. The use of women's groups and women contact farmers by the extension agents proved very effective. The Bank estimated the majority of contact farmers to be women.

– At the Safe Motherhood conference held in Nairobi in 1987, sponsored by the World Bank, UNFPA and WHO, Barber Conable, the then Bank President, announced the doubling of World Bank lending for population, health and nutrition over the succeeding years. Of 100,000 mothers in developing countries giving birth in the 1980s, 600 were dying, as opposed to 10 in 100,000 in the developed world. This commitment by Conable spelt the beginning of one of the World Bank's major contributions to women's health in the developing world.

– From among "Best effort" projects 10 to 15 were selected for review to illustrate what a best effort to involve women could accomplish. The WID Division assisted with project design and assessing project impact and costs. The first fruits of these activities came in the form of the first country studies specifically on women, namely those on Kenya (5) and Pakistan (6), both published in 1989. In that same year each of the Bank's country departments began country assessments and action plans for selected client countries. By 1990, 23 such assessment plans were being prepared, those on Bangladesh, India and Nigeria had been discussed with their respective governments , and the Bangladesh study (7) had been published.

The work of reviewing the Bank's activities in the field of women in development has been a recurrent exercise. The Women in Development Division first undertook the review of a small sample of 117 economic and sector reports covering the period 1980-1987 (8), which excluded Staff Working Papers and internal reports and memoranda. Of the sample only 10 had substantial analysis or specific recommendations on women's issues; 57 per cent, though addressing relevant issues, such as small farmers and labor intensive production, made no mention of women; 13 per cent, though mentioning women, offered no analytical comment; 11 per cent specifically discussed women's issues but made no policy recommendations: 10 per cent of the sample provided some policy recommendations but with little analysis or discussion to support these.

However, a subsequent and much wider review of all 442 Bank operations approved in 1988 and 1989 (9) suggested that the women in development initiatives had begun to change the earlier picture. One in five projects approved in 1989 included specific recommendations on women, compared with one in ten in 1988 and still fewer in earlier years. The projects were concentrated in the high-priority areas of education, population, health and nutrition, and agriculture. In education there was a shift from 28 per cent in 1988 to 44 per cent in 1989 of projects specifying actions to improve women's education. In population, health and nutrition, project recommendations addressing women's needs increased from an occurrence of six in eight projects in 1988 to ten in eleven in 1989.

In yet another review of 254 economic and sectoral reports from the Bank, prepared during the same 2 year period, 25 per cent addressed women's issues in some detail, as compared with 19 per cent in the period 1980–1987.

The review process of the Bank's Operations Evaluation Department showed that projects that benefited women had a sound sociological analysis in advance, access to gender disaggregated data and a clear target population among other considerations. These OED reports are of particular value as they are undertaken after the project has been completed, wehreas economic and sector reports are statements of good intention.

Unfortunately all these reviews are not publicly available, but a good insight into the analysis applied by the Bank at this period is given in the Women in Development Division's overview report "Women in development issues for economic and sector analysis" (10) issued in 1989. An alternative useful overview of these rapid developments, following the establishment of the Women in Development Division, is given in the published booklet "Women in development: a progress report on the World Bank initiative" (11) which draws heavily on the above working paper.

Yet a further review of all economic and sector reports written during 1991 showed progress had been maintained: 62 per cent of these reports contaned substantive discussions or recommendations on WID issues (1990 – 41%; 1989 – 25%) and 72 per cent of the country macroeconomic reports regarded the subject as an important topic (1990 – 50%).

The Bank had by now widened its view to include five prime areas of attention: education, reprodctive health care, agricultural services, credit and related support for women entrepreneurs, and labour-force participation. Forestry, water supply and other sectorsd were looked at as dictated by circumstance. Guidelines on "what works" were issued for the agricultural extension and education sectors. (12)

The Bank now also distributed the expertise of WID by establishing co-ordinating Units on Women in Development in each of the operational regions set up in the Bank under the 1987 re-organisation, namely, Africa, Asia, Europe, Middle East and North Africa, and Latin America and the Caribbean. By June 1991 the Africa region had completed 14 WID country assessments and expected to have completed them for the remaining countries by June 1995.

Asia had adopted an experimental departure by recruiting full-time local programme officers in India, Bangladesh and Indonesia to monitor the WID projects in those countries.

In North Africa a US$140 million social fund project was launched in Egypt to establish income-generating and micro-credit schemes among women. Encouragement was also being given to voluntary organisations in the region to include women on their boards.

Latin America was suffering from a lack of gender disaggregated statistical data on women, but women's needs were specifically addressed in two projects in Colombia, and one project in each of El Salvador, Honduras, Mexico and Venezuela, although relatively few projects in this region were specifically WID projects.

One of the most startling successes in all the Bank's WID activities came in Nigeria where the Women in Agriculture (WIA) extension programme (a programme established to test ways of assisting women farmers) had grown from 425 WIA Agents in 1989 to over 800 in 1991.

Since that time there have been further reviews conducted of Bank WID activity and a strong evidence of continuing success in integrating women into the mainstream process of the Bank's lending activity. A comprehensive implementation review was carried out in Europe and Central Asia, Middle East and North Africa, and Latin America and the Caribbean regions, 3 of the now 6 regions a further re-organisation of the Bank created. Sectoral reviews have been conducted on agriculture in East Asia and the Pacific, and South Asia, and on environment in Africa. A Bank-wide review was conducted on the provision of enterprise development and financial services to women.

The findings from these reviews reinforced earlier conclusions. Gender issues are most effectively addresses by the Bank increasing women's access to assets, productive resources and labour markets. This access is best achieved through the following:

– education and training support for NGOs training and mobilizing women

– recruiting female project staff

– gender sensitising of both borrower country and World Bank staff, and

– the systematic assessment of project effects on women's productivity.

In 1992 the Bank invested US$2 billion in education, much of it on getting girls go into school. The then Chief Economist of the World Bank, Larry Summers, argued in a speech in Pakistan that educating girls is the highest return investment available to Pakistan.(13) Even so, by 1992 lending by the World Bank in education and population, health and nutrition were about equal. Of all human resource development lending the Bank had undertaken in the previous 48 years, 50 per cent had been lent since 1987. Likewise 66 per cent of all population, health and nutrition lending had been invested in the last five years. This has resulted in a focus upon poverty reduction through primary level service provision, and the emergence of lending priorities to increase productivity of women in the labor force through better health, education, training and access to new technology. The 1994 Annual Report of the Bank records that the "special operational emphasis" on its "women in development initiative" has resulted in 45 per cent of all Bank projects containing gender-specific actions and interventions. In 1992 this figure stood at 38 per cent and in 1988 at 11 per cent.

The research and review effort on women in development has continued apace. The Bank's Executive Directors have discussed several WID policy and best-practice papers: primary education in 1990; vocational training in 1991; family planning in 1992; and health – the subject of the World Development Report – in 1993.

The Bank's large, diverse lending program for human resource development is served by an operationally focused program of research and policy work that has been explicitly designed to help the Bank improve operational practice by addressing gaps in knowledge about 'what works' with 'what benefits' and 'at what cost'; disseminating knowledge about best practices; and fostering collegial exchange and a shared sense of purpose among staff dispersed throughout the Bank.(14)

This dispersal has been effected also in another way. The 1993 Annual Report of the World Bank is its first issue for many years not to comntain a separate section on women in development. Instead, the WID issues are addressed as a major component of the section of the report dealing with human resource development. The Bank has also moved away from the notion of "women in development" and refers now instead to "gender" in development. In conformity with this, the pioneering Women in Development Division has changed into the Gender Analysis and Poverty Group (GAP) (15), the term "group" reflecting the dispersed nature of the staff across the Bank.

The new Group produced an approach paper at the end of 1993, which was to serve as the basis for a full policy paper to be presented to the Executive Board in 1994. A special study on gender development is also being planned by the Group as its contribution to the Fourth World Conference of Women to be held in Beijing in 1995.

The Inter-American Development Bank's Activities

The Inter-American Development Bank (IDB) has had for a long time a close involvement with the rural poor of Latin America and the Caribbean and, given the world-wide phenomenon of the high proportion of women among the world's poor, the IDB's activities have inevitably involved women for much of its work. However, with the initiatives taken by the World Bank and other organisations since the United Nations Decade for Women specifically identifying Women as the focus of attention of their programmes and policies, the IDB also developed its response to the call to arms on behalf of the women of the world.

In 1987 the Executive Board of the IDB approved a new policy on Women in Development under which the IDB would

- take account of the demands placed on women by family and household duties
- provide training to technical personnel on women's needs and increase the number of women extension agents
- provide measures to facilitate women's access to credit, and
- support administrative, managerial and entrepreneurial skills of women. (16)

To carry out the policy the IDB set up an inter-departmental working group tp review the efforts of other institutions in WID and to make recommendations for action. Chief among those recommendations was that a Senior Adviser on WID be sought and appointed to promote activities targeted to women in Bank projects. In 1989 this Adviser was appointed. At the same time two initial, specifically WID projects were funded: one of US$ 250,000 to benefit low-income Haitian women operating microenterprises; a second of US$ 265,000 directed to women farmers in the Andean region to increase their production of grain. Both schemes were run for the IDB by NGOs..

The Senior Adviser's first task was the co-ordination of the inter-departmental working group, whose advocacy had created the position of Senior Adviser, in the drafting of an Action Plan to promote women's interests in the design and implementation of IDB projects. The guiding principle in drafting the Plan was to increase the impact of projects on economic growth and poverty alleviation of women.

In the meantime, work commenced upon a series of studies on women in Latin America and the Caribbean, which in 1990 formed a basis od a special section entitled Working Women in Latin America" in the IDB's annaul report "Economic and Socail Progress in Latin America". (17) The report contains an excellent bibliography on women in Latin America and the Caribbean. The report presents a ten-year overview of developments in the region and has a third section giving a very useful collection of statistics covering the same period. The studies upon which the Progress Report was based were themselves published as a volume (18) and became the subject of a seminar attended by IDB staff and outside experts to discuss them. The seminar found

- that official statistics undercounted the region's rapidly growing workforce of 40 million women
- that women were playing an increasingly important role in the urban informal sector and in food production, and
- that women receive disproportionately limited benefits in return for their contribution to the economy.

The seminar concluded that to increase the benefits women receive they need to be given greater access to land, capital, credit, technology and training. It was this conclusion that has become the focus of the IDB's WID policy.

As recorded in the 1990 Progress Report, refferred to above, there had already been a number of projects which the IDB had funded and which, by default, had had women as their beneficiaries. The report records that between 1978 and 1990, the period of activity up to then of the Small Projects Programme (SPP) of the IDB, some 23,000 women, mostly microenterprise owners, had received IDB assistance. That formed 20 per cent of all the beneficiaries of the Programme in that period. Of 222 projects run, 22 had been specifically designed for women. In 70 other projects women accounted for 25 to 50 per cent of direct participants. Included among these projects had been the request for technical assiistance from the governments of Barbados and Jamaica to strengthen their women's bureaux. The bureaux serve as catalysts for change in the government and as co-ordinators between women's organisations and the government.

Particular effort had been made also to support women's contribution to the reduction of poverty through Social Emergency Funds and to health care. The IDB had also tried to enhance women's benefits through education, and science and technology projects where there is a high proportion of women involved. In 1990 the IDB also moved to a large scale project, building on the experience of the SPP, to create three global microenterprise projects aimed at women.

The following year, 1991, the IDB's Women in Development Plan of Action, having been formulated by the Senior Adviser on Women and the working group, was introduced identifying three areas of activity: programming, project development and social investment funds, this latter one designed to mitigate the effects of economic adjustment on the poor. Women were particularly effected by the economic crisis in the region at that time. The Plan of Action recognised the key role of women in the alleviation of poverty and, whilst urging the continuance of the previous WID activity of the IDB, which primarily supported the financing of credit and provision of training to women microentrepreneurs, argues for the adoption of specific measures to strengthen the participation of women in all IDB projects. The Plan proposed the institutionalising of this approach by training IDB staff, strengthening organisations working on behalf of women in the member countries and improving public sector capability to effectively address women's needs and contributions in projects.

A review of progress of the Plan of Action (19) identified the challenge still facing the IDB whilst recording considerable achievement. A review of all loans completed in 1991-1992 revealed that some 12 per cent of the IDB's 1992 loans, not including small projects, had required a thorough analysis of women's potential for participation in the projects and the specification of concrete steps to improve their participation. In 1991 only 6 per cent of the IDB's loans, other than small project loans, had included specific WID actions. For both 1991 and 1992, 20 per cent of all project loans had addressed gender issues in the project planning stage, though they had not incorporated specific activity in the project implementation to promote women's participation. While 78 per cent of loans had not addressed women's issues at all in 1991, this figure had been reduced to 68 per cent by 1992.

Analyses of Women's and Socio-Economic Issues

As with the World Bank, the real impact of project work upon women – or anyone else – is not determinable until after the project has been completed and evaluated. In 1992 the IDB's Office of Ex-Post Evaluation was developing and testing a methodology for gender-disaggregated assessment of projects. The results of such assessments will be of real value to the cause of women in development.

Analysis of WID issues, meanwhile, had been incorporated, by 1992, into the IDB's Socio-Economic Reports (internal documents) for about half of the member countries and into several Country Programming Papers (also internal documents) prepared by the Bank since 1990, including those of Columbia, Honduras, Nicaragua, Peru, Paraguay and Venezuela. Based on the experience of a pilot programme initiative, conducted with the Colombian, El Salvador, and Trinidad and Tobago governments, a set of guidelines was being prepared to address WID concerns in all Bank programming

- to identify priority concerns of women in those countries

- to develop a strategy to address them, and

- to ensure that IDB projects in those countries were conceptualised to fully support the contribution of women.

To strengthen further the IDB's potential to meet women's needs in its projects, direct assistance from the Senior Adviser on WID issues had been incorporated into project orientation and analysis missions conducted in the areas of vocational training, rural development, health, environment, social funds and municipal development. To facilitate the indorporation of WID priorities into the IDB project cycle, sectoral WID Guidelines were prepared for Agriculture, Vocational Training, Credit and Microenterprise, and Social Emergency and Investment Funds.

In 1990 the IDB approved a technical co-operation loan to support a study on the role of women in food production in Central America. A series of seminars and training sessions have been held in the IDB since 1990 the topics including: "Working women in Latin America", "Women in development: Latin American perspectives", "Innovative approaches to the problem of street children", "Indicators for Women in Development", and "Women in Development: Caribbean perspectives". Other proposed topics for the series included "Women and social funds" and "Women and environment". (20)

The IDB has conducted research on the socio-economic status of women in sepcific countries and incorporated it into its Socio-Economic country Reports (ISEs), as mentioned above. It has also undertaken studies on women's employment, the role of women in agriculture and their situation in the microenterprise sector. All these reports have been conducted under technical co-operation projects. In 1994, from 5–7 April, a meeting was held in Guadalajara, Mexico, sponsored by the IDB, ECLAC and UNIFEM, which brought together more than 400 men and women, representing governments, NGOs, community groups, academic bodies and business associations, in the Regional Forum on "Women in the Americas: participation and action". The forum was called together to assist the IDB, and the other sponsoring IGOs (international governmental organisations), in setting priorities and devising concrete steps to strengthen the participation of women in their programs. The Forum produced an Agenda for Action with three major areas of recommendation for the IDB:

A. The promotion of equitable and sustainable economic and social reform, such that gender equality becomes part of social reform, through social reform and poverty reduction programmes, which specifically addresses the role of women.

B. The promotion of women's participation in public decision making through the IDB's programmes strengthening women's participation in this at local and national level, and

C. Strengthening of the institutional capacity of the IDB and its counterparts to implement its policy on women in development through improved technical and operational capacity. (21)

The Forum met as part of the programme of activities for the 35th Annual Meeting of the Board of Governors of the IDB, at which the Eighth General Increase in the Resources of the Bank was discussed. I hope the IDB succeeds in its endeavours, if only for the sake of women in development.

Conclusion

I hope I have succeeded, with this inadequate effort, in some small degree, to illustrate the considerable work the staffs of the World Bank and the IDB have undertaken in the cause of women in development. It seems, from my priviledges viewpoint, to be of a high order and high quality. At the end of delving and discovering the writing of this brief overview involved, my cynicism about the Decade is well dispatched. Instead, I have but one disappointment: the lack of exposure this great body of work has to the world beyond the office walls of these two organisations. Clearly, there is both great expertise in these organisations and the benefit of informed insight to the problems they identify and attempt to solve. It could only do the cause of women in development good, for this great expertise to be made available far more widely than is presently the case. But there perhaps speaks a librarian...

References and Notes

1 "Women in development: a change in emphasis. An interview with Minhchau Nguyen". [World Bank] Bank's World 13:1/2, Jan/Feb 1994. pp. 3–5.

2 World Bank. Recognising the "invisible" woman in development; the World Bank's experience. Washington, D.C.; The Bank, 1979.

3 World Bank. Office of the Adviser on Women in Development. Notes on Women in Development. Sectoral Overviews, Case studies, ets. Washington, D.C.: Office of the Advisor, 1979–1988. Numbered series. Unpublished, for internal use only.

4 Ibid. Notes on Women in Development. Sectoral Overviews. Nos 14 and 15.

5 World Bank. Kenya: the role of women in economic development. Washington, D.C.: The Bank, 1989. (World Bank Country Study)

6 World Bank. Women in Pakistan: an economic and social strategy. Washington, D.C.: The Bank, 1989. (World Bank Country Study)

7 World Bank. Bangladesh: strategies for enhancing the role of women in economic development. Washington, D.C.: The Bank, 1990. (World Bank Country Study)

8 Duncan, Ann and Masooma Habib. Women in development: a review of selected economic and sector reports 1980-1987. Washington, D.C.: Women in Development Division, 1988. [Restricted] For official use only.

9 Years refer to financial years, which in the World Bank run from July to June.

10 World Bank. Women in Development Division: Women in development: issues for economic and sector analysis. Prepared by Barbara Herz. Washington, D.C.: The Bank, 1989. (Policy Planning and Research Working Paper No. WPS 269.)

11 World Bank. Women in development: a progress report on the World Bank initiative. Washington, D.C.: The Bank, 1990.

12 World Bank. "How to get girls to school (and keep them there)". World Bank Annual Report, 1991. Washington, D.C. p. 57, Box 3-5.

13 Summers, Lawrence H. Investing in all the people. Washington, D.C.: World Bank, 1992. (Working Paper WPS 905) Originally prepared for the Quad-i-Azam Lecture at the Eighth Annual General Meeting of the Pakistan Society for Development Economists, Islamabad, Pakistan, January 1992.

14 World Bank Annual Report, 1993. Washington, D.C. p. 45.

15 Bank's World, 13:1/2, Jan/Feb 1994. pp. 3–5.

16 Inter-American Development Bank. Annual Report, 1987. Washington, D.C.

17 Inter-American Development Bank. Economic and Social Progress in Latin America: 1990 Report. Washington, D.C.: The Bank, 1990.

18 Not published as of August 1994.

19 Inter-American Development Bank. Women in development: implementation of the Action Plan, 1991-1992. Washington, D.C.: The Bank, [1992]. (Internal document)

20 Unpublished. The availability of seminar papers at the time of this writing, July 1994, was not known to the author.

21 Regional Forum on "Women in the Americas: participation and development". Guadalajara, April 5–7, 1994. Agenda for Action – draft. Guadalajara: IDB/ECLAC/UNIFEM, [1994].

THE WOMEN OF KAZAKSTAN: THE SOURCE OF CULTURAL DEVELOPMENT

Rosa A. Berdigalieva and Zarema D. Shaimardanova

National Library of the Republic of Kazakstan,

Almaty, Kazakstan (2000)

Introduction

From time immemorial the Kazak women, beginning from the legendary Tomiris and up to the heroines of modern times, have participated in the administration of the country and equally with the men defended their land. A virtuous Kazak will never chide a girl. We never put parandja (the veil) upon a woman. And in the years of the Great Patriotic war (1941–1945) only two oriental girls became Heroes of the Soviet Union and they are representative of the Kazak people: Manshuk Mametova and Alia Moldagulova.

In the modern independent Kazakstan women constitute more than the half of our population: 51,8 per cent. The level of education with the Kazakstani women is also higher than that of men. Out of 1000 people there were 129 degreed women and 117 men, or 1 per cent more. By the results of the December 1999 election to the higher and local organs of state administration of the country 8 women (8 per cent of the whole composition) passed to the higher legislative organ of the country – Majilis, and 639 (10 per cent) became deputies of the Maslihats, the regional legislative organs. Four women are the heads of the central organs of power, 5 occupy the posts of vice-ministers, the same number are deputies of akims in the regions; in the diplomatic corps there are 3 women-diplomats.

The women of Kazakstan are an extremely valuable political, economic and, especially, cultural resource. Their role in culture and art can be defined as the transference from generation to generation of the memory of the tribe, nation, mankind on the whole. In the system of education 75per cent are women, in the cultural sphere, the employed are more than 62 per cent women. Women are active creators of intellectual values carrying out the role of conductors and keepers of national tradition and memory.

Cultural Heritage of Women

The genetic memory of the country's administration, freedom of thought and freedom of expression has played its positive part in modern society, which led to the appearance of the leader-woman. The modern woman is characterized by the avid striving towards learning, and conceiving the mechanisms of business, participation in decision-making in the organs of state administration, in the sphere of business and cultural activity, at home and in civil society. Women demonstrate spirit and initiative, perseverance and ability to use their social links and contacts in order to realistically and effectively achieve substantial positive changes in the country.

In a young democratic state such as Kazakstan, culture develops in the following trends:

- preservation and development of Kazak national culture and cultures of other peoples of the country
- preservation and augmentation of historical-cultural heritage
- deepening and intensification of international cooperation
- integration into international cultural space and
- formation of home market of cultural production and services.

Women's associations and organizations are represented in all spheres of the cultural life from folk handicrafts to cinematography and make contributions to preservation and development of the Kazak culture. With the purpose of the fullest realization of their creative and organizational capabilities, women come forward with initiatives to create private authorized educational-cultural establishments. In the area of handicrafts creators are the craftswomen from distant places, united into "Sheber" aul, where they create on an equal basis with men. There, deep in the country and far beyond are well-known the names of Aiman Musakhodjaeva and Janiya Aubakirova, who became organizers and leaders of highly professional musical collectives.

In Kazakstani librarianship workers are practically 100 per cent women. It must be noted that the leading educational establishment of the country that prepares cadres for work in libraries is the Women's Pedagogical Institute.

At present, in Kazakstan, there are many problems in the work of the libraries: under-development of legislative-legal basis of library activity, their closure due to economic problems, difficulties in funding, technological backwardness, etc. However, despite of this all, women librarians of the country make an unusual world, where high civil duty, the realization of significance of their work as the source of cultural development, unanimity, a special devotion to work, desire to bring the book and thus knowledge and information to every resident of the country rein. In the Kostanai region was opened a   library that was organized on a voluntary basis. Another astounding example was that workers of libraries continue work even after the closing of the establishment, because they feel they are needed. Thus, in the Kzyl-Orda region the workers of the libraries, in response to the residents' request, continued working until people revoked the unjust decision.

In modern conditions every library in Kazakstan, beginning from the National Library, including the specialized republican, and city libraries and to the rural ones, became an informational and cultural centre. The practice of librarianship in the republic, which is more than 100 years old, has created conditions for such work. In the work of the libraries were formed the leading trends:

- providing various information services by using traditional forms
- providing information services through new technologies: the formation and usage of electronic data bases
- the development of network technologies and unification of national library resources
- inclusion into the international librarianship space and the world information exchange

- provision of preservation for library fonds as part of national cultural heritage and information resource of the country.

- development and deepening of the system of professional communication for exchange of ideas and experience (conferences, other forums, seminars, round tables etc.)

The National Library of the RK works on the project of the Republican Automated Library-Information System (RALIS), the purpose of which is to unite national library resources and the provision of world-wide access to them. At present the NL has 30 data bases of over 1 million records. Primarily, this is the catalogue of new acquisitions and the so called "Retro" catalogue, which includes the "Kazakstanica" fond. The data bases called "Kazakstan: the past and the present", "Khodja Ahmed Yassaui", "Abai".

"The History of Kazakstani Capitals", "The returned names" contain within themselves historically authentic information. The data bases "The Literary Kazakstan", "The Culture, the Art, the Literature of Kazakstan", "The Kazak Book before 1917", "The New Literature on Kazakstan", "Nursultan Nazarbayev – the First President of the Republic Kazakstan", and "The social sciences" are constantly updated. Of course, to preserve such volume of information is not easy at all: these data bases require continuous work and maintenance regarding software and backups. "Rukhaniyat" is a data base created by the Rare Books Department. It is the basis of the joint catalogue of manuscripts, rare and valuable books in the Kazak and Russian languages. The data bases on the history and culture of the regions of the country, "Education", "The Legislation of the Republic of Kazakstan", and a number of others including also acquired full-text data bases provide for a quicker provision of information to the user. Most of the leading libraries, such as the National Library, the Scientific Library of the KazGNU after Al-Farabi, the Eastern-Kazakstani, Pavlodar, Karaganda regional universal scientific libraries have their own Web-sites. The first multimedia products of the National Library – "The Musical heritage of Kazakstan" and "The Kazakstani Chronicle from the first Kazak newspapers in Arabic script" give an opportunity of preserving the information and ensuring access to it.

In the libraries are created libraries for family reading, also on ecology, history, and regional study. In the Northern-Kazakstani Regional Universal Scientific Library the population is attracted by the "Library of regional study" and "Library of historic-spiritual renessance".. In several regions (the Eastern-Kazakstani, Western-Kazakstani and Northern-Kazakstani) can be found "the Library of youth's leasure time" and "the Library of modern novel" that are spreading information among different groups of population, especially among the youth. The clubs of interest, in the libraries of the Akmola region, called "Panorama", "Girlfriend" and "Candle" are organized by enthusiastic women, the leader-women. The task of the "Olketanu" club in the Pavlodar region, organized by the "Library and regional study" programme, is to introduce and strengthen Kazak patriotism and the study of history and culture of the region. The same programmes work succesfully in the Pavlodar and Northern-Kazakstani Regional Universal Scientific Libraries. "The support and development of the state language" project is implemented in the Eastern-Kazakstani RUSL together with the organization of surveys, exhibitions etc.

"The day of the languages of the peoples of Kazakstan", organized in the Karaganda RUSL and with the affiliation of the National Library of the RK in Astana became the means of effective exchange of information at a round table with the representatives of the

Korean, Polish, Tatar, and Ukraine cultural centres, and for the organization of exhibitions and surveys. The implementation of "the World of Kazak literature" programme in the Karaganda RUSL gives information to readers about the whole stratum of Kazak literature upto the current trends and names.

The purpose of the informational centres, created in the centralized library system of the Pavlodar region and other regions of the country is the collecting, storage and provision for the population of information of socio-economic, legal, cultural and educational character. The Eastern-Kazakstani RUS carries out informational services for 17 organizations and establishments of the region. Realizing that information and knowledge lie in the basis of the political, economic and socio-cultural development of any state, the Association of Business Women of Kazakstan (October,1995) deems as its primary activity the provision of access to information to all women on the international as well as regional levels by means of using the libraries and data banks. The structure of the Association includes an information-consulting centre with data bases on legislation, economy, social, cultural, educational and other issues.

The acknowledgement of book as the primary source of knowledge and information became the main task for organizing of a great event, devoted to "the world day of book and copyright" (April 23rd), declared by the UNESCO and initiated by the NL RK. Besides the exhibition of the evolution of printed book of Kazakstan at the "Book of Kazakstan meets the third millennium" and a round table on the significance of copyright as the basis of protection of intellectual property, there were organized several charity actions. The biggest publishing houses of the country brought in and donated their books to the NL. During another event, "You read it yourself – give it to another" workers of many libraries of the city gave books from their own private collections to children's homes, homes for the elderly, etc. For the purposes of book popularization and importance of knowledge, in Atyrau city, was organized by the National Commission on Women's and Family Affairs jointly with the NL RK the move of 600 books of the NL RK to the children's home of the city.

The national culture contains within itself a system of ideas and conceptions that was forming in the course of all the history of the formation of a certain people and was recorded by this or that method. For each man the recorded memory presents the testimony of his inner participation, the gratitude to the preceding generations and the object for preservation. There in Kazakstan it was namely the women, on the basis of the NLRK who became initiators of the creation and development of the system of preservation of the libraries' documents, elaborating the Conception of the National programme for preservation and the draft project of actually the National programme. There have already been made some concrete steps for the preservation of written heritage with the use of modern technologies. We already spoke about the multimedia products, there is coming in its turn the third CD-ROM to be issued, representing the cultural chronicle of the country as seen by the first Kazak newspapers in the Arabic script and dedicated to the Year of Culture Support, declared by the Decree of the President of the RK this year, the last year of the ending millenium.

The history of many prosperous states testifies to the fact, that at the most crucial moments in the life of society the mobilizing strength was derived from a high civil attitude, the realization of common interests of the citizens of the country. The leaders, sincerely wishing to turn the events of history for better, always found the words, actions that united people of different strata and ages. The women-leaders of the libraries of the country direct their actions upon the harmonious development of society.

References

A woman at the State service and business. Comp. Batpenova G.D., Iskakova S.K., Kanapjanova R.M. Almaty: IPK, 1997. 148 p.

Cultural contexts of Kazakstan: Materials of the international conference dedicated to Auezov's 100th aniversary. Comp. by A. Kodar, Z. Kodar. Almaty: Nisa, 1998. 280 p.

Kazakstani libraries in 1998: facts and figures. Almaty: National Library of the Republic of Kazakstan, 1990. 86 p.

The State policy conception of women's condition improvement in the Republic of Kazakstan: Approved by the RK President's order of March 5, 1997. Kazakstanskaya Pravda. 1997 March 6.

Women and children of Kazakstan: Statistical guide. Almaty, 1998. 48 p.

WOMEN AND THE INFORMATION SOCIETY:
BARRIERS AND PARTICIPATION

Anne Goulding and **Rachel Spacey**

Reader in Information Services Management

Loughborough University

Loughborough, England (2002)

Abstract

The development and use of communication and information technologies, notably the Internet, have stimulated huge changes in the organisation of work and daily life in Europe, leading to a process of transition from the "Industrial" to the "Information" society. The ultimate aim of the Information Society should be the empowerment of all its citizens through access to and use of knowledge but at present some people, including women, are more distant than others from the opportunities presented by the Information Society. Thus, although the Internet has been hailed as an emancipating and democratising force it is not gender-neutral. Evidence of a gender imbalance in the use of the Internet threatens the vision of a democratic space to which everyone has equal access and in which everyone is equal. This paper reviews the literature on the topic of women, the information society and the Internet. It also presents selected results of Masters research projects undertaken in the Department of Information Science at Loughborough University. Specifically, the paper discusses female access to the Internet and explores some of the barriers that may prevent women having the same access as men. It also examines differences in male and female Internet use. The point is made that, very often, the negative aspects of the Internet for women are emphasised but stresses that there are, in fact, positive reasons for women to use the Internet and advantages to this method of computer mediated communication for women. Finally, the concept of Cyberfeminism is discussed. It is concluded that although there are negative sides to the technology, women must engage with the Internet if they are to help shape the Information Society.

Introduction

The development and use of information and communication technologies (ICTs), notably the Internet, have stimulated huge changes in the organisation of work and daily life in developed countries, leading to a process of transition from the "industrial" to the "information" society. One of the essential characteristics of information societies is a high level of information use among the general public (Moore, 1999). This means that everyone should have access to information for their own social, economic, political and cultural development. As Dearnley and Feather (2001) point out, information technology does not define the information society nor is the information society merely computing and associated activities such as the Internet. Nevertheless, ICTs do offer huge opportunities for improving the ways that communities and individuals operate by providing alternative, universal and often cheaper ways of accessing and disseminating information, and the Internet, in particular, has had a huge impact on the development of the information society.

The ultimate aim of the information society is the empowerment of all its citizens through access to and use of knowledge, but there is concern that some people, including women, are more distant than others from the opportunities presented by the changes being wrought by ICTs. Thus, although the Internet has been hailed as an emancipating and democratising force, it is not gender-neutral and it has been suggested that the information society is becoming increasingly divided into information 'haves' and 'have nots' with women, particularly immigrant women, minority women, women with disabilities, women in poverty and older women lacking the information resources available to others (see, for example, Houdart-Blazy, 1996). In contrast to this perspective, other commentators have drawn attention to the potentially liberating nature of the Internet for women (for example, Bahdi, 2000), arguing that through ICT women have the opportunity to network on a global scale and become in involved in society and community development in new ways.

This paper explores issues surrounding women and the Internet, and includes the results of Masters research projects undertaken at Loughborough University (Spacey, 2000; Heimrath, 1999). Issues of use and access will be explored as will the advantages and potential of the Internet as a networking tool for women. Finally, the concept of Cyberfeminism will be discussed.

Women and Internet Access and Use

A variety of research reports and surveys throughout the 1990s and early years of the 21st century documented the digital gender divide, discussed the difficulties faced by women in accessing the Internet and also explored subtle differences in male and female use of the technology.

Access

According to the latest figures from the UK's National Statistics Office, British men are more likely to have used the Internet than women(National Statistics, 2001). 57 per cent of men had used the Internet compared with 45 per cent of women. Intra-gender differences are of interest, however. According to NOP, among 15-25 year old Internet users females outnumber males, suggesting that younger women at least are comfortable with the technology (Kinnes, 1999). Although, the 'chickclick' phenomenon has apparently arrived in the UK (O'Rouke, 1999), the experiences of older women who have received less IT training and familiarity through education have not been well documented. It is important, therefore, not to be essentialist when considering women's use of the Internet because an individual woman's use of, and attitude towards, the Internet is dependent on a number of variables. Not all women lack the computing experience, confidence, skills and access to engage with the information society, indeed, some women have better access to the facilities and are more at ease with the technology than some men. While these differences must be analysed, we can surmise that, as a whole, women are in danger of being disempowered compared to men because of a variety of barriers that prevent women accessing and using the Internet to the same extent as men.

Barriers to women's Internet use

Women's Internet access is increasing, therefore, but a number of difficult and stubborn obstacles remain.

Time and money

Finance and time are barriers of a very practical nature that may prevent women accessing the Internet. Resnick (1995) found that, "the biggest barriers to women going online are time and money". Women generally have less disposable income than men and, in the UK, earn just 82 per cent of men's hourly earnings (Women and Equality Unit, 2002). The costs of going online can be more of a barrier for women than men, therefore. Finance may not be the insurmountable barrier it once was, however. The prices of computer hardware and Internet Service Provider (ISP) costs are falling and women now do not need to own a computer or pay an ISP for access at home as the Internet can be accessed in many public spaces including public libraries, Internet cafes and even supermarkets. In the UK, the UKOnline Centres initiative aims to provide access to ICTs in local, community-based sites including Internet cafés, public libraries, colleges, community centres and village halls (UKOnline Centres, 2002). The centres also offer training and support for new users which is essential for those lacking confidence in the use of ICT – another major barrier for those wary about using the Internet or even entering an unfamiliar public space. For those of us in developed countries, access to ICTs is generally not the problem it once was, then, although we should not forget that some members of society do not have access for a variety of reasons. It is also important not to generalise from a Western perspective and to realise that for those in developing countries, in particular, there are various barriers that need to be overcome before use of the Internet is widespread including the expense of connections and the lack of telephone lines and electricity. Women@Internet (Harcourt, 1999), an edited volume of contributions exploring women's use of the technology around the globe, gives an excellent overview of the potential power of projects using the Internet worldwide, but also highlights concerns relating to lack of access or inequitable access.

Even if a woman has access to a computer in her household or at hand, the lack of time to go online can be an obstacle to use. Married or partnered women still generally work a double-shift of paid work and domestic or caring responsibilities. All the surveys conducted over the last decade continue to indicate that women, even those with full-time paid employment, are still responsible for the bulk of the work of the household. With so many demands on their time, it is clear that women have less spare time than men to surf the Web. Furthermore, Spender suggests that women do not view using the Internet as aleisure pursuit as men do (Spender, 1995). This assertion is supported by other researchers in the area who argue that women view computers and their applications as tools but not as a leisure activity (see, for example, Martin, 1998 and Cunningham, 1994). So it seems that even when women can find the time to access the Internet and become proficient in its use, they might not necessarily see a purpose for it. As an article in the Washington Post reasoned, "It's not that going on-line is too complex a task for women […] to master. It's that they have yet to find much in the way of useful and compelling benefits fordoing so" (Maier, 1995).

Lack of confidence

The relationship between gender and computers has been much researched. It is argued that a variety of forces and pressures mean that women's relationship to ICT is often characterised as 'problematic' (Shade, 1998). Social stereotyping, for example, can give girls the impression that computers are not for them whilst negative school experiences can discourage female pupils from pursuing an interest in computers. Forces such as these can lead women to feeling under-confident and reluctant to use ICT.

In a 1996 study of female university students, Ford and Miller found that whilst the men in their sample enjoyed "browsing around the Internet", the women seemed "relatively disenchanted with the Internet, generally feeling themselves unable to find their way around effectively" (Ford and Miller, 1996).

Although this study is now some years old, the issue of under confidence or reluctance to engage with technology can still be a problem for women, especially when their experiences of using the Internet is a negative or damaging one due to the problem of 'flaming' and/or computer pornography.

Negative Experiences of the Internet

The literature identifies a number of facets of Internet culture that may deter women from going online including male monopolisation of discussion lists and bulletin boards and the flaming and harassment of female users by male users. Dale Spender (1995) devotes a whole chapter to the "male menace on the superhighway" in her book giving an overview of issues surrounding women and the Internet. Spender's earlier works on Man-made Language (Spender, 1985) and Invisible Women (Spender, 1982) are well known and in Nattering on the Net (Spender, 1995) she extends her argument that men dominate both linguistically and in conversation, to a study of male and female interaction on the Web. She asserts that, if anything, male domination is worse in cyberspace than in the real world.

The results of We's study support Spender's argument (We, 1994). She published the results of a participant count on three feminist newsgroups. Since feminist issues were not expected to be of great interest to male Internet users, female participation was expected to be overwhelming. It was found, though, that males dominated even on these female-oriented lists – up to 80% of posting were from men. This led We to conclude that on "almost any open network, men monopolize the talk" (We, 1994).

Another study of gender differences in computer-mediated communications found that on the exceptional occasions that women did post more messages than men on a list, the men became hostile and angry, threatening to unsubscribe from the list because they felt they were being silenced (Spender, 1995).

Herring also investigated the phenomenon of flaming in a study investigating the differing online communication styles of men and women (Herring, 1994) and found that whilst men accepted flaming as a regular feature of academic life, women reacted with aversion. Sutton argued that men consider flaming acceptable behaviour and because they dominate in cyberspace, they make the decision about what is appropriate (Sutton, 1996). Women, on the other hand are likely to be upset by "violations of politeness", according to Herring and therefore become discouraged from using Internet services such as discussion lists and newsgroups when they encounter behaviour which distresses them (Herring, 1994).

Whilst flaming can be unpleasant and distressing, it is not the only form of intimidation that female Internet users may encounter. Harassment via email and in Internet chat rooms is also common. The amount of pornography on the Internet has also received a lot of attention and is frequently cited as a factor that deters women from going online. In one user survey, nearly 10 per cent of women said that pornography was their greatest concern related to the Internet compared with just 3 per cent of men (GVU, 1998). Women can be dissuaded from using the Internet, therefore, because of the male-oriented culture and behaviours associated with it including male monopolisation of discussion lists and bulletin boards and the harassment of female users.

Women's Use of the Internet

Despite the problems listed above, there is an increasing number of women going online but whilst the proportion of female Internet users is clearly increasing, subtle gender differences are still apparent in the extent and purpose of use of the medium. An Australian study found that that the most pronounced differences in the use of Internet services were in the following areas:

- "surfing the Net" (80% of males compared with 69% of females);
- use of trading tools (23% vs. 14%);
- accessing news (58% vs. 38%);
- looking at sexual content (25% vs. 6%); and
- transaction processing such as banking and paying bills (36% vs. 25%).
  (Australian Broadcasting Authority, 2001)

The American Internet Life Report (Pew Internet & American Life Project, 2000) found that women were more likely to search for health/medical information, job information and religious or spiritual information. Somewhat surprising, women in this survey were also more likely to play games online. Men were more likely to search for news, financial information, product or service information, information about a hobby or interest, political information and sports information. They were also more likely to sell and buy stocks and shares and participate in online auctions. With other general Internet shopping, though, there was very little difference between the sexes.

The Internet Life Report was primarily concerned with how women use the Internet to maintain relationships with family and friends. The report concluded that, "women have used email to enrich their important relationships and enlarge their networks" (Pew Internet & American Life Project, 2000).

Email certainly seems to be a strong attraction of the Internet for women. In 1995, Resnick concluded that "communications ranks highest on women's online agenda" as her study found that emailing friends and family was the Internet feature used most by women (Resnick, 1995). Another 1995 study also found a high use of email; 30 per cent of respondents said it was their main reason for going online whilst 33 per cent cited research (Sherman, 1998). The academic nature of Sherman's sample probably biased the results of her survey but, nevertheless, the ability to use email appears to be a strong attraction of the Internet for women and although men also use this facility, "women cite the benefits of email more frequently than men do" (PR Newswire, 2000). This discussion of women's use of the Internet and, in particular, the focus on women's attachment to email, gives some indication of why the Internet has the potential to be a powerful tool for women.

Potential of the Internet for Women

As we have seen, women engage with the Information Society through the Internet in a variety of contexts (at home, through public access points and at work) and for a variety of reasons (leisure, citizen participation, work and consumerism). There is, however, a tendency to emphasise the barriers that women face which prevent them participating fully in the Information Society without acknowledging that the Internet can offer women the opportunity to become involved in new ways, empowering groups which have been under-represented in the past. Through the Internet, women can express themselves anonymously. It also presents them with new opportunities to develop and participate in additional forms of communication and organisation, creating mechanisms of information interchange and dissemination that encourage support and solidarity. A study at

Loughborough University (Spacey, 2000) investigated the role of the Internet as a feminist tool and selected results are presented below alongside consideration of other literature in the area.

Woman-friendly

Of the 100 respondents to the Loughborough study, 70 considered the Internet to be a woman-friendly resource (11 felt it was not and 18 did not know). For many, the feeling of control that the Internet gave them was the principal benefit. As one respondent commented, "I'm in control of where I go, what I see, who I talk to". The anonymity afforded by cyberspace was also considered very attractive. McCulley and Patterson (1996) found that electronic communication was viewed positively by women because it reduced their worry that they would be judged by their physical appearance. This notion was echoed by survey respondents, one of whom commented, "people are forced to judge you on what you say alone" whilst others agreed that the Internet can overcome gender prejudice because others do not know your sex.

Networking and access to information

Traditionally, the women's movement has made extensive use of networking. The costs of traditional forms of networking can be a problem, but electronic communication offers women a dynamic, efficient and rapid means of contact. The Internet thus makes it possible for women all over world to participate in virtual communities and to converse and share news, information, experience, knowledge, support and advice. This could enhance women's full and equal participation in all aspects of society. Although the negative aspects of the Internet for women are often emphasised, feminist research has also celebrated the positive aspects of the Internet, viewing it as a complimentary means of communication alongside the telephone, fax and even letter writing. As Gittler notes, "Information and communications have always played a vital role in the global women's movement. Electronic communications are facilitating women's networking and advocacy in ways not previously possible" (Gittler, 1999).

It is even argued that the Internet has advantages over and above these more conventional means of contact because of its power to connect women all over the globe in a matter of minutes, women who would probably never have the opportunity to meet anywhere apart from in cyberspace. According to some observers, the Internet has brought us to "a new age of discovery by women about women" (Youngs, 1999) as women with very different lives can be in contact. An action research project in Australia, for example, established an electronic discussion group which linked women in rural and urban areas, giving rural women information they would otherwise have had difficulty accessing and giving women in urban areas the perspective of those in rural districts (Lennie et al, 1999). The Internet thus creates opportunities for dialogue, exposing women to the issues and perspectives of other women living and working thousands of miles away. As Bahdi suggests, "the Internet creates the possibility for an expanded dialogue between women" (Bahdi, 2000).

The Internet therefore enables campaigns to be mobilised, information and knowledge to be disseminated and personal experiences to be shared. Email, for example, can help female users overcome geographic and social isolation. As one respondent to the Loughborough study argued, women are generally less mobile than men but the Internet can be accessed from home, opening up the possibility of virtual contacts and making vital information accessible. Bahdi suggests that one of the main ways in which the Internet empowers women is by giving them enhanced access to information about their rights

(Bahdi, 2000). The respondents to the Loughborough study suggested that, through the Internet, information could be found on women's activities that were not reported in the mainstream media. Thus, the Internet reduces isolation and enables women to keep informed of activities and issues of which they might otherwise be unaware.

Feminist Activity

For Youngs, the Internet has radical potential, "the new links offer women on an international basis new knowledges about one another and collective communicative opening to share experiences, views and goals and to strategize. The shared characteristics of such endeavours are potentially transcendent in a number of ways. And it can be argued that they represent consciousness-raising possibilities in new transnational settings" (Youngs, 1999).

There are countless examples of this radical potential translated into reality as women around the world use electronic discussion lists, newsgroups, projects and conferences to communicate with other women, share experiences and learn from one another. The Internet could thus be viewed as an important feminist medium and tool for effecting social change as it can empower and promote dialogue between women, giving public voice to women's interests:

"Every campaign feminists have ever thought of is present on the Internet. From what to do and who to contact for help in the case of sexual assault, to networks of women living in remote area, to campaigns about education or violence, to networks of lesbians, Women's Studies scholars, women's organisations, environmentalists; and the possibilities are endless" (Hawthorne and Klein, 1999).

This was certainly recognised by many of the respondents to the Loughborough survey, one of whom felt that a principal advantage of the Internet was that it "puts women in touch with other like-minded individual; somehow the connotations of this is more liberating for women". With specific reference to feminism, respondents felt that the Internet was useful because women's groups could share information and collaborate on projects. McCully and Patterson argue that, "The Internet will provide the nearest approximation our society can offer to a mass meeting of feminists" (McCulley and Patterson, 1996) and some feminists are even hopeful that the Internet will prove to be the tool that facilitates a revival in feminist activity and interest. As one respondent to the Loughborough survey stated, "I think the Internet has great potential in linking women together and being used as a feminist tool. I can foresee the Internet as a mechanism in a third wave of feminism".

A Web Site of One's Own

The Internet also enables women to participate in the Information Society in another way. Publishing, traditionally a 'Gentleman's profession', has now become much more accessible to women via the World Wide Web. The Internet offers women the opportunity to express themselves freely and "creates a public space for women's interests" (Bahdi, 2000). Women can use Internet publishing tools to develop their own publishing and media activities on the networks and, in contrast to the mainstream media, create gender-sensitive media products. These alternative communications outside the conventional media have the potential to counteract discrimination and stereotyping. Using Internet technology, therefore, women have created and used alternative communication channels to support their campaigning efforts, defend their rights, disseminate their own forms of representation and question dominant models of mainstream culture. Bahdi, for example, celebrates the power of the Internet for bringing women's issues to the attention of the mainstream:

"If the international community is slow to respond to women's global disadvantage largely because of the exclusion of women's voices from the public world, then the Internet is helping to bring women's voices into public space". (Bahdi, 2000)

Cyberfeminism

In the Loughborough survey, the following definition of Cyberfeminism was given:

"Cyberfeminism is a philosophy which acknowledges, firstly, that there are differences in power between women and men specifically in the digital discourse; and secondly, that Cyberfeminism wants to change this situation". (Hawthorne and Klein, 1999)

According to this definition, Cyberfeminism recognises that, for a variety of reasons, men and women are treated differently in cyberspace and this must be addressed. Some of the respondents to the Loughborough survey had difficulty with the above definition or the term 'Cyberfeminism' itself but 41 per cent of respondents identified themselves as cyberfeminists and commented further on a number of aspects of Internet access and use which they felt encapsulated the spirit and aims of Cyberfeminism.

For some, encouraging other women to learn to use the Internet and to make best use of the services it offered was an important feature of Cyberfeminism, both as an essential source of information for women and so that women's interests are taken into account. One respondent noted:

"I keep trying to get women and women's groups to develop their use of the Internet, their interest for Internet issues, their culture to include technology and get their daughters to do the same, so women could contribute to the development of ICTs".

Some of the respondents agreed that women face obstacles in using the Internet, as stated in the definition given, often due to different socialization and educational experiences. The issue of malecentred design and male domination of the Internet was also considered an obstacle to women's use, one that some respondents hoped Cyberfeminism would help overcome:

"I feel strongly that I am carrying on my feminist work by making space for women in the most maledominated areas of the Internet technology world".

Publishing sites on the Internet with a feminist or at least a female-oriented focus was considered part of Cyberfeminism and was seen as important to try to change the perceptions of both men and women and show that women are welcome in cyberspace:

"I think that creating relevant, women-friendly sites and linking up with each other is a very effective way of launching our own protest against the anti-women sites on the Web"

For some respondents, it was particularly important that sites devoted to women's culture were created "as a counter-culture to patriarchal sexist cultures".

Cyberfeminism was also taken as a term to explain feminist activism undertaken via the Internet and respondents offered numerous examples of this activism including bulletin boards, discussion lists, circulating electronic petitions and the development of Web pages for women's organisations. There has been concern expressed, however, that feminist activity undertaken on or via the Internet may distract women away from 'real world' feminism, as Millar commented: "Can organizing in Cyberspace result in social change in the real world? Or does prolonged use of these technologies simply sap our energies?" (Millar, 1998) Other doubts about the value of the Internet for women have been raised too. Hawthorne (1999), for example, stressed that "connectivity is not everything" and although she recognizes the benefit of the Internet for mobilizing support for campaigns and activism, she also understands that there is an ulterior motive behind the call for women to be connected, namely profit.

Conclusion

Although the Internet began as an instrument of the powerful, as Bahdi argues, the marginalized are now harnessing the technology to promote diverse causes (Bahdi, 2000). Women and feminists have not been slow to recognise the potential power of the Internet for information dissemination, gathering and sharing and for connecting with like-minded people in the pursuit of common objectives. There are still some formidable barriers to overcome in increasing women's use of the Internet and ensuring that they participate fully in the Information Society. Some of the more obvious problems have been discussed above but there are other quite fundamental issues to address, such as the question of language. Web site design can also be a factor rendering some Internet content inaccessible to a large proportion of women worldwide.

Despite the difficulties, women must engage with the technology now if they are to have a say in shaping the Information Society. Women have been excluded from important aspects of society and governance for many centuries; information society technologies could reinforce that marginalization if women do not master the technology and speak out about the future of the Information Society. Although there are concerns about commercialism, explicit, misogynist content and the power of the Internet to homogenize, on balance it is probably more dangerous for women to be excluded altogether than to try to work within a male-dominated electronic environment. Hopefully, by engaging with it we can change it for the benefit of women all around the world.

References

Australian Broadcasting Authority, 2001. Australian Families and Internet Use.(http://www.aba.gov.au/internet/research/families/index.htm).

Bahdi, R., 2000. Analyzing women's use of the Internet through the rights debate. Chicago-Kent Law Review, Vol. 75, No. 3: 869-897.

Cunningham, S. J., 1994. Guildelines for an introduction to networking: a review of the literature. The Arachnet Electronic Journal on Virtual Culture, Vol. 2, No. 3.

Dearnley, J. & J. Feather, 2001. The Wired World: an introduction to the theory and practice of the information society. London: Library Association Publishing.

Ford, N. & D. Miller, 1996. Gender differences in Internet perceptions and use. Aslib Proceedings, Vol. 48, No. 7/8, 183-192.

Gittler, A. M., 1999. Mapping women's global communications and networking. In: W. Harcourt, ed. Women@Internet. Creating new cultures in Cyberspace. London: Zed Books.

GVU, 1998. The GVU 10th User Survey. (http://www.gvu.gatech.edu/user_surveys/survey-1998-10/)

Harcourt, W., ed., 1999. Women@Internet. Creating new cultures in Cyberspace. London: Zed Books.

Hawthorne, S., & R. Klein, eds., 1999. Cyberfeminism. Melbourne: Spinifex Press.

Hawthorne, S., 1999. Unstopped mouths and infinite appetites: developing a hypertext of lesbian culture. In: Hawthorne, S., & R. Klein, eds., 1999. Cyberfeminism. Melbourne: Spinifex Press

Heimrath, R., 1999. Internet Perception and Use: a gender perspective. MA dissertation, Department of Information Science, Loughborough University.

Herring, S., 1994. Gender differences in computer-mediated communication: bringing familiar baggage to the new frontier. (http://www.cpsr.org/cpsr/gender/herring.txt)

Houdart-Blazy, V., ed., 1996. The Information Society. A challenge for omen. Women of Europe dossier no. 44.

Kinnes, S., 1999. Domain of women. Sunday Times Magazine, 19th eptember: 55-57.

Lennie, J., M. Grace, L. Daws & L. Simpson, 1999. Empowering Online Conversations: A Pioneering Australian Project To Link Rural and Urban Women. In: W. Harcourt, ed. Women@Internet. Creating new cultures in Cyberspace. London: Zed Books.

Maier, F., 1995. WOMEN.NOTFRANMAIER. Washington Post: Section C: 1. 10

Martin, S., 1998. Internet use in the classroom: the impact of gender. Social Science Computer Review, Vol. 16, No. 4: 411-418.

McCulley, L., & P. Patterson, 1996. Feminist empowerment through the Internet. Feminist Collections, Vol. 17, No. 2: 5-6.

Millare, M. S., Cracking the Gender Code. Who rules the wired world? Second Story Press: Toronto. Moore, N., 1999. Partners in the information society. Library Association Record, Vol. 101, No. 12: 702-703

National Statistics Office, 2001. Internet Access. London: National Statistics Office.

O'Rouke, I. 1996. C-cups through e-tailing. The Guardian: Media section. 8th November: 6-7.

Pew Internet & American Life Project, 2000. The Internet Life Report. Tracking Online Life: how women use the internet to cultivate relationships with family and friends. Washington D. C.: The Pew Internet & American Life Project

PR Newswire, 2000. PR Newswire: new study: wave of women online catches up to men... but they surf differently. (http://www.prnewswire.com/news/index.shtml)

Resnick, R., ed., 1995. IPA's Survey of Women Online. (http://www.netcreations.com/ipa/women)

Shade, L. R., 1998. A gendered perspective on access to the information infrastructure. The Information Society, 1998, Vol. 14, No. 1: 33-44

Sherman, A., 1998. Cybergirl! A woman's guide to the World Wide Web. New York: Ballantine.

Spacey, R., 2000. Women and the Internet: Is the Internet a feminist tool? MA dissertation, Department of Information Science, Loughborough University.

Spender, D., 1982. Invisible Women. London: Readers and Writers.

Spender, D., 1985. Man Made Language. Henley on Thames: Routledge and Kegan Paul.

Spender, D., 1995. Nattering on the Net. Melbourne: Spinifex Press.

Sutton, L. A., 1996. Cocktails and thumbtacks in the old West: what would Emily Post say? In: L. Cherny & E. R. Weise, eds. Wired Women, Gender and New Realities in Cyberspace. Seattle: Seal Press.

UKOnline Centres, 2002. (http://www.dfes.gov.uk/ukonlinecentres/)

We, G., 1999. Cross gender communications in cyberspace. The Arachnet Electronic Journal on Virtual Culture, Vol. 2, No. 3.

Women and Equality Unit, 2002. The Gender Pay Gap. (http://www.womensunit.gov.uk/pay%20gap/introduction.htm)

Youngs, G., 1999. Virtual voices: real lives. In: W. Harcourt, ed. Women@Internet. Creating new cultures in Cyberspace. London: Zed Books.

STRATEGIC PLAN FOR THE ROUND TABLE ON WOMEN'S ISSUES 2002–2003

Introduction

Round Table on Women's Issues (RTWI) states its purpose and scope relating them to IFLA's professional priorities as follows:

"IFLA works to strengthen the abilities and knowledge of library and information science professionals and paraprofessionals throughout the world in order to improve service to the user."
The Round Table on Women's Issues concerns itself extensively with questions and issues that have special relevance for women in the library profession and in the user community.

This is the most important purpose of RTWI and, thus, it develops programs designed to enhance the opportunities and the image of these two groups of women, relating to that "IFLA actively promotes standards, guidelines and best practices to provide guidance to libraries throughout the world in how to perform core functions well, and in many cases how to perform them in the same manner."

Mission

The round table works with many other groups within IFLA to promote, enhance and support professional advancement of women. RTWI further promotes the collection, research, publication and dissemination of information on the status of women in librarianship. This is done with relating women's issues with other, wide issues in IFLA's work, essentially: intellectual freedom, freedom of access to information, and social responsibilities. For this end, RTWI's concern is to identify discrimination in all forms, and disparities in resources, programs, and opportunities relating to women in librarianship, and to collaborate with and support other groups within IFLA interested in these issues.

Priorities and Strategic Goals

1. Provide a forum for discussion of issues concerning women in librarianship. (IFLA Professional Priority: Developing Library Professionals)

2. Provide opportunities for research into the role of women in librarianship and ensure its dissemination. (IFLA Professional Priority: Developing Library Professionals)

3. Communicate with groups within librarianship and other information professions who have similar concerns. (IFLA Professional Priority: Developing Library Professionals)

4. Promote the inclusion of women's issues in library and information science education. (IFLA Professional Priority: Developing Library Professionals)

5. Promote awareness of the round table within IFLA membership. (IFLA Professional Priority: Developing Library Professionals)

6. Encourage collection development and establishment of information services on women's issues worldwide. (IFLA Professional Priority: Developing Library Professionals)

7. Promote literacy and life long and distance learning for women. (IFLA Professional Priority: Developing Library Professionals)

Action Plan

IFLA Conference 2002, Glasgow, Scotland: Open Session on the theme: Women, Democracy and Participation in the Information Society. (Goals 1, 6 and 7)

Conference 2003, Berlin, Germany: An Open Session and a Workshop together with German associations. (Goals 1, 2 and 4)

Begin the planning of Open Session and other programs for the Conference 2004, Buenos Aires, Argentina. (Goal 1 and, especially, goals 6 and 7)

Publication of papers presented in RTWI programs since 1992. (Goals 3 and 5)

Publish the results of the Research on Women's Participation in IFLA and continue other research efforts. (Goals 1, 2 and 5)

Publishing the Newsletter twice a year in both print and electronic format. (Goals 1 and 5)

Continue promoting awareness of RTWI within IFLA membership by translating its publications into several languages and procuring interpretation services in its programs. (Goals 1 and 5)

Continue working together with other groups and issues programs within IFLA, specifically with the Section on Education and Training (Goals 3, 4 and 5) and solicit their cooperation.

....

Prepared: 26.9. 2001